✿

"In these pages you will meet profound,
uplifting people whose iron devotion to human caring
compelled them to risk everything to shelter, hide, and save
the vulnerable. You will not stop thinking about them after
you finish reading, for Mark Klempner gracefully, hauntingly,
invites the most intimate reflection on the moral struggles
echoing from the Holocaust into the troubled present."

—DAVID K. SHIPLER, Pulitzer Prize winning author of
Arab and Jew: Wounded Spirits in a Promised Land.

"I read Mark Klempner's book with great interest,
and with gratitude that he collected these accounts from a
generation of remarkable people who are now leaving us.
It is so important that we hear their stories and
tell their stories to young people again and again."

—LOIS LOWRY, Newbery Award winning author of
Number the Stars and *The Giver*

"We need to know that there are transformed people,
even in the midst of a world that seems to avoid renewal,
resurrection, and transformation. Hope becomes personal,
concrete, and believable in these marvelous stories."

—FR. RICHARD ROHR, O.F.M.,
Center for Action and Contemplation, author of *Radical Grace*

"A work of both agonizing history and hopeful
prophecy. . . . Klempner's beautifully intimate portraits
illuminate the sanctuary of the loving heart, the place
from which the Dutch rescuers performed their
courageous deeds in quietness and strength."

—REV. MARK I. WALLACE, Swarthmore College,
author of *Fragments of the Spirit*

✿

THE HEART HAS REASONS

❧

THE HEART HAS REASONS THAT REASON KNOWS NOT OF.

— *Pascal*

THE HEART HAS REASONS

Holocaust Rescuers and Their Stories of Courage

MARK KLEMPNER

THE PILGRIM PRESS

CLEVELAND

The Pilgrim Press, 700 Prospect Avenue, Cleveland, Ohio 44115-1100
thepilgrimpress.com
© 2006 by Mark Klempner

Photographs courtesy of the United States Holocaust Memorial Museum (USHMM), Washington, DC; Netherlands Institute for War Documentation, Amsterdam, The Netherlands; Ghetto Fighters' House (Beit Lohamei HaGetaot), Western Galilee, Israel; personal collections of the rescuers; and Mark Klempner.

Map of the Netherlands on page xii from *Victims and Survivors: The Nazi Persecution of the Jews in the Netherlands 1940–45* by Bob Moore (Arnold, 1997). Reproduced by permission of Edward Arnold.

Credits for chapter opening photos:
Hetty Voûte (page 19): Hetty Voûte at a picnic. Courtesy of the Netherlands Institute of War Documentation, Collection Hetty Voûte. ▪ Heiltje Kooistra (page 45): In May 1945, Heiltje Kooistra (back center) and her husband Wopke (to her right) pose in front of their house with their three children, the eight onderduikers, two Allied soldiers, and a visiting friend. Courtesy of the Ghetto Fighters' house. ▪ Rut Matthijsen (page 63): One panel of Rut Matthijsen's ID card. Courtsey of Rut Matthijsen's personal collection. ▪ Gisela Söhnlein (page 75): Gisela during the war. Courtesy of Gisela Söhnlein personal collection. ▪ Clara Dijkstra (page 85): Netty, the Jewish child whom Clara saved, pictured after the liberation. Courtesy of Clara Dijkstra personal collection. ▪ Kees Veenstra (page 105): Kees playing music at the secret cabin. Courtesy of Kees Veenstra personal collection. ▪ Janet Kalff (page 127): Janet Kalff during the war. Courtesy of Janet Kalff personal collection. ▪ Pieter Meerburg (page 133): Photo of Pieter taken during the Hunger Winter of 1944–45. Courtesy of Pieter Meerburg personal collection. ▪ Mieke Vermeer (page 157): Mieke Vermeer as a young woman. Courtesy of Mieke Vermeer personal collection. ▪ Theo Leenders (page 169): Ted Leenders as a young man. Courtesy of Ted Leenders personal collection.

Printed in the United States of America on acid-free paper

10   09   08   07   06   5   4   3   2

Library of Congress Cataloging-in-Publication Data [to come]
Klempner, Mark, 1955–
     The heart has reasons : Holocaust rescuers and their stories of courage /
Mark Klempner.
          p. cm.
     Includes bibliographical references.
     ISBN-13: 978-0-8298-1699-0
     ISBN-10: 0-8298-1699-2
     1. Righteous Gentiles in the Holocaust—Netherlands—Biography.   2. World War, 1939–1945—Jews—Rescue—Netherlands.   3. Jewish children in the Holocaust—Netherlands.   4. World War, 1939–1945—Personal narratives, Dutch.   5. Netherlands—Ethnic relations.   I. Title.

D804.65.K55   2006
940.53'18350922492—dc22

                                                                      2005028965

ৰৢ

FOR *James R. McConkey*

ঌৡ

CONTENTS

⤴

FOREWORD

☙

THE HOLOCAUST HAS BECOME UNIVERSALLY RECOGNIZED as the ultimate measure of radical evil. It confronts those who study it with the insurmountable task of trying to explain the existence of harm-doing on an unimaginable scale, and above all, the motivation and nature of the perpetrators. But if the Holocaust is a story with all too many perpetrators and victims and all too few heroes, the goodness of the rescuers is as difficult to explain as the evil of the perpetrators.

Rescue as part of national resistance, as in Denmark, or communal civil disobedience, as in Le Chambon, France, at least allows us to see the production of goodness as a group project, in which individuals acting in concert could find inspiration, support, and strength from one another. The individual rescuers, such as those in Holland who made their lonely decisions to risk everything to help strangers, acted with a moral autonomy that is both astonishing and humbling.

Without hyperbole or hagiographic fanfare, Klempner examines a small group of these remarkable Dutch rescuers, allowing us to hear them explain their lives in their own words and to sense the ethos in which they lived. The cumulative effect of their individual accounts is deeply moving, while simultaneously avoiding a false note of redemptive triumphalism. I have spent much of my professional career trying to put a human face on the ordinary men who committed acts of unspeakable evil. Like no other work I have read, *The Heart Has Reasons* puts a human face on those who committed acts of inestimable goodness.

— *Christopher R. Browning*

The Netherlands

BEGINNINGS

&

We need to know people who
have made choices that we can make, too,
to turn us into human beings.

—RICHARD BACH

THIS BOOK IS ABOUT TEN DUTCH MEN AND WOMEN who helped save
the lives of thousands of Jewish children during the Nazi occupation of
their country. But this chapter is chiefly about how I came to record
their stories, and what those stories have meant to me personally. The
importance of any rescuer's testimony as a historical document speaks
for itself. But my interest in these particular accounts is not only historical but—unabashedly—inspirational. As the son of an immigrant
who narrowly escaped the Holocaust, I found that these narratives
helped me come to terms with my family's past; as an American trying
to navigate the challenges of our times, they've helped me to find my
ethical bearings. In short, working with these people, recording their
experiences, and getting to know them over the past ten years has
changed my life. I hope that their example may do the same for others.

Fifteen years ago, I was a Los Angeleno with fraying nerves and a
rapidly plummeting attitude. As I drove around the congested city, I
wondered what had gone wrong. How had we, citizens of the most prosperous nation in the world, become so mistrustful, so incapable of caring
about one another? Even the best of my fellow Los Angelenos seemed
to be living in fear, on edge—the wealthy in Beverly Hills sequestered on
gated estates with surveillance cameras and grounds security; the poor in
East L.A. making do with deadbolts, chains, and barred windows.

Though I was doing all right as a musician, the self-aggrandizing nature of the music business was getting to me. All the individual acts of selfishness I had witnessed began to blur together, leaving me vulnerable to becoming another burned-out L.A. cynic. I suspected that if I spent another decade in "the industry," I might turn into someone I didn't recognize, someone I wouldn't have wanted to know when I was younger.

I had come of age in the early 1970s, and like many Americans at that time, I took Eldridge Cleaver's words seriously: "You're either part of the solution, or you're part of the problem." In October 1969, my father, recognizing an unjust war when he saw one, announced to the family that he was going to join the upcoming march on Washington. My sister and I, though barely into our teens, convinced him to let us come along. Upon our arrival at the national mall, he hoisted me up on his shoulders, and I surveyed the seemingly endless multitude united in their opposition to the war in Vietnam. It was at that moment, I believe, that I first became moved by the spirit of activism, "the power of the people" to effect social change.

As Richard Nixon's malfeasance became exposed in the years that followed, I rallied and campaigned for causes and candidates I believed in; I stuffed envelopes, circulated petitions, and knocked on doors. I worked as a crewmember on the *Clearwater* to help clean up the Hudson River. Later, I answered a suicide prevention hotline. My spiritual studies had led me to believe that all life is connected, that everything I did, no matter how small, affected the whole. Through both my attitudes and my actions, I tried, as Todd Gitlin puts it, "to bend history my way."

By the early 1990s, however, the United States had changed in ways that I couldn't have imagined, and so had I. I see my personal changes as a sobering lesson in the power of society and culture to affect and mold an individual. Like Anne Frank, I'd always felt that people were basically good, but being a studio guitarist in Hollywood during the '80s had eroded my capacity to believe even that. This was a dangerous development, for once you stop expecting people to be good, you'd be surprised at what they begin to show you.

How do you continue to care about others when they only seem to care about themselves? That was a question I found myself increasingly unable to answer. Then, in 1992, someone set fire to my neighbor's car in the middle of the night; I awoke to the sound of the wind-shield exploding. The next day I learned that the perpetrator also set fire to a homeless person sleeping in a nearby alley. What lack of human connection could have resulted in such horror, right at my doorstep?

One year later, I was living in Ithaca, New York, attending college for the first time, having left the music business after the L.A. riots. At Cornell, the answer to Rodney King's question, "Can we all get along?" seemed to be a resounding *yes*, but I knew I was in a rarefied environment, far from the drive-by shootings, brutal policemen, and the world-class greed of my former home. Life in Ithaca, a small university town, is strongly influenced by both the idealism of many of its inhabitants and the rugged beauty of the natural world that surrounds it. I remember thinking, as I wandered amid its waterfalls and gorges, that here I might actually get back my peace of mind.

While at Cornell, I applied for the Conger Wood Fellowship for Research in Europe—mainly, I admit, because it would mean a trip to Europe. But as soon as I started brainstorming about what, exactly, I wanted to research, my thoughts swerved in a serious direction: I would interview people who had rescued Jewish children during the Holocaust. Immediately the project occupied some large psychic space, but I didn't yet recognize that the rescuers might have—or be—the answer to the crisis of meaning and purpose that had overtaken me in L.A. Rather, I was drawn by the peculiar attraction and repulsion I had to my family history, a history that now seemed a little more imaginable whenever I pictured that homeless person on fire.

I'll never forget how anxious I made my grandmother when, as a child, I unknowingly drew a design that resembled a swastika. My mother, seeing my bewilderment over this unexpected reaction, explained to me that my drawing reminded Grandma of something terrible. At that age, I couldn't understand how a mere set of lines on a page could make someone so upset. Later, I learned that she had lost nearly her entire family to the Nazis: she had come to the United States in 1936, while her parents and ten brothers—all of whom were studying to become rabbis—had remained behind.

My father, at the age of eleven, escaped Europe on the last boat out of Poland. On August 25, 1939, he and his two brothers, one sister, and his parents, boarded an ocean liner bound for New York. One week later the Nazis invaded, and all sea travel became *verboten*. My grandmother, Lillian Klempner, once sat me on her lap and, turning the pages of photo albums from the old country, showed me wedding pictures, sepia-toned young couples, smiling women, and plump children in their little white shoes. "Hitler took them all," was all she said.

And so I am among those people in their 30s and 40s who, as writer Daniel Mendelsohn has noted, are the last generation to be directly touched by the Holocaust. "There is, in our relationship to the event," he writes, "a strange interweaving of tantalizing proximity and unbridgeable distance . . . the dead are close enough to touch, yet frustratingly out of reach." As with many members of this "hinge generation," the Holocaust was not spoken of in my home, but, rather, was conveyed by strained silences and disconnected emotions.

Psychologists note that children of survivors often feel compelled to express the suppressed feelings of parents and grandparents, having inherited the original trauma as a "wound without memory." This has been true of me. I grew up in a well-lit world of modern conveniences, TV dinners, and expectations of upward mobility that were realized when my family moved from the Bronx to Schenectady, New York, when I was eleven. In a split-level house with a neatly trimmed lawn, over a hundred miles from our relatives in Brooklyn and Queens, the past had been left behind and assimilation was in full swing.

But the shadow of the Holocaust is long. That overarching emptiness seemed to hold the key to the legacy of woundedness I felt in my family. Whenever I tried to open the door, though, some kind of emotional force field stood in my way. I would get hold of a book on the subject, but then one glance at a picture from the death camps would send me back to my "normal" life. Still, I couldn't stay away forever.

Only after I undertook this project did I realize that interviewing people who risked their lives to save the lives of others, those who radiated hope during that time, rather than fear, might be a way to finally face the void rather than be driven away by it. I also found myself looking to the project for answers to my own moral quandaries. I had watched myself grow more angry and suspicious while living in Los Angeles; how was it that the harrowing ordeal of the Nazi occupation had unleashed such altruism and courage in the rescuers?

Upon having the good fortune to receive the grant from the Cornell Institute for European Studies, I wrote to Yad Vashem, the institution established by the state of Israel whose mission includes locating and honoring those people who selflessly aided Jews during the Nazi years. I asked Mordecai Paldiel, the director of the Righteous Among the Nations program, if he could supply me with names and addresses of the Dutch "righteous." From a list of eighty rescuers, approximately half agreed to be interviewed; these, in turn, often directed me to friends who were also rescuers.

Many people associate Holland with rescue attempts after reading the diary of Anne Frank. I soon learned, however, that the Jewish survival rate in the Netherlands was the worst in Western Europe: different estimates by historians place it between 11 and 36 percent, as compared to about 60 percent in Belgium, and 75 percent in France.

The physical terrain, the strong Nazi presence, and the gradual, covert way the Nazis went about implementing the Final Solution in the Netherlands proved to be particularly deadly when compounded with the Dutch inclination to seek consensus and accept compromise. The vast majority of Dutch people cooperated with their Nazi occupiers and complied with the avalanche of Nazi regulations, paving the way for the eventual murder of their Jewish cocitizens. As members of the Dutch legal system stood by and the mass of Dutch citizens remained silent, the Nazis ran roughshod over the country's constitution, trampling all the protections and privileges that the Jews had enjoyed for centuries.

Those who decided to help Jews in Holland had to be willing to disobey the Nazi measures and resist the Nazi machinations to relegate Jews to subhuman status. They had to cross the line from being law-abiding citizens to enemies of the state. They had to act from the heart, come what may.

Who was willing to do it? The women and men who speak in the pages of this book. They are never boastful, but proud in some quiet way, and reticent to varying degrees. Their explanations of their actions often make it sound as if what they did was the most natural thing in the world. Most of them continued to be morally engaged after the war as well, offering through their example a luminous alternative to the empty materialism and superficial values in which so many of us have become enmeshed.

Spending time with the rescuers was, for me, a transforming experience. They welcomed me into their homes as though *I* were someone special—a characteristic inversion—and showered me with hospitality and kindness. I soon was looking at them not only as people who had made history, but also as people who could teach me a different way to live. I've come to think of them as the radiant specks around the black hole of the Holocaust, and they've become a radiant presence in my own life as well.

BACKGROUND

A talent is formed in stillness;
a character, in the world's torrent.

—GOETHE

MOST OF HOLLAND'S NINE MILLION CITIZENS were bystanders to the Nazi persecution of the Jews. Though millions wanted to do something, and hundreds of thousands gave assistance to those who were doing something, only about fifty to sixty thousand—less than 1 percent—stood up to the Nazi injustices through active resistance. Of that number, only a small fraction—perhaps a tenth—dared to actually rescue Jews. So that's less than one-tenth of 1 percent of the population shouldering the task of saving one hundred forty thousand innocent people.

How did the rescuers come to make the choices they did? What choices were available to them, and to the Jews, during the Nazi occupation? Though the narratives of the rescuers directly engage these questions, it's helpful to know more about the circumstances that were the backdrop for the rescuers' choices. By surveying that vanished historical and cultural landscape, it becomes easier to understand why so many sympathetic Dutch citizens did nothing, and it also puts the heroic actions of the rescuers into sharper relief.

The night before Germany attacked the Netherlands, Adolf Hitler came on the radio and gave his solemn pledge that Dutch neutrality would be honored. Twenty-five years earlier, the Dutch had managed to stay out of the First World War; many hoped that they would be able to stay out of this one, as well. On May 10, 1940, however, people all over the country were awakened in the early morning hours by the drone of fighter planes, punctuated by the sounds of anti-aircraft flak. The Dutch army fought desperately with heavy losses, but their defenses were easily overrun by the panzer divisions of the invading Wehrmacht. Through the use of paratroopers, the Germans were able to seize every important airfield and most of the strategic bridges by dawn.

Three days later, when the Nazis announced that they were planning to bomb Rotterdam by air, the Dutch command stationed there expressed willingness to surrender the city. The offer was ignored. Hours later, a formation of Stuka dive bombers set out on an air strike that left one of Holland's oldest cities in charred ruins. The firebombing of Rotterdam, the first large-scale airborne attack in history, is remembered firsthand by survivor Ralph Boucher:

> I saw the planes still diving and releasing hundreds of bombs. Flames and black smoke were now visible over the center of the city. . . . The fires grew steadily worse and by evening the whole center of town was one vast sea of flames, so huge that young trees in front of our house were bent by the strong winds sucked in by the fire. This continued into the night and all of the next day.

Closer to ground zero, the firestorm reached hurricane velocities, ripping doors and windows from their frames, flinging burning rafters into the air, and razing buildings and factories. Amid the fiery chaos, hundreds of civilians were killed, thousands more wounded, and tens of thousands were left homeless.

Within five days, the Dutch High Command officially capitulated, and Queen Wilhelmina and most of her cabinet fled to England. Many Dutch felt betrayed by her departure as hundreds of German troops goose-stepped into the Netherlands, their jackboots, equipped with steel taps, making a thunderous clicking as they approached. As days stretched into weeks, however, it became clear that the queen was better off in exile than imprisoned in her own castle, as King Leopold of Belgium was in his. During her hasty escape, Wilhelmina had also had enough presence of mind to take the entire national treasury with her. Safe in her London headquarters, she began to issue stirring addresses on the BBC-broadcast Radio Orange, urging the Dutch people to stand strong.

The Germans, even before having arrived on land, had airdropped leaflets declaring: WE THE GERMAN PEOPLE HAVE COME TO LIBERATE YOU. Most Dutch were offended by such propaganda, but the Germans hoped to win them over with a show of civility and by appeals to a shared "Aryan blood." The prospect of the Dutch being among the winners, through the very real possibility of a German victory, and according to their high ranking in the Nazi racial hierarchy, did draw a small number of them into the Nazi fold. Most, however, wanted nothing to do with their occupiers, though they also wanted to avoid antagonizing them. There were some among the Jews, of course, especially the recently arrived German-Jewish émigrés, who guessed correctly where all this was leading.

Two extreme Jewish responses were therefore seen early on. In Amsterdam, where the Jewish population was concentrated, more than a hundred Jewish people committed suicide during the first weeks of the occupation, putting their heads in gas ovens, or jumping out of windows rather than be subjected to what they feared the Nazis had in store for them. There were also some Jews who, either alone or in gangs, directly fought the Germans with whatever weapons they could get their hands on. This was tantamount to suicide, considering the tens of thousands of heavily armed German combatants.

The majority of Holland's one hundred forty thousand Jews adopted a wait-and-see attitude, however, as did the rest of the Dutch populace. The easiest option was to go about one's life as before, keep a low profile, and hope that the Germans had the sense to realize that there was no point in arresting quiet, law-abiding Dutch citizens. The Germans were quick to exploit such hopes; their deceptive policies led Jews to believe that decent treatment was possible for those who acted with the utmost restraint and compliance. Still, Dr. Arthur Seyss-Inquart, the forty-eight-year-old Reichskommissar put in charge of the Netherlands by Adolf Hitler, stated the Nazi position quite clearly in an early public address: "We shall hit the Jews wherever we find them and those who side with them will bear the consequences."

Less than five months into the occupation, the Germans required all government employees to fill out an "Aryan attestation." This form called for detailed information about the applicant's family background, especially any Jewish ancestry. Though there was some protest, not just from the government employees, but also from several churches and universities, in the end, all but twenty of the two hundred forty thousand Dutch civil servants dutifully signed and returned the form. Dutch historian Peter Romijn reports:

> From the German point of view, the registration went as planned. Anyone who was of two minds about signing the attestation, and who sought guidance from their superiors, found none. The Supreme Court refused to sanction refusal to sign, most members arguing that in view of the state of war the Germans had the right to take such measures. Because of the position taken by the Secretaries-General and the Supreme Court, any chance of making a collective protest was lost.

Jewish girl in the Netherlands standing next to a "Jews Forbidden" sign. Courtesy of the United States Memorial Holocaust Museum, Washington, D.C.

Soon after demanding the Aryan attestations, the Germans began to issue the first of hundreds of regulations aimed at denying Dutch Jews their civil liberties. In the beginning, the devil was in the details, sometimes ridiculous details: "Jews cannot walk on the sunny side of the street." Hardly worth fighting against, but greater restrictions followed: "Jews cannot go to the park." "Jews cannot attend the cinema." "Jews cannot play sports." By the time the deportations started two years later, Jews could not travel or change their place of residence. They were prohibited from marrying non-Jews; they could not even visit non-Jews. They could not drive cars or make telephone calls. Many of them could no longer practice their professions. As they became increasingly stigmatized and desperate, they also became increasingly isolated from non-Jews. Through such means, the Nazis sought to establish the Jewish people as a subhuman species, repellant and deserving of persecution.

Who was enforcing these regulations and carrying out the Nazi agenda? When the rescuers recount roundups—known as *razzias*—and other operations, there was no single generic Nazi group that carried them out, but rather a startling array of NSB storm troopers ("Black Police"), German common police ("Green Police"), Waffen-SS (Schutzstaffel, meaning, "Defense Echelon"), Gestapo ("Secret State" police), SD (German intelligence officers), Sipo (German security officers), Kripo (German criminal police), Wehrmacht (German soldiers), and still others such as detectives, espionage agents, and the Dutch police, who were all taking their orders from the German authorities. Holocaust scholar Christopher R. Browning has remarked that in the Netherlands the bewildering assemblage of Nazi groups essentially competed with each other to see which could do away with the Jews most quickly.

The NSB storm troopers require special explanation, for they were not Germans at all, but rather Dutch. The Nationaal Socialistische Beweging was a Dutch fascist party, founded in 1931, dedicated to establishing a powerful central government with emphasis on order and discipline. During the occupation, NSB members often proved to be more dangerous than the Germans because they spoke the language, knew the neighborhoods, and served as eyes and ears for the Gestapo. Many a fledging rescue attempt ended in tragedy due to an NSB informer; such people would sometimes take the Gestapo up on its offer of a reward—typically seven-and-a-half guilders, worth about fifty dollars today—for each Jew whose whereabouts they betrayed.

Before the war, the NSB had been able to capture only about 8 percent of the vote; after the Nazis arrived, however, their leader, Anton Mussert, formed an alliance with the German occupiers and suddenly became extremely powerful. He and his followers enthusiastically assisted the Nazis in all of their operations, especially the rounding up and deportation of Jews. Within a couple of years, the Nazis had made the NSB the only legal political party and declared Mussert the leader of the Dutch people.

. . . .

Nationaal Socialistische Beweging (NSB) marching in a rally in the Netherlands.
Courtesy of the Netherlands Institute of War Documentation.

In January 1941, the Germans announced that all Dutch citizens over the age of fifteen had to register and be issued identification cards. This request was, as Holocaust historian Raul Hilberg points out, "the first step to ensnare the Jews in a tight network of identification and movement controls." Dutch historian B. A. Sijes estimates that out of a Jewish population of one hundred forty thousand, only about fifty Jews refused to register.

By this time, Jews were increasingly being taunted and beaten up in the streets, not yet by the Germans themselves (who were covert and methodical about carrying out their plans), but by NSBers. On February 11, a gang of NSB vigilantes entered the Jewish Quarter of Amsterdam and proceeded to break the windows of storefronts and attack people at random. This time, however, a Jewish *knokploeg*—the Dutch word for a kind of paramilitary gang—attacked the attackers, and one Dutch Nazi by the name of Hendrik Koot was severely wounded.

The following day, the Nazis ordered the establishment of a Jewish Council to act as an intermediary between themselves and the Jews.

They appointed the chief rabbi of the Ashkenazi community, as well as its president, Abraham Asscher, to lead the Council, along with one of the rabbis from the Sephardic community. When both rabbis declined, Asscher suggested Dr. David Cohen, an influential, though not widely liked, secular leader in the Jewish community who was already presiding over an agency that assisted Jewish refugees. (Cohen had snubbed the rabbinate by hardly including any rabbis on the board of this and another major Jewish organization that he had founded.) And so Asscher and Cohen chaired the Council, which immediately began to issue announcements to the Jewish community based on orders from the Nazis, the first being that all Jews must surrender their weapons.

On February 14, even as the death of Hendrik Koot was receiving wide coverage in the Nazi-controlled newspapers, another incident happened, this time in an affluent neighborhood in South Amsterdam. Some members of the Green (German) Police surrounded Koco's, a popular Jewish-owned ice cream shop believed by the Germans to be a base for a Jewish knokploeg. The previous week, after the shop had had its windows smashed, its owners rigged up a contraption to spray ammonia at any unwelcome intruders. When they used the device against the entering German police, the owners and others present were arrested. But this was just the first step in the Germans' exponential formula of retribution.

On Saturday, February 22, when many Jews were quietly observing the Sabbath, hordes of Green Police cordoned off the Jewish Quarter and arrested hundreds of Jewish men, dragging them off the street or pulling them from home and synagogue. After being marched in columns to Jonas Daniël Meyerplein, a public square, the men were forced to run through a gauntlet of policemen swinging their truncheons and then ordered to squat down for hours with their arms outstretched. The next day, the police raided again, bringing the total number of arrests to over four hundred.

This first brutal roundup sent shock waves throughout the entire country. British historian Bob Moore writes, "For the first time, the Germans had shown their hand: the tactics of the oppressor, which had been so evident in Germany since 1933, were now being applied in the Netherlands." The Communist party called for a protest strike, an idea that spread in a great flurry of whisperings to other groups and workers of all kinds—not only in Amsterdam, but in Utrecht and elsewhere. Though the Communists had initiated several previous strikes in opposition to Nazi policies, this was the first time that a strike had been called specifically to protest the Nazis' treatment of the Jews. Thousands of workers walked off the job, bringing shipping, unloading, transportation, and other services to a standstill.

The Nazis responded with a crackdown that resulted in at least seven deaths and the arrest of more than one hundred strikers. The next day, however, the strike grew bigger. Thousands of longshoremen, metal workers, and others refused to go to work, severely crippling the economic and industrial infrastructure that the Nazis were so vigorously exploiting. In the armament industries alone, more than eighteen thousand workers were absent from the factories and assembly lines. However, when the Nazi authorities claimed that the strike was being instigated by the Jews and threatened to arrest and possibly shoot five hundred additional Jews the next day, the strike's leaders, heeding advice from the Jewish Council, called an end to it.

The February Strike was the only mass protest over the plight of the Jews to be carried out in all of occupied Europe and perhaps the only mass strike in history on behalf of a persecuted minority. For many Jews, it was the most cherished moment of the war, providing a tangible sense of solidarity with their Dutch cocitizens that cut through the isolation and denigration in which the Nazis sought to envelop them. Still, it was ultimately ineffectual.

During this winter of 1941, the Jews in the Netherlands must have been desperately weighing their options. Clearly "fight" was futile; what about "flight"? Many Jews were thinking about leaving the country or going into hiding, but both possibilities were fraught with difficulties. All legal means to emigrate had been cut off by the Nazis, and those who tried to make a run for it found danger in every direction.

Holland is flanked by Germany to the east and the north. To the south lie France and Belgium, both of which had been invaded at the same time and were also under German occupation. To pass through these lands, money would be needed to pay off the right people, and even then there would be no guarantees. Nevertheless, about fourteen hundred Jews escaped to Switzerland via Belgium and France, and another thirteen hundred managed to get to Spain or Portugal. To the west of Holland is

A group of children hiding by a haystack in the Netherlands.
Courtesy of the United States Memorial Holocaust Museum, Washington, D.C.

the open sea, and by crossing it one could reach England. Some Dutch tried to do this in small boats and canoes, but only about two hundred were able to make it without being intercepted by German patrol boats.

To go underground posed a different set of difficulties. The Netherlands is only twelve thousand, nine hundred square miles— about the size of Maryland—and in the 1940s it was already densely packed with a population of nearly nine million people. The Dutch take pride in themselves, saying that God made the world but that they made Holland, because their ambitious system of dikes reclaimed large tracts of land that were once underwater—including what is now Amsterdam. It is an exceedingly flat country, with no mountains and very little forest. Its excellent network of roads, stretched across the level countryside, enable anyone with a vehicle to be anywhere within its borders within a few hours. However, an environment so meticulously planned and developed does not lend itself to hiding. On the contrary, it may be seen as a natural trap. In the 1940s, only the rural areas provided some open space where one could walk around without great risk of being observed.

It has often been noted that the Jews were well integrated into Dutch society, having lived harmoniously in the Netherlands since the seventeenth century. That is true, but not in the sense that the term "integrated" is often used. Though Jews enjoyed full Dutch citizenship and encountered little anti-Semitism, they, like other religious groups in Holland, had their own separate political representation and functioned parallel to other groups without necessarily having much contact with them. Often they lived in the Jewish sections of Amsterdam, or in other enclaves. As a result, many Jews didn't know many non-Jews. This made going underground extremely difficult.

The best bet for would-be *onderduikers*—that is, people who wanted to "dive under"—was to find some shelter on the property of a sympathetic farmer. Unfortunately, this required contacts that most city dwellers, especially those Jews who lived in the Jewish Quarter of Amsterdam, simply didn't have. This left only the option of finding a hiding place somewhere in the city, where the houses were built close together. Such proximity to one's neighbors reflected the close-knit nature of Dutch life, but made it difficult for someone to remain undetected for long. What's more, curtains were typically left open, leaving the common living areas of the home in plain view.

To hide under such conditions required a high level of secrecy. Some special situation—an attic, a basement, a crawl space—would probably be necessary. But of course one could not live in such a space self-sufficiently; hiding would require the cooperation and assistance of other people. Possible helpers had to be approached very cautiously due to the possibility of betrayal. After all that, there was still no assurance that even the most sympathetic person would be willing to take the risk.

On 20 January 1942, at the Wannsee Conference in Berlin, Reinhardt Heydrich, designer of the Nazis' mechanism for mass murder, presented his strategy for the deportation and extermination of every remaining Jew in Europe—*eleven million* was the targeted number! Within an hour-and-a-half, consensus was reached by the enthusiastic quorum of fifteen high-level Nazis (eight of whom held Ph.D. degrees). The Holocaust was officially underway.

Children in Westerbork.
Courtesy of the United States Memorial Holocaust Museum, Washington, D.C.

It's difficult for us to imagine today that there was a time when names such as Auschwitz held no particular resonance. Before the Holocaust, however, the horrors of high-tech genocide were, as Dutch historian Louis de Jong states, "beyond the belief and the comprehension of almost all people living at the time, Jews included." The Final Solution was a massive undertaking, requiring multiple layers of administration and the varied skills of many professionals. Yet, despite the complexity of this "apparatus of total destruction," the basic formula behind it can be stated in four words: denigrate, isolate, deport, and kill.

Seyss-Inquart already knew the routine (albeit on a small scale) from his experience as Commissioner of Security and Police in Austria after Hitler forcibly annexed it to Germany in 1938. Under his orders, Jews in the Netherlands began to be rounded up in the summer of 1941—first to be detained in Amsterdam, and then sent off to Westerbork, a transit camp located almost one hundred miles northwest near the Dutch town of Hooghalen. Of the many officials below Seyss-Inquart, only one warrants our special attention: Ferdinand Hugo Aus der Fünten, who was principally responsible for coordinating and implementing Seyss-Inquart's plans for the Jews in Holland. We will hear more about Aus der Fünten in chapter 8 from rescuer Piet Meerburg, who helped to free captive Jewish children right from under his nose.

All the Nazi officials were part of a well-defined hierarchy that maintained an unusually strong presence in the Netherlands. In France and Belgium, the Germans were content to rule through a puppet government with the army as the ultimate authority. But in the Netherlands, the elite SS and Nazi party representatives were involved in every aspect of the transformation that they envisioned. One indication of this is that five thousand German police were stationed in the Netherlands, and only three thousand were stationed in France, despite the fact that the former is a much smaller country and contained only half as many Jews. Browning believes that the Nazis exercised tighter control there than in any other Western European country because they saw the Dutch as a kind of Nordic-Germanic people to be absorbed into their inner realm.

Despite their large numbers, however, the Nazis could not have done it alone. They relied on Dutch government employees and numerous public agencies and utilities to carry out their objectives. They used the entire governmental infrastructure as a platform from which to pursue their master vision for the Netherlands, which involved not only the extermination of the Jews but the Nazification of Dutch society and the full exploitation of all Dutch resources. Despite their misgivings, all but a few Dutch officials cooperated with the wishes of their Nazi occupiers. Dutch civil servants supplied Jewish addresses; Dutch policemen forcibly removed Jews from their homes; Dutch tram conductors transported Jews to the train stations, and Dutch railway workers operated the trains to Westerbork. Though there were some who tried covertly to resist—for instance, in Amsterdam, Police Inspector Schreuder organized a team of his men to inform Jewish people of upcoming raids that the police themselves had to conduct—others performed their jobs with zeal.

In the spring of 1942, Jews were ordered to wear the yellow star of David. There were scattered protests from the non-Jewish community: some non-Jews donned homemade stars that said "Protestant" or "Catholic." Leaflets protesting the policy were distributed in the tens of thousands. Such responses were not unusual in Holland—statements of protest in regard to the Nazis' treatments of the Jews were plentiful throughout the war, and petitions and protest letters were sent to everyone from Seyss-Inquart on down. De Jong informs us that the Netherlands Institute for War Documentation houses over seventy thousand different issues of more than twelve hundred underground newspapers. In such documents we find human rights and decency preserved on an ideological level, and certainly they served as morale boosters. However, these "paper tigers" did not do much more than that, at least as far as the Jews were concerned. They may even have inadvertently misled the bewildered Jewish public by reinforcing the notion that in a civilized society, in solidarity with their non-Jewish cocitizens, such injustices could not long continue.

Most Jews, instead of realizing that they had better scramble to save their lives, underestimated how long the war would continue and how much damage the Germans would be able to do before it ended. They also misjudged the Allied forces in thinking that they would take action against egregious human rights violations, when actually their objectives remained strictly military, and, as has often been noted with bitter regret, they could not even be persuaded to bomb the railway tracks to Auschwitz. In the words of Elie Wiesel, "The blindness of the Jews was equaled only by the indifference of the Allied leaders to their plight."

And so Jews put on their stars and "set off for the streets, embarrassed, proud, ill at ease, or indifferent." Most felt that since they had already registered as Jews, they might as well wear the star, although the stars unmistakably marked them for discrimination, deportation, and, when the time came, death. None of the scribbled letters of protest, or the noble, measured phrases of the petitions, or the rough-and-ready prose of the underground newspapers could save them then. On 14 July 1942, a major razzia took place in Amsterdam, and the next day, to make room for the new arrivals, the first trainload of Jews left Westerbork for Auschwitz. Death trains, filled to capacity, were soon leaving Westerbork regularly. To expedite turnover, the Nazis requested additional train service from Amsterdam to Westerbork, and the Dutch Railways complied by adding train number 11537, departing Amsterdam 2:16 A.M., arriving in Hooghalen 5:58 A.M.

Even as the Jews were being called up to work in "labor camps," able-bodied Dutch men were being conscripted to work in Germany, mostly in factories, so that the Germans they replaced could be drafted. Failing to get an adequate response from their call-up notices, the Germans started rounding up Dutch men by the tens of thousands—a two-day raid on Rotterdam alone yielded over fifty thousand deportees. Before the war had ended, over ten times that many had been used to provide manpower for the Nazi war effort. It turned out that these men, unlike their Jewish cocitizens, were made to do purposeful work.

For the Jews, the requirement that Dutch men provide labor, and the roundups of Dutch men that followed, added to their confusion. They had already seen how everyone had to register, but it was the Jews who were singled out for discrimination. Now, all Dutch men had to provide labor, and so did all Jewish men and women. But how would their treatment be different?

Most Jews did not learn what was in store for them at their "labor camps" until they were already there. And then they were forced to write letters to their family members on the outside, saying that everything was fine. The following is one example, a letter written in December '42 by an inmate at Auschwitz III, the I.G. Farben factory where two out of every three prisoners perished:

> I have now been here four weeks, and I am well. I am in good health. Work is not particularly heavy. We start at seven in the morning and we work till four in the afternoon. Food is good: at noon we have a warm meal and in the evening we get bread with butter, sausages, cheese, or marmalade. We have central heating here and we sleep under two covers. We have magnificent showers with warm and cold water.

In Amsterdam, those same relatives were encouraged by the German authorities to write back. De Jong reports: "Tens of thousands of such letters were handed to the Germans. Of course, not a single one was ever delivered."

To understand how such deceptive tactics could have been official, albeit secret, German policy, one need look no further than Hitler himself:

> When you lie, tell big lies. . . . [The masses] more readily fall victim to the big lie than the small lie, since they themselves often tell small lies in little matters, but would be ashamed to resort to large-scale falsehoods. It would never come into their heads to

fabricate colossal untruths and they would not believe that others could have the impudence to distort the truth so infamously.

And so the air in Amsterdam was thick with propaganda and deception, along with rumors, guesses, warnings, assurances, and secondhand reports. Most Jews, facing a gaping uncertainty each day and trying their best to cope with the mind-splitting worries, simply muddled through, hoping for the best.

For those who had still not decided what to do, receiving a deportation slip brought matters to a head. Some reported as required while entrusting their children to others. Some families tried to dive under together or, failing in that, tried to split up and secure separate hiding places. In any case, finding "safe addresses" was very difficult.

It must be remembered that in 1942 the German forces appeared invincible. Not until the battle of Stalingrad a year later did Hitler suffer his first major defeat. As Browning points out, "This is not a point that one can say the Allies will win the war, or even that the war is going to be over soon. Those who hid Jews in the Netherlands in July '42 were making a very extraordinary decision considering that there was no timetable and no guarantee of liberation."

Who were these people, willing to help their Jewish cocitizens, despite the risk and uncertainty? They were people who could not cut their consciences according to Nazi specifications, who could not accept the mountain of newly enacted Nazi laws. They were people who were unafraid—or, at least, undeterred—by the threat of torture and death. Some of them acted alone, but often they managed to find others who shared their feelings and convictions. And, in some cases, they organized into groups.

The largest general resistance network involved in helping people to hide was the LO, an acronym for the Landelikje Organisatie voor Hulp aan Onderduikers, which was started in December 1942 by Reverend Clomp of the Orthodox Calvinist Church. His aim was not specifically to aid the Jews, but to assist Dutch men trying to evade the Nazi summons to forced labor assignments.

In terms of sheer numbers, the LO assisted more Jewish people to hide than any other organization. However, hiding Jewish people was more

Young Jewish girl in hiding in Utrecht, drinking tea.
Courtesy of the United States Memorial Holocaust
Museum, Washington, D.C.

involved and dangerous than hiding those who were trying to evade forced labor. People willing to take in Jews were hard to come by, and security issues became much more complicated. And so, since assisting the Jews "was thought to present special problems which a mass organization could not handle," the LO often referred Jewish onderduikers to specialty groups.

These humanitarian cells had begun their rescue activities earlier, and some of them concentrated on saving Jewish children. In sharp contrast to the Nazi regime they would attempt to outwit, they were grassroots, informal, and non-hierarchical. There were only a handful of them, none with more than fifteen or twenty members. Three of the main groups of this type were the Utrecht Kindercomité; the Amsterdam Student Group; and the Naamloze Vennootschap (NV).

Among the rescuers profiled in this book, Hetty Voûte, Gisela Söhnlein, and Rut Matthijsen were part of the Utrecht Kindercomité; Piet Meerburg was the cofounder of the Amsterdam Student Group; and Mieke Vermeer was part of the Naamloze Vennootschap (NV).

Because of the secrecy required in the running of such groups, especially the need to avoid keeping written records, there were no doubt other groups that have escaped the attention of historians. For instance, in chapter 6, Kees Veenstra, who had never been interviewed before, speaks about a nature study group for young people that became a rescue group, and yet I have found no mention in the historical literature about the group's secret function.

Whether the rescuers acted independently or as part of a group, they had to play many roles. Hetty Voûte, Gisela Söhnlein, and Kees Veenstra were primarily involved in helping to find safe addresses for the young people, and then transporting them to those addresses. Clara Dijkstra, Heiltje Kooistra, and Janet Kalff all took Jewish children into their own homes, thus providing three such safe addresses. Mieke Vermeer made regular visits to the houses where the children were hiding, bringing the host families food ration coupons and money. Rut Matthijsen helped to raise that money, and Ted Leenders stole large supplies of ration coupons from government offices. Piet Meerburg, as organizer of the Amsterdam Student Group, developed intricate security measures to ensure that the whereabouts of the Jewish children would not be found out, even if he or other members of the group were arrested.

Raul Hilberg writes, "Few Jews survived in Holland, but those few were saved as a result of the most strenuous efforts, for Holland was the one territory of the occupied West in which the Jews did not have an even chance to live." The people profiled in this book were the ones who made those strenuous efforts. All together, they and the other children's rescuers throughout the Netherlands were able to save more than four thousand young lives.

H E T T Y   V O Û T E

Invincible Summer

In the depth of winter,
I finally learned that within me, there lay
an invincible summer.

—ALBERT CAMUS

DESPITE HAVING SPENT NEARLY TWO YEARS in prisons and concentration camps, Hetty Voûte is one of the most cheerful and self-assured people I have ever met. Her self-confidence goes hand in hand with a certain playfulness, and may also be the basis of her dry, no-nonsense, candor. Her very manner seems to be saying, "I'm here; I'm glad; I have no regrets, no apologies, and no need to mince words." She's both tough and tender—sometimes in the same breath.

We met in Amsterdam on a subdued December morning. Hetty lives in an elegant apartment on one of the loveliest streets in the city, just a few blocks from the Anne Frank House. Entering the quiet hallway, I passed a vase of fresh flowers and climbed the softly carpeted stairs to her inlaid oak door. A stooped yet stately woman with a heart-shaped face and hazel eyes, Hetty welcomed me with a warm smile.

As she stepped into the kitchen for a moment, I surveyed her bookshelf filled with literature in Dutch, English, French, and German, and noted some knickknacks and wall hangings that appeared to date back to the war. The room's combination of sophistication and comfort was, I soon learned, emblematic of its owner; Hetty's cosmopolitan manner is interfused with a completely sincere and natural hospitality.

Hetty returned with a pot of coffee, and we spent the afternoon in conversation. Her rich alto voice possesses an easy authority; in the course of a few minutes it can rise to a throaty laugh or lower to a whisper. She took her time answering my questions, pausing whenever she needed to, for as long as she wished. Surely there was a connection between her utter fearlessness during the war, and the sense she projects of being completely comfortable in her own skin.

When describing her wartime experiences, Hetty sometimes uses the word "unbelievable," and yet she takes her own bravery completely for granted. We, on the other hand, looking back at the Holocaust, have grown accustomed to hearing of its grisly extremes. It is Hetty's actions that now seem unbelievable to us.

I am the seventh child of an ordinary Dutch family. I'm from 1918, just at the end of the Great War. I had five brothers and one sister, and I was the youngest. At the time of the war, I was living at home in Utrecht and going to college. We had seen the war coming for several years. One of my brothers worked for the Dutch airline KLM, and he was in Berlin on Kristallnacht. So he knew *exactly* what was going on there.

Then the Germans invaded the Netherlands. It was a blitzkrieg—a lightning offensive—very sudden. After five days of fighting, Dutch boys were coming back with their legs shot off. When one of them said we had capitulated to the Germans, the people wanted to kill him. It was such a deplorable message.

At the beginning the Germans were very civil—you didn't know what to do. They behaved courteously and correctly, and many people thought they were not so bad. Early on, Seyss-Inquart issued a statement saying that he would respect the laws of the Dutch people as much as possible. That's why two of my brothers started an underground newspaper. They wrote things like, "Don't be fooled by them—they say they are here to liberate us, but they are stealing everything out of our shops." Whenever I saw my brothers, their fingers were always black from assembling the news. I learned from those articles what the Nazis were up to, and I decided to throw "the stubborn ounces of my weight" against them. That little poem by Bonaro Overstreet expresses very well how I felt at the time:

You say the little efforts I make
will do no good: they never will prevail
to tip the hovering scale
where Justice hangs in balance.

I don't think
I ever thought they would.
But I am prejudiced beyond debate
in favor of my right to choose which side
shall feel the stubborn ounces of my weight."

At first there wasn't much I could do except to deliver my brothers' illegal newspaper. But I didn't miss an opportunity to mock the Nazis. In college, we had a very nice end-of-the-year dinner, and there was a girl sitting next to me who was a member of the Nazi women's auxiliary. When the appetizer was served, it was just a hard-boiled egg, and she complained about it. I said in a loud voice, "One Führer, One Reich, One Egg." Everybody laughed, and she got up and left. I enjoyed that. Childish stuff, but still . . .

In the fall of 1940, my friend Olga and I moved to Noordwijk, a little village by the sea, in order to do some marine biology research required for our course of study at the university. For this we had to go down to the beach, but the Nazis forbade it unless you had a special pass called a *Strandausweis*. I told them that we needed to go down to the water each day to examine the plankton—that we could tell from the plankton whether the men should go out and fish. That last part was nonsense, but the Nazis cared about the fish supply, so we got our Strandausweis. Every month I had to go to the office of the military commandant to renew it, and that, it turned out, became my entrée into really doing something in the Resistance. You see, there on the wall was a very nice map showing the locations of all the anti-aircraft guns on that strip of land. I'd take a good look at that map, and then report what I had seen to a boy I knew who had a secret radio transmitter. He would then send the information to British intelligence.

As a child, I used to have a Jewish girlfriend who would invite me over to her house on Friday night. I remember the glow of the candles and the marvelous songs her family used to sing after the Sabbath meal. I thought of them on 14 July 1942 when there was a big razzia in Amsterdam. The Nazis sealed off a whole block and went running through with their rifles and Doberman dogs shouting, "All Jews out!" We heard how they broke down doors, barged into houses, and roughed up anyone who got in their way.

Many Jewish people were arrested, but afterwards, there were some children left behind, just wandering the streets. A young woman named Ad Groenendijk went walking through the Jewish Quarter and thought, who is going to care for these little ones? She gathered four or five of them up and brought them to the home of our friend Jan Meulenbelt. His mother immediately said they could stay there until other arrangements were made.

Jan called me and said we had work to do. Up until that point I thought that the war was some kind of a play—very déclassé, you know, very badly acted. But after seeing those children without mothers and fathers, I knew it was all too real. For several months, I'd been helping to find places for Jewish children whose parents had to report for "labor assignments." But this was different: the parents had just been snatched away with no thought given to the children. Very quickly, about ten of us students joined together to try to find hiding places for them.

The Jews had always felt safe in the Netherlands. They lived in a neutral, tolerant country where there hadn't been a war in ages. They were so much a part of Dutch society that you often didn't know who was Jewish and who wasn't. Then when people started disappearing, you thought, "Oh, they must have been Jews." Very strange.

Nobody wanted to believe the worst, so there was a lot of underestimating. Early in '42, I remember suggesting to one couple that they go into hiding, and they said, "No, we're young. If we have to work in Germany, it won't be a picnic, but we'll get through it." But after the razzia, parents would come to us and plead, "Can you hide my children?" You'd say yes, and then they'd say, "And my sister needs help too." And then the sister would have a cousin. So from July '42 on, from early morning 'till late at night, we were busy. But once you started, you simply had to go on. Sometimes I would fetch two or three children in one day, and deliver them far into the country. By the end of August our group had found hiding places for 140 children. But those Jewish parents were unbelievably brave to part with their children. They figured it was the best bet for their children's safety, but, still, you can't believe that they actually gave them to us.

Probably they could tell that our motives were pure. We were just doing it for the children. You can't let children be taken away. There was nothing to be afraid of, we thought. It was all so innocent. Yes, the Germans were always threatening us, but they didn't reach us. It was just the Germans telling you, and you never believed them.

Later we became known as the Utrecht Kindercomité, but when we were actually doing the work, we were just a group of Utrecht students. A tight group we were, however, and it was marvelous being part of that group. We all knew each other, and we trusted each other completely. Each of us had something special. You felt at home; you felt safe. In a way, it was a great time. It was *terrible*, but that was exactly the reason why you could reach heights that would be impossible to reach in everyday life.

Jan Meulenbelt was our leader—he kept everything moving forward, but if people ran too far ahead, he would whistle, and they would stop and listen to him. He really knew how to give a pep talk, and he could be quite persuasive when he wanted to recruit someone into the group.

Once we went to the room of a fellow student named Frits Iordens, who later did everything from rescuing children to organizing an escape route for downed pilots. But at that time, he was studying law, and trying to stick to the books, though he loved to play the piano and violin.

Jan started talking to him about the group, but he said, "Sorry, I came to the university to study, and that's what I'm going to do." But Jan kept on, and after a while Frits sat down at the piano and began to play something really beautiful. I could see that Jan was starting to get to him. Finally, Frits, between piano arpeggios, said, "OK, Jan, I'll do it. I'll do it."

For me, it wasn't really a choice: I knew I had to do it. I never had any second thoughts—if anything, I felt that I needed to do more. I liked taking risks, and I didn't mind getting into something a little dangerous. Some people had the same sympathies as I did, but they were too timid to get involved. And that was all right, for they were not the right people to do it. You had to be a kind of daredevil type, I think. Something like that.

Of course, all kinds of people were needed in the Resistance. There was one German-Jewish student who had taken some art courses in Berlin. She didn't work with us on hiding children, but she was great at falsifying documents. And sometimes doing nothing was doing something. When I was transporting a really Jewish-looking boy or girl, no one on the train said a thing, though they knew exactly what was happening. That was helping with the Resistance too.

Then again, there were people like this one couple—I invited them to join our group and the girl said, "You must look at this in a more astral way. Try to imagine that you are far off in the stars, and that you then look down from there on what goes on here." I had no time to argue. I said, "You can just go burst!" and walked off. Sometimes people would tell me, "The Germans are unstoppable; whatever you do won't matter." I answered, "It will matter to the children that we save."

To find places for the children, I'd just knock on doors. Whenever I saw a big farm, I thought, Oh, they could very easily hide children there. Then I'd ask them if they'd be willing to do it. Most people would say no, sometimes in ridiculous ways. I remember one well-to-do farmer who said, "If it is God's will for the Nazis to catch the Jewish children, then they will catch them." I answered back, rather rudely, "If it's God's will for your barn to burn down tonight, then it will burn down. And your neighbors won't help to put the fire out, either!"

But most people were sympathetic, and at least offered suggestions. For example, there was a blacksmith in Utrecht I knew very well, but he worried that taking in Jewish children would endanger his own children. But he gave me the names of people he thought were reliable. It's something you quickly got a feel for: this one I can trust; this one I can't trust. And if they started asking for money, you never did it.

My father didn't want to know what I was doing, and my mother never asked, though she helped me in everything. After the war, my father told me, "If I had known what you were doing, I would have *locked* you in your *room!*" He didn't dare do anything himself, and that was a shame for him. My sister and brother-in-law, whom I loved very much, thought that what the Germans were doing was despicable, but they were too afraid to do anything. Once or twice they brought children to addresses, but they didn't keep on with it. She said, "Oh, my heart was beating so fast on the train. I don't dare to do it again." I said, "No, you're right. If you don't dare to, please don't. You will do it in the wrong way, so it's better not to do it at all." But they would hide papers and other materials for me, and I could always bring a child to them for a night or two if I had to.

Early in 1943, I began working closely with Gisela Söhnlein, whom I had first met in the fall of '42 when she brought children to us from Amsterdam. In contrast to my dark features and tomboyish ways, Gisela had wavy blonde hair and sparkling blue eyes, and she could be quite a stylish dresser. Still, we hit it off right away. When she moved to Utrecht, she became part of the Kindercomité, and we spent every day finding safe addresses, taking the children there, bringing supplies, faking papers, falsifying everything.

Each month we would go around and pick up the ration cards for the children—that way we could get them bread, butter, sugar, flour, tires for the bicycle, as well as shoes and clothing. Sometimes those cards were counterfeited, but usually we would have to take the papers for each child to one of our contacts working in the distribution offices, and then he would make the changes in identity and address, and give us a ration card for that child. But imagine having to obtain two hundred of these cards a month. . . . When I was arrested and locked in my cell, I thought, "Ahh, at last—rest."

On 11 June 1943, we tried to take action against some people we had trusted who turned out to be "wrong." But we were all such amateurs that it came off rather badly. Soon we had the SD—the German intelligence operation above the Gestapo—searching for us. What did we know about dodging the SD? I was caught the next evening when I went to the train station in Utrecht to pick up my bicycle.

They took me to the local police station and left me under the watch of a Dutch policeman. I knew I had to warn the others, but I didn't know how. I sat there on the hard bench, pouting at the policeman. I said, "I've done nothing wrong, and I can't understand why this has happened. Today is my birthday, 12 June, and I must call my parents. They are waiting for me!" It *was* my birthday; he could see that from my ID. He said, "Oh, no. It's absolutely forbidden . . . if they know it." I said, "They will never know it." Finally he said, "If you go to the next room, you will find a very old-fashioned telephone hanging on the wall."

So I quickly called my brother and said, "I've been arrested by mistake, but perhaps you can do something about it." My mother soon came to the police station and cried, "My poor little baby, my youngest daughter!" I said to her, "Mama, the best thing you can do for me now is to be strong." And that's what she did.

Meanwhile, my brother had passed the news to Jan, and Jan called Gisela and told her to come hide at his place. But on the way over, the SD caught her. Later we were in prison together, and I was *so* glad. Gisela was always laughing and happy—the perfect person to be with in a terrible situation. I don't think I would have made it without her. But with her, it was always fantastic.

When the SD came back, they sat me down at a table beneath the glare of a single light bulb hanging down from a frayed cord. At first they said nice things and did nice things, trying to get what they wanted. The main thing they wanted were the names of the boys: Jan Meulenbelt, Rut Matthijsen, and the others. If they caught them, they would have killed them, so I kept my mouth shut. When I wouldn't talk, they took off my spectacles and began to slap me in the face. I much preferred that to being treated nicely—it made it easier to not give in.

After a while, I started making up a really complicated story—I figured, the crazier it sounded, the more they'd believe it. After most of the night had passed, one of them sat down at a typewriter and said,

"I'm typing out a warrant for the arrest of your parents." I said, "If you think they know more than me, then you must do that." But my legs were shaking under the table. To keep them still, I pressed them up against the wood, but that just made the whole table start shaking, which was even worse. They never did arrest my parents though.

They sent Gisela and me to the dreary prison at Hertogenbosch for a few days, and then to Haaren prison, which was a Catholic seminary that the Nazis had turned into a prison. As I was leaving the police station, someone said, "Oh, you will be away from everyone, and all alone, and it will be awful." I said, "No, it won't be so awful. My brothers have already been through this." Two of my brothers had spent time in a prison, so, as far as I was concerned, it was the thing to do.

When we got to Haaren, I found that it was life also, though a very different kind of life. I heard someone in the cell above mine—a boy up there walking. My cell was quite small, with a window that was all bricked up, but there was still a very tiny opening that let in some light. And there was a sink with running water. I found that if I stood on a ledge, and put my mouth at the place where the vent went through the ceiling, I could speak to the boy in the cell above mine. The problem was that if I heard the guard, I had to immediately jump down. The prisoner in the cell below me must have thought that I was practicing a circus act.

But I was able to talk to the boy above me in this way, and I learned that he was a British paratrooper who had been dropped on the full moon as part of an espionage operation called *Englandspiel*. I thought that was *very* exciting. He told me that he had come to find out about the location of anti-aircraft guns. I told him about my Strandausweis and the map in the Gestapo headquarters, but that didn't do us any good, because I had eaten the Strandausweis, photo and all, soon after I had been arrested!

But we didn't only talk about serious things. He told me about all the latest songs and films from England. Gisela had also made contact with the boy in the cell above her. It was *so* exciting that it didn't even seem like such a bad thing that we were in prison. Of course, we didn't know about the concentration camps and gas chambers, or the full extent of what the Nazis had in store for us. We only knew that we had to resist them in every way we could, and part of that was to not let them get to us. That was where our silly songs came in.

I did a lot of singing with Gisela—it was then that I started to call her Piglet. That's because on the first day of prison, a letter was slipped to me from a boy I knew in another cell. It's a very nice thing when someone welcomes you to prison, and I stuck it on my wall using some moistened bread. He called me Pooh, and he said that he was Christopher Robin. And then right away I named my friend Piglet, and we've been Pooh and Piglet ever since.

When I am nervous I like to sing, so the first day in prison, I started singing. And then Piglet heard me, and she started to sing back to me. She was only a few cells away, and that was the way we would communicate.

I got hold of a little pencil, and I would write letters to Piglet on scraps of paper. Whenever I sent her a letter, there were always three songs we would sing, all Sinterklaas songs. That's the holiday we celebrate a few weeks before Christmas—it's a time when Saint Nicholas comes from far away to bring gifts to all the children. So the moment I gave the letter to my neighbor, I sang "The Boat of Sinterklaas is Coming." And then when he gave it to his neighbor, Piglet would sing, "My Heart is Awaiting It." And then when he gave it to her, she would sing, "Look What I've Got in my Shoe This Morning." So, when I sent a letter to Piglet, I knew *exactly* how long it took for her to get it.

Once, just as I was finishing a letter, one of the guards saw me. He grabbed me and dragged me out of my cell, but he couldn't get it—I ate it. Well, they did get part of it out of my mouth, but they couldn't read it any longer, though they spent hours trying. And then they searched me, but they couldn't find anything. So they made me undress—*that* they enjoyed very much. Meanwhile, Piglet started to sing a children's song. I had, in fact, hidden my little pencil in one of my socks. As I was taking off my socks, I grasped the pencil with my toes, and they never did see it. I was standing there with my clothes in a pile beside me, with Gisela singing, "I'd like to go around the world, and see all kinds of things."

While still in Haaren, I embroidered an old piece of burlap using some yarn I had torn from my sweater. In the center was a little pig and bear behind bars, framed by the words: STAND FAST, MY HEART, IN ADVERSITY. Those were the words we lived by, but later we took up a more personal motto: POOH AND PIGLET ALWAYS TOGETHER.

You see, without her—and, I think, she without me—I don't think we would have made it. We thought exactly the same way. We could always see the humor in a situation, and then it wouldn't be as bad. And, you know, calling each other Piglet and Pooh—that was marvelous. To be Piglet and Pooh is something abstract. You can say, "Pooh feels unhappy." You don't have to say, "I feel unhappy."

The Germans made us feel powerless. To match our wits with them, to do something about that sense of powerlessness, was very attractive. Once I asked for soap and a wash cloth, and instead they interrogated me again. A Nazi officer named Gottschalk said, "You are a Jew. Wash yourself by spitting in your hands." I answered very cooly, "Herr Gottschalk, I have exactly as much Jewish blood as you have." And instead of beating me, he didn't say anything! So I'm sure he had Jewish blood. I had hidden two boys with the last name of Gottschalk, so I guessed he must be Jewish also. From that moment on, I was given things to wash myself. But I learned what it was like to be treated like a Jew. You were humiliated so terribly. I thought, I won't let myself be humiliated.

In prison, the boy above me wanted to break out with another paratrooper who was a few cells down. He asked if I could get him a map of the region, and I immediately began working on it. I love challenges. They make me feel fine, especially when you find that you can't be beaten by them. Whatever happens, you'll always be the master of it. That's the way I was thinking.

On our floor, there were a couple of prisoners who came around to bring us our meals. They gave us a lot of attention, because at that moment we were the only women in the prison. So I told these boys I wanted a map, and one of them was eventually able to get me a *marvelous* map which showed the location of the seminary and all the surrounding villages. I then had the problem of how to get it to that British boy. My bed had iron rails, and when I broke one off, it was sharp. So I used that to scrape a little hole next to the vent going up, and I was able to slide that map right up to him.

Soon afterward, the two of them made their escape, and Gisela and I were immediately suspected of having helped them. The Germans searched our cells, and they saw the hole I had made in the ceiling. For that, they sent both of us to the concentration camp in Vught, in the south of the Netherlands. Meanwhile, those boys were able to make it back to England, though they had a horrendous time.

At the camp in Vught, the Germans made us work in a big tire factory in Den Bosch that they had converted to manufacture gas masks. We had to make gas masks from six in the morning until six at night, and I sat at the end of an assembly line and molded the nose onto each mask. From there, the masks went into a vulcanization oven where they would be baked and come out hard. But I dug my nails into the nose-pieces while they were still soft, so that when they came out, nobody would be able to breathe while wearing one! For that, I was sentenced to the bunker: the prison within the concentration camp.

In the bunker, I sat with the boys who were going to be shot, and they gave me their last letters to their sweethearts and families. Later, I was able to get those letters through. One boy gave me two buttons from his shirt, and I kept them for the whole rest of the war, when I was able to pass them along to his parents, along with my memories of his final hours.

When the Allies came too near, we were crammed into railroad cars and deported to Ravensbrück, a women's concentration camp in Germany about eighty kilometers north of Berlin. They let us out at the nearest station, and as we trudged along toward the camp, I picked some flowers from along the side of the road, thinking they would brighten up our barracks. But Ravensbrück was no place for flowers.

When we got there, it was overfull, so we couldn't go in. They made us sit on a pile of coal for two days and two nights in the rain. Everyone was black and dirty and dripping wet, but still, there was this kind of laughter inside me, as if it couldn't be real, as if we were on another planet.

When we were let in, there was a big street, a *lagerstrasse,* and in the evening you had one hour when you could go walking there. And you heard *all* tongues around you: Russian, Norwegian, Polish, Danish, Hungarian, Romanian, French. At first you just heard voices, but then slowly you started hearing if it was a Hungarian or a Romanian, and then we got to know several of these women, and the Russians sang so beautifully.

The whole time during the war, we kept making up songs. We used tunes that we knew, anything we could think of—folk songs, Charles Trenet, German, English, or Dutch songs. We made up new words, and told the story of what had happened each day. It was a kind of diary all through the camp time. My friend sang a lot, and she sang very well, and I could always, very easily, sing in harmony with her. She would sing high and I would sing low. The moment she started, I quickly made the second voice, and that's the way the two of us would sing.

The sad thing was that very few people sang along with us. It was always a big mass of people being unhappy. There were lots of them who didn't want to sing. They liked us to sing *for* them, but they didn't come along with us on it.

And I can understand. When we came to Ravensbrück, it was like hell—all these skeletons clinging to you because perhaps you had something for them to eat. It was really *unbelievable* when you came in. There were about fifty thousand women in a camp built to hold five thousand. From all nationalities.

I had always wanted to go around the world and meet all kinds of people, and there I thought, I needn't here: I have them all. The Allies were so near that we said, "Two weeks and it will be over." But that is not what happened. We arrived in September of '44, and it wasn't until April of '45 that it ended.

We had to live in dirty barracks with the lice and sleep on hard mattresses filled with a little fetid straw. The thin blankets were never enough, so we would cover ourselves with rags. During the day, many of the women had to do shoveling or other hard labor, but we worked at the Siemens factory, which at least was indoors. For lunch we would get a watery soup with some cabbage in it, and for dinner, more soup and a piece of hard bread. We were always hungry, and cold too—it often snowed during the winter.

But somehow I accepted my fate when I was in the camps. I wasn't arrested for nothing—I had *done* something. I met many Jewish people in Ravensbrück, and we had exactly the same life. But for them, it was much worse. They were being destroyed solely because they were Jews.

And that was awful! There were lots of them who died there. In December '44 they installed gas chambers, and each week, all the old women who could not work any longer were put onto trucks and taken away. Then on Sunday night, the others waited for us to sing for them. We thought, we can't do it. But then we thought, we have to. One must simply go on.

I got a terrible ear infection in Ravensbrück, and Piglet—this is Gisela—always managed to get a little scrap of a letter to me in the infirmary. Those letters were marvelous. I want someone to tell me, why are they so moving? I still have them, and whenever I read them now, I always start to cry. She would write, "It's my mother's birthday today, and I've been singing her favorite songs the whole day long. Come with me to the woods and we'll kick through the leaves . . ."—always things like that, you know? She somehow managed to get them to the Dutch nurse in the infirmary, who would then slip them to me.

So we had all kinds of ways of getting through: the singing, the letters . . . Did you know you can make dominoes from bread? And if you want to sew, tear the threads from your clothes. My friend once had a Sinterklaas present made for me by the Polish women, who were very good at sewing. You had to pay them with bread to do something like that.

There was a group of Greek partisans who had fought in Albania together with the English army. They were arrested and had been sent a long way by train to Ravensbrück. They spoke some French, and we did too, so we would sit around at night telling stories as we picked lice from each other's hair. We had lovely conversations, and when we talk now with other women who had also been in Ravensbrück, their experience was so entirely different from ours. They only know about rain and dirtiness, and we only know about the *exciting* stories that we heard there.

Yes, our morale was higher than many of the other prisoners, but we were just young and bold with no responsibilities. There were a lot of Communist women there whose husbands had already been shot. There were so many who already had such sad things behind them. But we were just sorority girls. It was *easy* for us to live through it. Because of our good spirits, we were able to cheer up other people. And that makes *you* feel better, for you can't cheer someone up without being cheered up yourself. It's not that we had a good time there, but it was a very *special* time. You can never compare it with ordinary life because it brought you to the limits of what you could endure . . . and still there was a song to sing.

Each morning and evening we would line up for the Appell. We had to stand at attention for hours in the cold as they called out our numbers. Someone would be missing, and they would kick us, and hit us, and start all over again. Then one day I looked up and saw a gull winging across the sky. Unbelievable! Where did it come from? Where did it go? To see that gull with the sun on its wings . . . it was like a vision of another world. For truly in Ravensbrück you had the impression that you were no longer on this earth.

Toward the end, the Germans knew they were going to be defeated, and all their devils broke loose. They stopped feeding us, and day and night they were burning the dead bodies. I shared a bunk bed with four other women, and when I woke up one morning, the Hungarian girl who had been sleeping next to me was dead. The worst of it was that you didn't really react any more—you just said, "Oh, she's dead."

At the beginning, we didn't think that we ourselves would turn into skeletons—but we had. I thought, it's a pity for my parents. It will be hard on them if I die, but Gisela kept believing that everything would be all right. That really helped me.

We were liberated on 28 April 1945 through an arrangement that Folke Bernadotte, the Swedish diplomat, made with the Germans. It was incredible; absolutely incredible. A Red Cross official who came into the camp talked to us, and it was so fantastic to have someone talk to you like a human being. We were given fresh bread and lentil soup, and there were doctors on hand to take care of us. I didn't have the most urgent need, although I weighed just less than forty kilos—that's eighty-eight pounds! Then we were taken to Sweden by van and railroad and ferry.

When the ferryboat arrived in Malmö, we hobbled down the gangplanks, squinting with delight in the springtime Swedish sun. Despite our exhaustion, we smiled and waved at the welcoming party of Red Cross workers, and soon were plying them with questions. "How long will we be here?" "Can we contact our families?" "Is the war really over?" When someone asked, "Will we get a hot bath with soap?" the answer, incredibly, was yes. We learned that there was still a bad food shortage in the Netherlands, so we wouldn't be returning home anytime soon. Many people coming out of the camps had tuberculosis, and I found out that I was one of them. So I had to part with all my friends, and go away to a sanatorium near Stockholm.

It took a long time before I could accept that life should go on. Everything was all clean and white with Swedish nuns in their starched caps coming in to adjust your pillow. But it all seemed make-believe somehow, and when I looked in the mirror, I hardly recognized myself. When I really had to think about something, I thought myself back into the concentration camp. That seemed more real to me than freedom.

It was hard to be apart from Gisela, but I thought, I might as well make the best of it, since my recovery will take a long time. They gave me a dictionary and some books, and I thought, here's an opportunity: I'll learn Swedish. I was in my bed all day, so there was also time to knit things for all my little nephews and nieces who were born in the meantime. I had a strong will to live, so it was not so difficult.

There was no communication between Sweden and Holland for months, and no one was traveling back and forth. At the end of August '45, the first camp survivors began to return, and by that time my family knew I was alive because I had a nephew who went to the Dutch embassy in Stockholm, and he saw my name on a list of Dutch women who had been liberated from Ravensbrück.

Sometimes you felt guilty when you were with someone who had lost a husband, or a child, or parents, or everyone. More than ninety thousand women perished in Ravensbrück, so you'd ask yourself, why did I survive? Over the course of the war, two of my brothers were arrested and sent to the camps. One had been in the Dutch East Indies, and ended up in a Japanese camp. My other brother who was doing espionage was caught halfway across the North Sea on his way to England, and sent straight to a German camp. We all came out of the war alive, so we were very lucky. But you'd ask yourself, why is my family so well off?

That same nephew who told my parents that I had come out of Ravensbrück returned to the Netherlands to find that all his brothers had been killed. That's how life was then. But I don't really feel guilty over having survived. I'm glad about it. It could have been quite different. Often I think each day is a present.

By the time I made it back to the Netherlands to live, it was April of '46. In a way, I had forgotten about my old life. When the war started I was twenty-two, and by the time I returned I was twenty-eight. But it wasn't until I got home and started looking around that I realized how many years I had lost. I planned to finish my education, but then I met a very handsome young man who had been in the Japanese camps. I thought, well, I'm not going to get involved right now; I need to concentrate on my studies. You see, he was soon going to leave for the Dutch East Indies, and he wanted me to come with him. But when I went back to college, I found I was not able to read the books anymore. It was too abstract, too small. I just couldn't relate to it.

Meanwhile his passage to the Dutch East Indies was delayed for three months, and then for another three months. After that time I thought, well, it could be great to live with him in the Dutch East Indies, so we got married and soon afterwards set sail for the Malay Archipelago. And that was very exciting, for the people there wanted to be free, and our country was telling them that they were not ready for it. So they began to fight for their freedom. I was on their side, although most people said, "It's our country, and we made it great, so it should remain our property." But I knew what it was like to not have your freedom, and that's what they had been going through for ages.

While in the Dutch East Indies, we had four children, one after another, and I thought being a mother was *marvelous*. By the time our youngest was born, the native people had won their struggle and the country was renamed Indonesia. However, a chasm began to develop between my husband and me, even though he and the children were my whole life at that time. You see, I had stopped talking about what had happened to me during the war. At my final medical checkup before I left for the Dutch East Indies, my doctor had said, "Forget about all that as fast as you can." So as I closed the door behind me to leave his office, I also closed the door of my memory. But later the memories started returning, and I couldn't keep them back.

For my husband, however, it was an obsession *not* to talk about what happened. I began to realize that he had been much more wounded in the camps than I had. You could never say a single word—he did not want to hear it, and he would never speak of it. But as the children got older, I simply *had* to discuss it with them. To not be allowed to do so was very difficult, and, in the end, we went our separate ways.

I can see now, through the prism of experience, that he was absolutely right to find another woman. There was so much I wanted to talk about, and he was just shutting down more and more. I think that now I would understand him much better. Perhaps I should have handled it differently, but I didn't know enough then. Kierkegaard said that life must be lived forward, but can only be understood backward, and that's true.

The Germans put you through so much. How do you feel about them now?

For a long time I was very angry, but now . . . I always tell people, "I read as many German books as English books, and I love German literature and poetry." But an old kind of feeling sometimes comes over me. When we were going on holiday and our train had to stop in Frankfurt, a German lady started talking to my youngest son. It was as if she were somebody from the camps, and I felt so sick that I threw up. And sometimes if I'm on the highway and there's a German driving too close behind me, I have to pull over to the side of the road to calm down. It's something I can't master, that feeling.

But, for some reason, when I think back to the war, it never makes me feel bad. I've never even had a nightmare. Sometimes I think I'm not a deep-feeler, or something. I don't know.

I'd have to say I'm happy, but what is happiness? Cows are happy. During the war, we were happy because we did something. I think that if we had not done what we did, we would have been unhappy about it our entire lives. My grandchildren say, "We don't know if we would have done the same." Yes, but we had a *chance* to do something!

Overall, our group saved nearly four hundred children. Many more, of course, needed our help, but you simply did all you were able, and you couldn't stop with it. It was work—hard work. Also, the families who took in the children needed help to be able to afford the additional expense. So I would go around begging for money.

Hetty Voûte as an older person. Courtesy of the Ghetto Fighters' House (Beit Lohamei HaGetaot).

I think it's true that many Dutch people don't want to talk about the war because they are ashamed of how they acted—or rather, didn't act. When I came back in '46 I knew a lot of people who were absolutely not interested in hearing my stories. Looking back, I think they may have been uneasy over not having done anything. And I can understand—the ghosts of their choices must have haunted them.

And then there were the people who believed that if you did the right things in life, all would be well with you. When they heard that the Jews were in trouble, they thought they must have done something. That's a foolish, foolish way of thinking. But that is the way a lot of people thought, and that's the curse for the Jews: they always say it's their own fault. And that goes back to the original accusation that the Jews killed Christ, and the way that was used as a justification for killing the Jews. And that's what Christianity has done. It's terrible—all through the ages! Terrible!

I was brought up Remonstrant—it's a very free-thinking Protestant belief that goes back to the 1600s. And Gisela, my friend, was nothing. Atheist, absolutely nothing. When we were growing up, my mother always read to us from the Bible. I'm very at home with it—such wonderful stories. In prison I was able to have a Bible. Once while I was there, I sent Piglet a letter in which I quoted many things from it. She wrote back, "That's all well and good, but everybody already knows it, and you didn't have to get it out of the Bible." Still, when we were liberated from Ravensbrück, the official who talked to us also blessed us at the end, and we both liked that very much.

I think it's marvelous to have real faith, but I can believe no longer. Not a sad thing, but it's simply the way it is. I must say though that sometimes I have prayed very deeply, because it helped me. Yet I knew there was no one there, at least not in the way that some believers imagine. Take the Roman Catholics: they kneel before their saints and light candles and such. Marvelous if you believe in it, but to me it's all superstition. Never mind though—it's beautiful. Were you raised up with the Bible?

A little bit. My grandparents were religious Jews, but my father lost any faith he may have had because of the Holocaust.

I can understand.

He thought that if there was a God, He wouldn't have allowed it.

Yes, but what is your conception of God? I once had a friend who came to me and said, "I've lost my faith in God." After she explained, I said, "Oh, I haven't believed in *that* God for years." I think it's so terribly difficult to know what God is. What do you want from God? Is He responsible? Where is He? Inside you, I think.

So many people went along with what the Nazis were doing. How did you grow up to be a person who defied them?

I think that both of my parents were rather independent. They were never impressed by what other people said. They always went their own way and thought their own thoughts, and that's the way they raised us. My father took a strong stand on certain community issues. He didn't care what kind of flak he got. And when I went to school, I was the same way.

I think my family was an important factor in my being able to face the camps the way I did. I had a marvelous youth. I had a strong mother, and a very special father. And five brothers and a sister. We really had a fantastic home. The same was true of my friend Gisela—we both came from happy families.

It occurred to me to ask Hetty whether her parents had taken in any malnourished German and Austrian children following World War I. Miep Gies, who was one of the hungry little girls sent to the Netherlands through this humanitarian program, speaks of it as a crucial factor in her later decision to help Anne Frank and her family. The experience taught her that one can be "a good little girl" and still suffer for no reason at all, and also that there are people who understand, care, and are willing to help. When I mentioned the post-World War I program to Hetty, her face lit up.

Oh, yes, we had them. For years after the Great War, there were little girls who came, and they became our friends. I was still very small, but sometimes my mother would tell me that a train was coming with starved little girls and boys, and that they would go to a big room, and Mother would get to choose which one she wanted to take home with her. She would tell us a story about how she once went up to a small, black-haired girl, and asked, "Do you like playing with dolls?" She shook her head no. "Do you like to embroider?" "No," the girl said with a pout. "How about cooking?" "No!"—this time she spoke up. Then my mother said, "You are *exactly* like my own children— come home with me." And that little girl became a great friend of ours, and, afterwards, her family also came to this country, and we had other girls as well. Yes, we often had children come like that. They would stay for months. There were already seven of us—one or two more made no difference.

And that's the way it always was in my family. When somebody needed help, we would help them. In those days, there were no real social services; it always came down to someone helping in a very personal way. I remember that there were several families nearby with hardly any money. Every weekend my mother would say, "You just take these envelopes, and go there, and there, and there." And when Sinterklaas came, we were always preparing baskets of food, and we would bring them around to those people. It was just something I grew up with.

Later, all my brothers were involved in the Resistance, but I didn't realize how unusual that was. After the war, someone told me that only a few people had been working against the Germans. I said, "That's nonsense. Wasn't everybody doing it?"

What kinds of activities are you involved with these days?

I run a foundation with my children to help Icelandic horses. These beautiful horses are brought here and kept all cooped up, which offends them, for they need a lot of space. So then they become bad-tempered, and the owners castrate them to make them less aggressive. My children and I worked it out with the minister of agriculture to use certain grasslands, so now the young foals can run free, and they're very happy. If they're not confined when they're young, they'll be fine after that, so we keep them for four years, and then return them to their owners.

We also have a special tract of land for the retired horses. They can spend their old age there after they're no good anymore for riding or competition. They just canter about and have a lovely time playing together. It's *marvelous* to watch them. Icelandic horses come in so many different colors: chestnut, bay, palomino buckskin, smoky black, silver dapple, blue dun. At first, people said, "If I give you my horse, I'll never be able to get my hands on him again!" But that's absolutely not true. These horses only don't like people when they're forced to be around people all the time. Once you let them run free, they'll come up to you and be very friendly. It's people who make them nasty—as we always find everywhere.

I am also helping Beit Lohamei HaGetaot, the Ghetto Fighters' House in Israel, to create a Dutch exhibit. Some time ago, a lady phoned me and said, "For so long I've been looking for you, and at last I have found you!" I said, "I think you have a nice bright voice, but I haven't the faintest idea who you are." And then she came to visit, and I opened the door and she said, "Oh, exactly the same eyes!" She walked into this room, and said, "Don't you remember? You were standing under the clock at the Amstelstation and I gave you my two little children—a boy and a girl." I said, "I stood so often under the clock at the Amstelstation." But as we talked, her situation slowly came back to me.

She told me how the people who had escaped from the ghettos and camps in Poland went to Israel and formed a kibbutz in the Western Galilee. When they were still in the ghetto, they had promised each other that those who survived would preserve all the things they had made and written—diaries, paintings, knitting, everything. So in 1949 they built the first Holocaust museum. But it was only about the people of Eastern Europe, and this woman, who is from Holland and spent time in a camp, thought it should include the Dutch too. She asked if I would get involved, and we started to do it together. Many of my things will be on display, like that embroidery of Piglet and Pooh.

There was an unveiling recently of a very special stained glass window that was installed at a church in Vught. The window symbolizes the solidarity between the women who were in the concentration camp there. You see one woman lying on the ground, and the other ones helping her to get up. It's a beautiful window, and when it was first shown they had a program that included music that had been sung in the camps. A choir sang some of the songs that Gisela and I had made up. My granddaughter was there, and it was very emotional for her. For the first time she could picture how life was when I was a young woman, as she is now.

People say, "Never again," but how can we prevent something as terrible as the Holocaust from repeating itself?

It already has. Not on the same scale, but we've already seen the Khmer Rouge regime massacre its own people in Cambodia, the Iraqis gas the Kurds, the Serbs in Bosnia butcher the Muslims. We've seen the continuing slaughter of the Tibetans by the Chinese. And just a short time ago, the Hutus in Rwanda took up their machetes, and hacked almost a million Tutsis to death! Who was willing to do something about it?

Recently I was asked to speak at a college in Israel. In the audience there were both Jewish and Arab students, and at the end an Arab boy raised his hand and asked, "Would you have helped my people if they were in trouble?" And I told him that at that time it was the Jews who needed the help. If it had been another group, I think I would have helped them also. You can't let people be treated in an inhuman way around you.

So you're saying that we must stand up for those who are being persecuted, whoever they are.

Otherwise *you* start to become inhuman. It's a simple notion, but people tend to care only about their own people, don't they?

Yes, and it saddens me. . . . So, if I, as a Jewish person, say, "Never again," thinking only of the Jews, I am part of the problem. I probably won't take action on behalf of other groups.

Yes, and one group alone might not be strong enough to protect themselves from a bad situation; everything depends on their getting help from the others.

Any other ideas as to how we can help bring about peace and justice in the world?

I think only by being an example yourself. That's the only way to teach anybody anything. . . . Shall I make you a bowl of soup?

LIKE ALL CHILDREN of those who barely escaped the Holocaust, I have often asked myself the "what if" questions, such as: What if my father and his family hadn't made it onto the ship that took them out of Poland? When considered deeply enough, these questions become as confounding as Zen koans. For me, they also summon up the few shards of pre-Holocaust family history to which I've been privy.

My father once told me that after they left Glowaczow, just a few days before their departure on the ocean liner *M. S. Batory,* the cousin they were staying with in Warsaw tried to persuade the family to remain another week. "It will be so long before we see each other again," she pleaded. "Why not take the next ship?" My father, only a boy at the time, insisted that the family stick to their plan. According to the YIVO Institute for Jewish Research, no further passenger ships left Poland until nearly six years later. By then, nine out of ten of Poland's 3.3 million Jews had been murdered.

My father has enjoyed a full and comfortable life over these last six decades. But without that ship, his life would have ended in another era, in another country. It would have ended before he learned to speak English, before he worked in the clothing store with my grandfather,

Hetty and Gisela in Sweden after the liberation.
Courtesy of Gisela Söhnlein personal collection.

before he enlisted in the U.S. Army to go back to Europe and fight the Germans. It would have ended before he went to Brooklyn College on the G.I. bill, before he met my mother there, before my sister and I were born. If not for that ship, he would have suffered exactly the same fate as all my other relatives in Poland.

Or maybe, just maybe, he would have met up with someone like Hetty or Gisela . . .

two

HEILTJE KOOISTRA

Faith Like a Rock

Whomever the Lord has adopted and deemed worthy
of His fellowship ought to prepare themselves for a hard,
toilsome, and unquiet life, crammed with very many and various
kinds of evil. It is the Heavenly Father's will thus to exercise
them so as to put His own children to a definite test.

—JOHN CALVIN

TO FULLY UNDERSTAND HEILTJE KOOISTRA'S NARRATIVE, some background is needed about the "hunger winter"—the period towards the end of the war when the Nazis reduced, and then cut off, the food supply to those 4.5 million Dutch still under their control.

Early in the occupation, the Nazis issued ration coupons that the Dutch had to present when purchasing food. Though they appropriated all the choice foods, the rations were still considered adequate for nutrition, if not for taste. By November 1944, however, they lowered the rations to one thousand grams per person, or just over two pounds per week. The result was widespread undernourishment, especially in the densely populated cities of Amsterdam, Utrecht, and Rotterdam where people did not have gardens or livestock. Processions of hungry people began journeying into the farmlands to beg or barter food directly from farmers.

In December 1944, the ration was decreased to five hundred grams per person, per week. "So this at last is the phantom of starvation," read a newspaper article in De Telegraaf. "It attacks unexpectedly, in a cool and businesslike manner. Older people feel it first in their hearts, for they see that their children are hungry, really hungry, and there is no remedy." A later article evoked the eerie silence that had fallen over the cities: "Those who are hungry shout, but those who are starving keep still. The traffic has stopped, all enterprises are paralyzed. Footsteps are smothered by the thick snow and this immense silence is penetrated by one single thought: that of the daily bread which is lacking."

By February 1945, the ration had been lowered further to a life-threatening 350 calories a day. Before Red Cross packages and U.S. food drops brought relief in early May, more than eighteen thousand Dutch people had starved to death.

I first heard about Heiltje Kooistra from her friend Hetty Voûte, who told me that I must talk with her. At the time of the Nazi occupation, Heiltje and her husband Wopke lived with their three young daughters in a small house in Utrecht, a house that soon became the scene of much secret activity. Now in her eighties, Heiltje still lives in that same small house on the same quiet street.

She came to the door smelling of soap and rosewater, a tall woman in a vivid blue dress. Her face was broad, without any sharp angles or gauntness, and her hands, as she offered them to me in greeting, were plump and soft. My first impression was that of a sturdy woman who was also very gentle.

As she told her stories, Heiltje seemed, at first, to be all about practicality, but a different side came out when she recounted the fun she and her husband used to have with their secret guests after the day was done. And something extraordinarily different emerged when she began to speak about her religious beliefs, and how these came to bear on her rescue activities.

As I was leaving the house, she showed me a book by Clara Asscher-Pinkof, a widely read Dutch author who survived the Holocaust and later wrote about her experiences. This book, *Star Children,* is about the Jewish children of Amsterdam, most of whom did not live to see the liberation. Heiltje opened the thin volume to an epigram: "If you trust deeply in God, you can draw to yourself a miracle." Below, the author had written, "Wopke and Heiltje have brought a miracle close at hand." In the story that follows, Heiltje reveals something of the contours of that miracle.

As soon as the Germans occupied our country, my husband began resisting. He was from the province of Friesland, and the Frisians are legendary for standing up against tyranny. They've always been resisting—whether it was the Spaniards, or the Saxons, or all the way back to the Roman invasion by Julius Caesar. True to his roots, he refused to submit, and he held very strong convictions about how people should be treated.

He actually started a resistance movement here. He recruited people by scrawling messages on the sidewalk. I didn't know everything that he was doing—it was better for me not to—but when the Nazis started rounding up the Jews, the caretaker of the local synagogue gave him some addresses of Jewish children and adults who needed to dive under. After that, he went out into the farmlands and tried to locate households where these people could go and hide.

One night he came home downhearted, and said, "No matter how much I talk, they always ask if *I* have taken in any Jewish people. And when I tell them no, I don't get anywhere." I said, "Maybe we should try it ourselves—that would convince them." He agreed, and that's the way it started.

We decided to take in a friend of some friends: a diamond cutter from Amsterdam. Our friends couldn't take him themselves because they lived in the back of a store, and there were too many people coming in and out. Still, our house was not ideal: we shared a wall with our neighbors, and everyone knew everyone on this street. But we said we would be glad to meet him. Immediately, it sort of clicked. It has to click somehow; otherwise you'll never be able to get along with someone in the long run.

After we had taken in this Jewish man, my husband had more success finding safe addresses for the other people on the list. Then, a few months later, a doctor who lived in a nearby village told us about a certain couple who were roaming around in the countryside with their possessions on their backs. Could we help them? We told him he could give them our address, and they eventually made their way to us. They looked very tired, and they smelled of manure from having hidden in a pasture for a couple of days. Their clothes were rumpled, and they still had pieces of straw in their hair from having slept in a haystack. We had only expected two, but they had a daughter also—a thin girl with watery blue eyes, and a wan face.

Now that we had four onderduikers in the house, we became very vigilant. It was always, "What was that sound?" "Who's at the door?" We constantly had to consider how things looked from the outside. Across the street was a butcher, and he had customers all day long—anything suspicious would surely have been noticed.

Sometimes, when the onderduikers needed to come out of their rooms to take a break, we would put a sign on the front door that said DIPHTHERIA. This was because the Germans were very afraid to enter any house where someone had an infectious disease. Then we took the girl, who was very frail and pale, and sat her by the front window. She was our poster child to show that there really *was* sickness in the house.

The onderduikers had to stay inside all the time, except, once a day, one of them could go down to the cellar to listen to the broadcast of Radio Orange from England. They could never, ever, go out on the street. My husband was extremely strict about that.

It was forbidden to have a radio, and you could get into even more trouble if you were caught listening to the BBC. So we kept the radio in the cellar, and each afternoon at four o'clock one of the onderduikers would open the trapdoor and climb down there. The ten-minute Radio Orange broadcast was all crackly, but it meant a lot to us to be able to get news from the world beyond Nazi control.

Once, the neighbor's child was ill and a doctor had come over to make a house call. When he was finished, he left from the back, and just as he was walking along the side of our house, one of the onderduikers raised the trap door, and climbed out of the cellar! I saw the doctor take a look at him, and then stride away. What should I do?

I went running after that doctor. I didn't know what to say, because by saying anything I'd already be taking a dreadful risk. But if I didn't speak to him, I'd never know whether he could be trusted. He turned around, gripping his black leather bag, and fixed me with his deep-set eyes. "My, my, what a doctor sees. I see so much." Then he walked away. It was horrible.

We had a few sleepless nights, but, in the end, nothing happened. I later realized he was trying to reassure me, but he couldn't say anything either. Those unexpected crises were the most trying, and they would happen quite often.

A few months after we had taken in the couple with the straw in their hair, we decided to take in another couple. We had learned so much about the plight of the Jews from this first family that we felt that we had to do more. This time my husband went by train to meet our new arrivals at the Amsterdam Central Station. Again, he expected two, but he found they had a son and daughter. He said, "We only have room for two adults." The mother started to cry so hard that Wopke said, "Don't worry. We'll start out with you and your daughter, and your husband and son can come later." And that's what happened.

Occasionally we thought that perhaps we were taking in too many, but everything went fairly well. Their daughter Ellis called this the "chewing gum house," because you could always stretch more people into it. So eventually we had two families, plus the first man, plus myself and my husband. And our three children—but they never knew.

Even Hetty Voûte doesn't understand how we could have kept the onderduikers a secret from our daughters, but we did. Part of it was the precautions we took. No matter what room they were in, the onderduikers always kept the doors latched from the inside with hooks and eyebolts. And, of course, they had to keep very, very quiet.

The children were never supposed to see the onderduikers, and they didn't know about them for three years. I think our eldest daughter saw someone on the stairwell once, and she may have heard things in the house. But she wasn't eager to solve the mystery—I think she liked to fantasize about what might be going on.

Some people have suggested that there was a tacit understanding among the girls that this was not something they could speak about. Or that maybe they thought that if we *knew* they knew, it would worry us, and then we might ask the onderduikers to leave. Well, that may have been true in some households, but not in ours. Only by living here could you fully understand what our arrangement was like.

I must admit that it wasn't very good for my children. For instance, they all had to sleep in one small room on one mattress. At night, we would put a chamber pot in the room, and lock them in. If one of them needed us, she would have to bang on the door, and then I would get up and unlock it—after I made sure that the hallway was clear.

At six in the morning, the onderduikers who were upstairs—in the front room and the back room—would go downstairs to the room off of the hallway and spend the rest of the day there. That was where the family of three slept—they called it their Hilton. The three people who had had to sleep on chairs would then go into our bed so that they would be able to rest properly on a real mattress. (They used to tie chairs together and put a board between them to get a little bit of length.) In the upstairs back room was the family with the two children. The parents slept in a daybed that was uncomfortable, so they too would go into my bedroom later in the day to rest. It was a little like a game of musical chairs every day, only with beds.

In the downstairs hallway there were three doors: the room where the onderduikers would be during the day, the door to the kitchen, and the door to the toilet. Every Saturday my father would come to visit. Once he was heading for the toilet and, by mistake, he opened the door where the onderduikers were. There were eight people sitting around a table! He immediately closed the door, and acted as if he hadn't seen anything.

After he left, I went into the room and visited the people. Their faces were so long that you could have slipped them through a letter slot. When they told me what had happened, I was sure my father would never say a word. But I was sorry that he knew about it, because now he would worry about us. In those days, knowing such things could be a very heavy burden. After the war, he told me that he had understood immediately that they were onderduikers. Later we learned that where he was living—with my sister and her husband on their farm—they also had hidden three Jewish people. So, you see, everyone was very secretive about what they were doing.

Once, during the war, a woman I knew came to the door and asked very nervously if we might possibly take in an onderduiker. I said that we didn't have any room, since the house was so small. I just stood there and said that, not able to explain that there were already three people hiding in the front of the house, and five people stashed in the back!

You might think it was a lot of work to take care of eight extra people. But the onderduikers pitched in: the women did a lot of sewing, and they would knit and crochet using yarn from old sweaters that they dyed to look like new. They all helped with the cooking—peeling potatoes, cutting vegetables—and also with the mending: for instance, the diamond cutter would fix the children's shoes.

There was a heater in the back room, and in the winter, after our children had been playing outside, I would take them into that back room to warm up. The onderduikers in that room knew when the children were coming, and they would crouch under the table, which had a tablecloth that reached almost to the floor. So they would just stay under there and keep really quiet while the children came in to warm themselves. The onderduikers loved that little bit of contact—they were very, very excited to have the children come in. And the children would be dressed in the clothes that the onderduikers had made for them. They all delighted in seeing the children gambol about in those gay clothes.

It would have been very hard to get enough food for everybody, but in addition to our own food coupons, the Resistance gave us food coupons that they had spirited away from the civic offices. There was also a gentleman from Amsterdam who always brought over food coupons for the family of four. Most days we would put potatoes onto the stove at two o'clock in the afternoon, and when the food was ready, we would eat in shifts. Then at the end of the night, I piled up the dishes in the sink, and two of the onderduikers would come out of their room and wash them.

Once the children were asleep, the onderduikers all came out and we'd sit around downstairs and talk about everything under the sun. Often we'd discuss the Bible passages that Wopke had read to them earlier in the day—it was part of his routine to slip into the back room before the children got home from school and read them something from the Old Testament. So in the evenings, we had some great conversations about Abraham and Sarah, Joseph, Moses, Daniel, and the way God works in the world.

At other times, we were more frivolous: I remember a night when we talked about nothing but food and cooking. One of the women told us about a cake recipe that called for a dozen eggs! We were tantalized beyond belief to hear her description of the fluffy whipped egg whites and layers of chocolate, topped with powdery sugar.

We all used to tell stories, but especially my husband. He would tell tall tales, and could really plop it on. One of the men used to sell cigars, and the other one had also been a salesman. Together they had an endless supply of traveling salesman jokes. I can't remember ever laughing so hard as during those evenings. We would all sit there and just shake with laughter until Wop would make us quiet down. Or he'd play really loud on the barrel organ to cover up the sound. My husband was a very good musician. He would play some lively tunes, especially on evenings when we really needed to laugh out loud.

We kept our spirits up mostly through positive thinking. The onderduikers had so many worries, and being cooped up all day didn't help any. We all had to deal with quite a bit of doom and gloom, and there were some very hard periods. If you didn't think positively, if you didn't convince yourself that you were going to make it, then it was almost impossible to keep on.

Towards the end of '44, we had the "hunger winter." We didn't know it would only last for the winter; it slowly closed in upon us and after a while we couldn't imagine not living in hunger. Things hadn't gone well for the Allies at the Battle of Arnhem, and, though the south would soon be liberated, the land where we were—north of the great Rhine and Waal rivers—remained under tight German control. By that time, my husband couldn't show his face on the street anymore because of the forced labor roundups and his connections with the Resistance, so he was hiding in the house also. Not only was food scarce, but there was no coal, and you couldn't get wood, so it was very difficult to stay warm, let alone to cook.

I would go on my bicycle to other villages and bring back milk and eggs. When these were no longer available, we ate sugar beets and tulip bulbs. But the day came when we had no food at all. We didn't want to worry the onderduikers with this grave news, but finally my husband asked all of them to come sit around the table. "We really don't have anything to eat anymore," he said. Of course, when you have news like that, there's always someone who caves in completely. I looked around at the downcast faces and said, "We may not have food, but there's still plenty of water. If we had no water, then we'd really be in trouble."

After the war, Ellis' mother would say, "When I had completely lost hope, you'd always say something to make me feel better." I'm convinced that that power didn't come from me—it came from God. It was He that made me say, "Think about it: there's still water!"

I had other moments when I felt God put words in my mouth. Once I was hanging the wash out in the backyard, and my neighbor came over to talk to me. She was a very nosy person, and it was lucky that we had not become overly familiar before the war because if she had gotten into the habit of coming over here unannounced, it would have made life impossible. I usually did the laundry in dribs and drabs, but I must not have been thinking clearly that day, for I had washed quite a large quantity. Well, this neighbor made a comment about it. Without hesitating for a moment, I said, "Oh, yah, well, I am doing the laundry for my sister, because she lives on a farm, and if I do the laundry for her family and the hired hands, they give us cheese and butter." I said just the right thing, though it was a tricky situation. I had never thought of myself as a liar before. Yet, statements like that just came to me, and I am convinced that they came from above. It sounds a little odd to talk about divinely inspired lies, but I believe that's exactly what they were.

The Germans never did discover what was going on in our house. On the corner lived an NSBer, a collaborator. We benefited quite a bit from this man because he always knew when the house searches were going to take place. Next door to him there was a family with six boys, and they were always roaming the neighborhood talking to everyone. So we would hear from them when the next house search was happening, and then we'd get busy preparing for it.

I would stuff all eight people, plus my husband, under the hallway floor. It was my husband they were especially after, because he was on their wanted list. But if they also found some Jews, that would be all the better. So I'd pack everyone under the hallway, in a space my husband and one of the onderduikers had dug out. It had sewage pipes running through it that provided a nice place to sit, though they could break with too much weight.

Once during a house search, one of the onderduikers couldn't handle the tension. He started to have a nervous breakdown right there in the hiding place. It didn't help that it was so dark, with everyone crammed in like sardines. My husband said, "If you won't be quiet right now, I'll have to choke you to death." He would have done it, too, for it would be better to give up the life of one person and save the rest, than to have everybody get caught. Anyway, it worked—the man suddenly snapped out of it.

And so, I have to give credit to the strict discipline of my husband. He was very strict with himself, but also with the others. Without that, tragedy would have surely struck. It was like a standard of safety that everyone had to follow. Our lives were all connected, and we depended on each other in no uncertain terms.

It would have been very difficult if any of the onderduikers had become pregnant, but thankfully I was the only one to conceive during the war. I know just when it happened, too: *Dolle Dinsdag*—"Crazy Tuesday," which was 5 September 1944. When the Allies landed in the south, the Germans fled eastward, and we mistakenly thought that the area below the great rivers had been liberated. Rumors circulated that the wave of liberation would soon reach us here in the north. None of it was true, but there were many babies who were born nine months later, just after V-E Day.

I sometimes think back to those last months of the war, and wonder how I was able to manage. I used to do the laundry outside in the cold of winter! *That* was really impossible—kneeling with my knees in the snow, scrubbing and wringing things out. But after the war ended, we were "sitting in roses," as we say here in Holland. Everyone made it through, and our son was born healthy and strong—a crown on the work we had done. We felt that everything had been accomplished.

❦

Why did you help the Jews? What was behind it?

We respected the Jewish people, that's why. I feel a bond with the Jewish people because Jesus himself was Jewish. If you love Jesus, how can you not love the people and tradition out of which Jesus came forth? You can't be a Christian if you don't honor the Jews, for Judaism is the root of the Christian religion. Also, my father traded a lot with Jewish people, and they used to come around our house quite often. He was a farmer, but he also traded. My grandfather went to many Jewish weddings and funerals; he had many Jewish friends. So I was raised with a love for the Jews.

Would I have done the same for another group? One helps where there is a need. The main thing to keep in mind is that it is not a sin to have problems. People who are in trouble are often not to blame for their circumstances. They need to be treated with compassion, not wariness.

People were terribly afraid, and that's why many of them didn't help. After the war, they told me that they couldn't possibly have done what we did. If the Nazis had come to search their house, they would have broken down. I never in my life have held it against anyone for not helping. In order to do it, one has to be able to do it.

In my case, I think it made it easier that I came from a brave family, especially on my mother's side. When they needed to fight, they could fight. I grew up hearing about how strong my mother was. She died when I was less than two years old, so I didn't actually get to know her. My aunt moved in after my mother died, and she played a large part in raising us. My father never remarried.

I remember my grandfather doing a lot for people, since he didn't have a farm to work, and he lived during more prosperous times. He would help people when they had to go to the hospital, or when a woman was having a baby. Later he took in children from Hungary who were malnourished and needed to be strengthened; I don't recall how many, but it was after his own eleven children had already grown up. My father also tried to do things, but he had less money and less time, so it was more difficult for him.

After the Second World War, we ourselves participated in feeding hungry children from countries that had suffered. It was part of a program at our church. We helped children from Holland, and once we ourselves took in a child from Hungary. Because Hungary had fought

Heiltje Kooistra as an older person. Courtesy of the Kooistra family.

against the Allies, some people asked us, "Do you think that this child's family might have been Nazi collaborators?" but we didn't think like that. Even if they had been, would that be a reason to not feed him? Children of Nazis are children, not Nazis. Árpád was his name, and he stayed with us for a year. Some other members of our congregation were good at sewing and knitting, and they made him clothes. When it was time for him to return to Hungary, we sent him back with a big chest full of clothes and goodies, and fancy food like a big fruitcake. His mother knew Dutch, so afterwards we kept up a very nice correspondence with her. She would always end her letters, "Kisses from Árpád."

My religious beliefs are the result of my having been raised in the family that I was, and also of my having been brought up in the Calvinist

Church. However, your beliefs aren't only formed from what you hear at church. I have some very strong convictions that sometimes put me at odds with the church. Still, my faith has continued to grow over the years. During the war, I had the feeling that God was guiding me, and that was enormously important in the development of my faith.

We took turns going to church in those days, but our minister never really said anything to encourage people to help the Jews. My husband used to get very angry about that. There were churches that were not doing what they should have, and ours was one of them. Some churches, such as the ones in Friesland, did quite a lot, but ours didn't get involved. It depended on the minister.

My ties with the church have definitely lessened over time—organized religion is something I can do without now. Anyway, your faith doesn't depend on church attendance: you have to act by your own lights. I said to my husband, "Why don't you write them a letter to say you are leaving, because I will follow." So he wrote the letter, and we said goodbye to the church.

There are those who think that the church shouldn't take a stand on political issues, but during the Nazi years we saw where *that* leads. The church is one of the few institutions that can act as a counterweight if the government behaves immorally. I don't see how the church can steer clear of politics if it is truly pursuing justice, parity, and peace.

Then again, you don't want the government meddling in religion, and if a politician starts talking about God, you must ask yourself, what are his motives? Did you know that Hitler believed that his conduct was in accordance with the will of the Almighty Creator? So be wary when a politician uses religious rhetoric, and remember that the first one to quote scripture in the gospels was Satan.

Do you have any other advice for religious people trying to effect social and political change?

There's a saying that I keep on my refrigerator: "I'm only one—but I *am* one. I cannot do everything—but I *can* do something. What I can do, I should do, and what I should do, by the grace of God, I will do." It's far better to do something than to do nothing, even if it only involves taking a small step. I speak from experience: one thing leads to another.

Did you take in any children after that Hungarian boy?

No, we just couldn't anymore. My own children required a lot more time, and they would protest if they didn't like something. I welcomed that, because it was a sign they were thinking for themselves. When they were little, they would go along with anything, but that didn't last forever.

Do you still keep in touch with the Jewish people whose lives you saved?

We've been terribly spoiled by all of the people that we put up during the war. The family of four moved to Scheveningen, a beach resort town, and we were very welcome to come and vacation with them whenever we wished. The parents have died now, but I still have a strong connection with the children, Ellis and Bob. Ellis emigrated to Israel, but she sometimes comes to Holland to celebrate New Year's Eve with me, and I have been to Jerusalem several times to visit her. With the other family of three, the bonds were also strong, but their lives ended quite early, even the daughter.

How do you feel now about what you did during the war?

I'm glad we were able to help, and grateful to have been given the opportunity to put our beliefs to the test. Still, I wouldn't want to expose my family to something like that again. It was very hard on us in many ways. But that's the price you pay—there's never any good without some evil. Helping those people during the war was one of the good things, but for my own children it was not so good, and my husband suffered terribly afterwards because of the strain he had been under. I don't want to complain, but it did have its cost. But once you make a choice, you have to accept the consequences.

So you have some regrets about what you did during the war?

No, I would do it again. I would not *not* do it because of the consequences. I believe we did what we had to do. It was our destiny.

WHEN THE NAZIS INVADED the Netherlands, their hard, unyielding approach must have come as a complete shock to Dutch citizens, who had never experienced anything like it during their lifetimes. Hitler's way of operating allowed for neither compromise nor mercy, and he had fashioned the Third Reich in his own image. Yet, if we look back to the Eighty Years War (1568–1648), one of the most defining periods of Dutch history, the circumstances of the Nazi occupation take on the quality of a déjà vu. The Dutch national anthem dates back to this time:

A shield and my reliance,
O God, thou ever wert.
I'll trust unto Thy guidance,
O leave me not ungirt.
That I may stay a pious
Servant of Thine for aye
And drive the plagues that try us
And tyranny away.

The verse recalls the oppressive grip of imperial Spain during which King Philip II sought to purge all heretics—which, to him, meant non-Catholics. But the Protestant reformer John Calvin—born Jean Cauvin in France in 1509—was extremely influential in the Netherlands during this period, and a band of his staunch followers declared that they would rather die than have a corrupt Christianity forced down their throats. In 1566, Philip II appointed a new regent, Fernando Álvarez de Toledo, to bring about law and order in his colonial territory. Destined to become the quintessential villain of Dutch history, this Duke of Alva arrived with an occupying army and demanded that all Dutch sign an oath of loyalty to the Spanish king and the Catholic Church. When several prominent landowners presented him with a petition calling for religious tolerance, he had them beheaded. Such actions, along with the financial damage he inflicted through tariffs and fines, soon led to open revolt.

It was at this time that William of Orange rose up to rally the disgruntled Dutch Calvinists to fight a battle for freedom that would continue for generations. The Spanish Crown sank millions of ducats into this long-distance war of attrition but, in the end, had little to show for it except a ruined economy—their own. After eighty years, Spain finally relented and the Dutch were free to live as they wished. In the meantime, the identity of the Dutch, and especially that of the Dutch Calvinists, had accreted around that epochal struggle.

In a sense, Heiltje Kooistra is one of the spiritual heirs of the Dutch Calvinists of the sixteenth century who opposed the Duke of Alva. Nearly four centuries later, she and her husband recognized that Hitler represented a threat not only to the Jews, but also to the hard-won freedom from religious persecution that their Calvinist forbears had secured.

As Calvinism moved into modern times, it split into two major sects: the strict *Gereformeerden* (Dutch Orthodox Church) and the more assimilated *Hervormden* (Dutch Reformed Church). The Gereformeerden, also known as "blackstockings," still number as many as six hundred thousand today, and, as at the time of the war, remain concentrated in the north, especially Zeeland and Friesland. Farmers by tradition, one can often see them on Sunday, dressed in black, walking to church so as to avoid driving on their Sabbath. They are known for their unwavering adherence to their religious principles, which, most noticeably, involve a rejection of worldly pleasures and pursuits.

Though the blackstockings tend not to associate with strangers, during the Nazi occupation they were among those most willing to take in Jewish people. During the occupation, many of them felt that in order to be true Christians, they must help, and such behavior became the norm in their communities. In the words of one blackstocking rescuer, "If you didn't have an onderduiker in your house, you weren't a proper peasant farmer."

But the decision to help may also have been influenced by John Calvin's high regard for the Jews and Judaism. Unlike Martin Luther, who, especially towards the end of his life, excoriated both Jews and Catholics, Calvin had emphasized that the Jews are God's chosen people and affirmed that both the Hebrew scriptures and Christian gospels are divinely inspired and seamlessly coterminous. That, combined with his writings that recount a God who, working through men, "broke the bloody scepters of arrogant kings" and "overturned intolerable governments," may have roused these farmers, as well as other Calvinists such as Heiltje and Wopke, to put their faith into action. Indeed, his exhortations to revolt against iniquitous authority had become inscribed as one of the doctrines of the Calvinist Church.

A third, more subtle, factor may also have come into play: saving Jews was a way to know that you yourself were saved. Calvinism puts its faithful into an interesting theological predicament: God has already predestined who will gain divine favor and fellowship and who will be cut off from it, but mortals are not privy to that knowledge. However, an indication of the sealed judgment can be discerned by observing each individual's words and deeds. True believers are urged to heed the voice of their conscience and act rightly. Though righteousness is, in theory, its own reward, it carries the side benefit of providing a welcome clue that one is among the elect.

This history and theology may help to explain why Calvinists were so highly represented among the people who rescued Jews in the Netherlands: though numbering only 8 percent of the population, they constituted about 25 percent of the Dutch Resistance.

In 1942 when the deportations first began, both Calvinist and Catholic churches united in writing a declaration of protest. When the Germans demanded that the statement not be read from the pulpits, the Reform Calvinist Church gave in, but the Catholic and the Orthodox Calvinist churches went ahead anyway. Shortly afterwards, the Nazis arrested seven hundred Catholics and, later, five hundred Protestants, all of whom were considered Jewish according to the Nuremburg Laws, although they had converted to Christianity. These Catholics and Protestants whom the Nazis redefined as Jews became part of that great stream of people being deported to Westerbork and terminal destinations in the east.

three

RUT MATTHIJSEN

Chemistry of Compassion

It is more difficult to
crack a prejudice than an atom.

—ALBERT EINSTEIN

THE RESISTANCE DID NOT CONSIST ONLY OF BIG PERSONALITIES, nor were all of its members stationed on the front lines. Rut Matthijsen is a serene, soft-spoken man, long accustomed to the hush of laboratories through his work as a biochemist. His measured words and studied answers to my questions revealed a lifelong habit of precision and reserve, even as his brown eyes beamed affably behind the powerful lenses of his glasses.

During the war, Rut usually worked behind the scenes, applying his emerging scientific skill to a variety of technical problems that beset the Utrecht Kindercomité, and the Resistance in general. His quiet confidence, combined with a detail-oriented, analytical mind, made him especially suited to tackle these challenging tasks. His business acumen also came in handy, as he attempted to raise money to literally "save the children."

In 1942, I was a college student taking summer courses in chemistry at the University of Utrecht when a fellow student asked me if I would allow the room where I slept to be used during the day. "There are people coming from Amsterdam," he explained, "and they need a stopping-off place that's close to the station." Sensing that he might be referring to onderduikers, I said yes. Curious to meet my transient guests, I went home the next day and found members of the Utrecht Kindercomité with some Jewish children in tow. These people were inspiring—unlike some chem students.

Soon I was spending most of my time helping them transport Jewish children to safe addresses. Once the fall semester started, the group got smaller, even as the number of children who needed to be hidden was increasing rapidly. Many of our fellow students said, "Sorry, I have to study." But a core of ten or fifteen stayed on. A sense of group responsibility arose quite spontaneously between us, and a tremendous bond formed. I trusted them with my life, and they trusted me with their lives as well. You wouldn't do anything without thinking about how it might affect the others.

Meanwhile, the Nazis were trying to make over the universities, just as they had made over the government. When they suspended the Jewish professors, there were protests, and the students in Leiden and Delft organized strikes. The Germans then closed both universities, though Delft was later reopened. But in Utrecht we didn't have a strike—we thought we weren't ready for that yet. And so, a few months later, all Jewish students were suspended. Still no protest. But by then I had withdrawn from the university to devote myself to rescue work full-time. I wasn't able to concentrate on my studies, anyway.

At first I did what Hetty and Gisela were doing—delivering children, distributing ration coupons—but such work was more dangerous when done by a young man, and I'm not sure I possessed the requisite sangfroid. For instance, once when I was on my way to an address in South Amsterdam to bring food to some families that were hiding Jewish children, I was stopped by an officer who was interested in what I had in my suitcase. When he found it was full of cheese and sausage, I was arrested on the minor charge of being a black market profiteer. I might have tried to talk my way out of it, but I hadn't prepared a story in advance. Then I panicked at the thought that when they found the identification cards in the suitcase, they would turn me over to the SS. To prevent this, I jumped out the window.

That landed me in the hospital with a concussion, and an armed guard outside my door. A resistance friend arrived, and with his help we were able to persuade the police to drop the charges against me. But I still had to spend an additional five weeks in the hospital to recover.

I found a more valuable direction for my energies when I teamed up with another group member to do falsification work, which led—surprisingly—to a source of income for the children in hiding. You see, the foster families were, of course, taking on a big responsibility, but besides the danger of it, many of them had very limited resources. We realized we needed to assist them with the children's upkeep, but we were all students, and none of us had much money. We gave what we could—for instance, my stamp collection brought in three hundred guilders—but it wasn't enough. So that was an ongoing problem.

We got a big boost when the Archbishop Johannes de Jong of Utrecht gave us ten thousand guilders from his "special needs" fund. So by the fall of '42 we could say to the prospective foster parents, "If you take a child, yes, there will be risks, but we can provide support: fifty guilders a month if necessary." That was about how much university students would pay to rent a room in a nice house, so it certainly helped to make it more feasible. However, considering the number of children we were trying to support, our coffers were soon empty again.

One evening, Geert Lubberhuizen and I got together to try our hand at forging some identification cards. Geert was an older chemistry student who had also been the editor of *Vox Studiosorum,* the Utrecht student newsweekly. He stuck his neck out in '41 by writing a scathing critique of an anti-Semitic movie the Nazis were showing. The SD immediately came after him and shut down the paper for good measure.

When he joined us in the Kindercomité, he was keeping a low profile, but he thought he could work with me on forgery and falsification.

IDs were a big problem in those days. Beginning in November 1941, everyone had to go to the municipal building with two photos. One photo went into a central card file in the Hague, along with your fingerprint and signature. The other was attached to a preprinted card, and your fingerprint and signature were put on that as well. If you were Jewish, they would stamp your card with a big black J. An officer would then sign it, and finally he would stamp it again with a special stamp. The fingerprint was covered by a transparent seal, and that also was stamped.

Once the photo was attached, it was very difficult to remove it without tearing the paper. So you had to scrape off the front while leaving the backing, and then attach the new photo. Sometimes there would be a photo that was built up in layers. Then it could simply be peeled off. But often it was all in one piece, and then you had to scratch it very patiently—it could take a whole day to clear it away. After that, of course, you needed the right stamp.

To do that, we made a photographic enlargement, and then it had to be drawn exactly using a draftsman's pen. We would then reduce it and have a die made from it out of zinc and India rubber. After that, we would attach it to a block mount and test it out. We had certain tricks to get a better image, but that was usually good enough.

We also worked on special projects, such as official letters for some of our hidden children verifying that they had been bombed out of Rotterdam. This was a good cover for them as well as their foster parents because many non-Jewish children were left homeless after the bombing and had been sent away to live with relatives. All the streets in the center of Rotterdam had been destroyed, so it was easy to invent plausible former addresses.

So as the Germans came up with their identification cards, distribution cards, food ration coupons, and other official documents that were required for this or that, we would try to match them. Mostly it was a matter of removing the ink that was there, and printing something new over it—easier said than done. I always kept a magnifying glass in my pocket to be able examine documents that needed to be forged. The Germans would insert tiny markings on the originals to distinguish them from forgeries, so I had to be sure not to miss any of those details. Some documents couldn't be forged, such as the IDs, which were printed on paper with changing colors. In that case, we would use brand new ones stolen from the stock in the town hall, and fill them out as needed.

Geert and I often worked late into the night, and I remember him saying at one point, "I think it's very awkward for us to always be begging for money—why don't we make something that we can then sell for a decent price? People would be glad to pay for it, and afterwards they could say, 'This I bought for the cause.'" Well, that was the beginning of his printing press idea.

One of Geert's codenames in the Resistance was "Bas." We sometimes had a hard time finding him, for he was going all over trying to buy things to set up a printing operation. One day Anne Maclaine Pont, another member of our group, left a note on his door that said, "Where is Bas?" When he got back, he scribbled, "Bas is busy," and then went out again. She returned later, and added, "Bas is as busy as a bee." When he came back that night, he chuckled at the note and decided to call the press *De Bezige Bij,* meaning "the busy bee." Later he moved to Amsterdam, and had many people helping him, but at the beginning he had no one but me. You could say that *De Bezige Bij* was born in Utrecht, and I spent those first months rocking the cradle.

The first thing we published was a poster containing the poem "De Achttien Dooden," "The Eighteen Dead," by Jan Campert. He wrote it as an elegy for fifteen members of a Dutch Resistance group who had been shot by a firing squad along with three of the February strikers. It gives you a glimpse into the mind of a man who has been captured, and knows that his time left on earth is very short. Campert wrote it when he, too, was in prison, after he'd been arrested for helping to hide Jewish children.

A cell is just two meters long
And scarce two meters wide
But smaller is the little space
In which I shall be laid.
Though I have not yet seen it,
There, nameless, I shall lie,

And eighteen more beside me,
Tomorrow all will die.

I knew the task that I began
Would be awash with pains.
But yet the heart could not resist:
It never shuns whatever risk.
It knows that in this land
Proud freedom once prevailed,
Until his cursed hand
Decreed it otherwise.

The vermin-catcher of Berlin
Piping his evil tune
Hunts down a generation free
Till all of us are gone.
No more I'll see my loved one,
Or share with her my bed,
Why then this fight for freedom?
What difference to the dead?

I watch the early morning rays
Sift through the window high
Lord, now let Thy will be done,
May death come easily.
And if it be that I have sinned,
Forgive me, as I pray
To face, unbowed, the firing squad
That ends my life this day.

Someone managed to sneak it out of the prison, and copies were
being passed around in the Resistance from hand to hand. Anne
Maclaine Pont took it to Geert and said, "Can't you do something with
this?" By the time we printed it in March '43, Campert had already
been killed. But the poem quickly became the anthem of the Dutch
Resistance, and it's still read widely in the Netherlands today.

Our initial run was fifteen thousand copies and we sold them for a
donation of five guilders or more. Within six months we had raised seventy-five thousand guilders. Geert went on to publish books by some

of our best Dutch writers and poets—all the ones who refused to become members of the *Kultuurkamer*, the Nazi-controlled organization of approved "culture workers"—plus some powerful foreign works by such authors as John Steinbeck, who was a newcomer at that time.

But he published some lighter things too. We put out several books of political cartoons, making fun of Hitler and Nazism. For instance, one cartoon depicted German soldiers overrunning the Netherlands. The caption read, "They've returned to show their appreciation." You see, some of those same children who had received food and shelter here in the Netherlands following the Great War came back in their Nazi uniforms twenty-five years later to terrorize us. Another cartoon showed Hitler's mother at the time of his birth, looking shocked at her loudmouthed, mustached baby.

It wasn't difficult to sell that book, or any of the other things. People didn't have much to buy during the German occupation, so, in that way, at least, it was an opportune time to ask them to open their wallets. All along, we distributed the money to the families who were hiding Jewish children, not only to our own contacts, but those of the Amsterdam Student Group as well. We also gave some money to other groups, such as a theater troupe that had also defied the *Kultuurkamer*. They were really hard pressed, for they were banned from working and had their families to feed.

When Geert moved the operation to Amsterdam, I remained in Utrecht but we kept in contact. I used to warn him not to attend meetings of the Resistance there, because the Gestapo was very active in Amsterdam. Later he joked, "That boy saved my life again and again, because whenever I was invited to a big Resistance meeting, I'd say 'Sorry—Rut tells me not to go.'"

After the war, Geert added up all the wartime revenues of *De Bezige Bij,* and the figure was close to eight hundred thousand guilders. He continued to run *De Bezige Bij* for nearly forty years, and it is still thriving today. As for me, when the war ended I returned to school to finish my chemistry studies, and then went to work in the lab of Organon, a pharmaceutical company. It was a good time to jump on the science train, and I learned on the job under the tutelage of some fine biochemists. I was fortunate to be part of the research team that discovered how to isolate, and later to synthesize, heparin, the anticoagulant drug.

What do you make of Germany's use of highly advanced technology to do such terrible things during the Holocaust?

Following the liberation, I was shocked to learn that the stories about the gas chambers were true, and that industrial giants such as I.G. Farben—which was later broken up into Bayer, Agfa, and BASF—had been directly involved. My uncle was a chemist, and we also worried a lot about the atomic bombs that had been dropped on Hiroshima and Nagasaki. There you saw how the latest technology had brought the war to an end. But to a terrible end.

My uncle said, "We should join the group of scientists that refuse to do atomic research." I think this was in 1950 or something. But it occurred to us that if certain ethically minded scientists refused to do the research, then other scientists would take it up. How would our refusal improve the outcome?

I believe that science, ultimately, is neutral. The same physics that makes nuclear weapons possible also makes nuclear medicine possible. The Zyklon B that was poured into the gas chambers was a fumigant, very handy for killing bugs and rodents. The problem was not with the Zyklon B, but with the use that was made of it.

The same holds true for most science and technology. Consider a factory that manufactures guns. If those guns are used by the police to protect citizens, then you say, "Well, that's OK." But if they get into the hands of criminals? To prevent this, you don't talk to the scientists and engineers—you go to the lawmakers and the government agencies.

In 1962 there was a drug that worked very well as a sleeping pill for elders. Then some marketing people thought, "We can sell it to pregnant women, for they don't sleep well either." It was marketed that way, but the research had not been done, and it caused terrible birth defects. So we need clinical trials, and regulations, and so on, because scientists can't imagine all the possible uses that might be made of their research. The people who apply the science have to come up with uses that will benefit humanity. And if they don't, we need laws to stop them, or at least to ensure that the public won't be harmed.

Of course, I'm not saying that the scientists themselves bear no responsibility. In 1941, when the Germans wanted an identification card

Rut Matthijsen recently. Courtesy of Mark Klempner.

that would be impossible to counterfeit, the design was actually the work of a Dutch technician named Jacob Lentz. The odd thing is that this fellow was not a Nazi, he was not a member of the NSB—he was an overly ambitious civil servant. This was a case where he should have been thinking about the implications of what he was doing, but instead he was trying to rise to a higher position by impressing the Germans. We'll never know how many lives were lost as a result of his "perfect" ID.

How can we educate our children about the Holocaust?

Children must be taught in stages, because at different ages you need to give them different arguments. And you must do it very carefully, or else it will go awry. Let's say a teacher shows pictures from the concentration camps to the students in her fifth-grade class in order to teach them about the Holocaust. The children ask, "Who has done that?" The teacher says, "The Germans." And then, for years afterwards, the children think negatively about the Germans. That is not preventing racism: it is propagating it.

I hear teenagers—*three* generations removed from the war—making anti-German remarks. That's crazy. Germany is the strongest member of the European Union economically, and from a moral point of view they are doing their very best at the moment. So I wonder how these young people, including my own grandchildren, became anti-German. Could it have something to do with well-intentioned adults trying to be sure they will not forget the past?

The same thing can happen when Jewish children are taught the history of anti-Semitism. What good will it do them if they learn to hate Christians and Muslims? You know, before the war, we didn't give much thought to what religion someone followed. We were all just people, Dutch people. Then the Germans came and made a strict division between Jewish and non-Jewish. Years later, when I went to Israel to receive the Yad Vashem award, I was asked, "Why did you help the Jewish people?" The emphasis being on the word *Jewish*. But that was Adolf Hitler's emphasis. I helped them because they were people.

WHEN INDIVIDUALS OF CONSCIENCE such as Rut Matthijsen were impressionable young college students, they surely were influenced by the uniquely defiant atmosphere that existed at Dutch universities during the occupation. The universities were the only institutions other than the churches where one could sometimes find authoritative voices urging people to resist the Nazi injustices. The words and actions of several brave professors still stand today as courageous examples of speaking truth to power.

In the fall of 1940, at the time of the Aryan Attestations, Professor Scholten, a jurist at the University of Amsterdam, circulated a petition that emphasized "the simple fact that there is no Jewish question in the Netherlands," and that "it is a matter of indifference whether a scholar is Jewish or not. . . . In the Dutch view, all learning is service to a single, universal truth, involving all mankind, and it is from this service that education derives its moral value and social importance." The petition was signed by as many as half the faculty at Amsterdam, and, after being circulated at other universities throughout the country, was sent directly to Seyss-Inquart.

Concurrently, the students at Leiden University circulated their own petition, which amassed as many as two thousand signatures. Dr. Telders, a professor of international law at Leiden, said to his colleagues at that time: "Naturally, it is far easier to let events run their course, but can we really reconcile such passivity with our duty as Dutchmen?" In November 1940, when all Jewish professors at the public universities were dismissed, Professor R. P. Cleveringa, the Dean of the Law School at Leiden, gave a speech on the eve of the departure of one of its Jewish faculty members, the distinguished jurist E. M. Meijers. As Presser reports, Cleveringa did not mince words when talking about the Germans:

> Their actions are beneath contempt. All I ask is that we may dismiss them from our sight and gaze instead on the heights, up to that radiant figure in whose honour we are assembled here.

Cleveringa ended his address by expressing the fervent hope that Prof. Meijers, "this noble son of our people, this man, this father to his students, this scholar whom foreign usurpers have suspended from his duties," would soon return.

As with the public anti-Nazi declarations of the churches, such free speech wasn't free: Cleveringa was arrested the next day and imprisoned for eight months. Still, thousands of copies of his speech were distributed underground and became part of the rapidly proliferating Resistance literature.

Later in the war, the German authorities began rounding up college students after a paramilitary group known as CS-6 fatally wounded a Nazi officer. Before dying, he identified his assailants as students, and the next day the first campus razzia took place. On 6 February 1943, six hundred students were arrested at university libraries and sent to Vught concentration camp. Another twelve hundred were arrested a few days later.

The Nazis viewed the remaining Dutch students as a source of slave labor, and planned to deport about seventy-five hundred of them to Germany. Things were not going well in Stalingrad, and they needed able bodies to work in the factories at home so that more Germans could be sent to the Russian front. This led in March '43 to an Aryan Attestation redux in which all students were required to sign an oath of Nazi loyalty on the threat of being suspended from school and sent to Germany.

The Dutch government in exile called for noncooperation, as did many of the professors. Activist students urged their classmates to refuse to sign and counseled students who were wavering. Despite the additional threat that parents would be held responsible for the decisions of their college-age children, no more than 16 percent signed.

After that, the Germans gave up trying to Nazify the Dutch universities, and more or less shut them down. Students all over the Netherlands hustled to dive under with the help of the LO. The lives of the Utrecht students, however, were in less danger, for a handful of them had previously carried out a raid on the office of university records and burned all the registrar's files. The raiders—in a rare departure from their usual activities in the Utrecht Kindercomité—were Frits Iordens, Geert Lubberhuizen, Rut Matthijsen, and Anne Maclaine Pont, along with a friend of theirs named Gijs den Besten.

Rut recalls, "We figured the Germans would use the same 'salami technique' on the students as they had on the Jews: slice by slice bringing us under their control. So we decided to take preemptive nonviolent action." Rut was the youngest of the raiders, and it was he who observed that the heavy card stock used to record each student's name and personal information would not burn easily unless it were well exposed to air. The students spent the night crumpling cards until the pile was higher than their heads, and then set them on fire before exiting the building at 4 a.m. By the time the fire brigade put the blaze out a short time later, the students' records were smoke and ash.

four

GISELA SÖHNLEIN

On Wings of Song

*Each of us in this world must cross over
a very narrow bridge. And the most important
thing is not to be at all afraid.*

—REB NACHMAN

GISELA SÖHNLEIN WAS HETTY VOÛTE'S "PARTNER IN CRIME" and companion in the concentration camps, Piglet. After the war, both Hetty and Gisela married men who had also survived the camps, and they settled down in different places to raise families—Hetty in the Dutch East Indies; Gisela in Waalre. The bond between them, however, proved indissoluble. "Hetty was the daredevil," the now-octogenarian Gisela explained on the phone, "but I kind of caught it from her."

When we met at her house in Waalre, I found Gisela to be more reserved than Hetty, but just as forthright and hospitable. A small woman with smiling eyes and a hearty laugh, she welcomed me into her home with a warmth I was coming to expect of the rescuers. Her last name means "little sun," which was her nickname in the Utrecht Kindercomité, and it still fits her today.

Throughout the afternoon, my "egometer" registered zero. Though she was happy to answer my questions, and even sing me some of the songs she and Hetty had made up, she seemed entirely content, with no need whatsoever to talk about herself. I found this refreshing, and when I thought back to the self-aggrandizing way people related to each other in the entertainment industry in Los Angeles, it seemed a small miracle. Over the years, we have kept in close touch, and she has helped in many ways with this book.

I grew up in Utrecht, but when the Germans invaded in 1940 I was a student living in a sorority house in Amsterdam with seven other girls. Right across the street was the Gestapo headquarters. In the summer of '42, they really started going after the Jews, and on July 14 they carried out a big razzia. All that night, I heard trucks pulling up, Germans shouting, dogs barking, and people crying. It was horrible, but there was nothing I could do.

Then the next day, my friend Hansje van Loghem, one of my sorority sisters, asked me if I'd like to help her and her boyfriend Piet Meerburg to hide Jewish children. I immediately said yes. I didn't know until then whether I would be brave enough to do something like that. But from that moment on, I never stopped.

Because of my Utrecht connections, I became a liaison between the Amsterdam Student Group, of which Piet was the leader, and the Utrecht Kindercomité run by Jan Meulenbelt. Hetty was in that Utrecht group, and we became fast friends. Then the Nazis said that anyone who had not signed the declaration of loyalty could not attend school, so I moved back in with my family in Utrecht, and Hetty and I worked together every day to help hide Jewish children. My stepfa-

ther was employed by the railroad, so I could travel for practically nothing on the trains. That came in handy when transporting the children.

I wasn't afraid to take the children on the train—I was a little bit
stupid, I guess, because I was young. But, come to think of it, no one in
my family was really afraid. When I told my mother what I was doing,
she said, "Oh! That's a good idea." She was a very positive person. Even
after my arrest, she always believed that I would be set free and that no
harm would come to me. My father was the same way. Our whole family believed that you should go ahead and help, and not worry about it.

How were we arrested? It's complicated. . . . There was a very nice
lady in the east of Holland whose house was big enough to hide about
ten Jewish children. They could go outside there, and swim in the river.
It was a very good situation for them, and we were trying to come up
with more situations like that. And then a certain minister offered us
the use of a big house in the south of Holland in a place called Esch,
but before bringing children there, we had to find someone to live in
it. One of the group members located an older couple who said they
would be willing to do it.

We didn't know them. They came there very quickly and said,
"Very well then, give us the children." So we began to bring them children, and we also sent an older Jewish girl over there to provide house-
hold help. It was she who overheard them arguing about whether to
turn the children in immediately, or wait for more to come. She ran
away after that, and hid in Utrecht. At the same time, some Jewish people managed to get a message to us from out of Westerbork—they said
that every Jew the couple had been in contact with was betrayed.

So what must you do at such a moment? If it was only a matter of
the children, we could remove them, but they'd met several members
of our group, and they knew our contact address. After discussing it for
hours, we realized we had to kill them! Imagine us, young college students, having to make such a decision. Rut Matthijsen knew about a
knokploeg that did that kind of thing, and we asked them to help us.

The day of the action, Hetty and I bicycled to Esch. The others
were already there—Rut was in the woods a little ways from the road,
keeping a watch over the four bicycles, while Jan was hiding with the
knokploeg near the house. It was a beautiful spring morning, and we
went to the front door and told the couple that we wanted to take the

children for a little walk. That was fine, but we saw that their foster son was visiting! What would happen to him? It was too late to change anything—we strolled down the path with the children, while Jan led the knokploeg to the door. A few moments later we heard gun shots. Hetty looked back and saw the foster son crawling out the door toward the neighboring farm. We put the three children on our bicycles, and pedaled hard to the train station. Soon we were speeding along the rails to Utrecht, where we safely delivered them to another address.

We learned later that the boys from the knokploeg had only been able to kill the man. The woman was severely wounded with a bullet in her lung, but it was only a matter of time before she had recovered enough to talk. They shot the foster son in the leg because they didn't know if he was part of it or not, but he knew enough to send the SD after us.

They caught Hetty the next day, and she somehow was able to telephone in order to warn us of the danger. I was about to have a Sunday meal with my family when Jan called and said that I should come meet him. Yes, but how would I get there? The safest way was by bicycle, but mine was still at the Utrecht station. When I went to pick it up, I felt the firm grip of a SD plainclothesman on my shoulder.

The arrest felt like a dull blow, just enough to daze me. That and, "What do I do now?" The plainclothesman left me at the Utrecht police headquarters, but the Dutch police didn't seem to understand at first that I was a serious case. They put me in a cell with another girl, and I got busy eating some addresses I had on me. When I learned that this girl would be released the next day, I asked her to pass on a message to my parents: "Look for me after the war."

Before long the SD returned, and the interrogations began: I was shown a photo of the man who had been shot, a terrible photo of him all keeled over with blood everywhere. I closed my eyes and cried a little, and told them that I had nothing to do with it. Still, the foster son had told them certain things. I concentrated on not giving away any information that could endanger the group or the children.

Hetty and I were reunited at the prison in Hertogenbosch where we spent a few tedious days, and then they shipped us to Haaren prison, which housed a lot of Resistance people. The prisoners there kept in touch through the pipes, and Hetty found a way to talk through the vents. She was given a harder time during the interrogations because she had dark features and looked dashingly defiant. I had more of a dumb blonde look, like someone who wouldn't know anything. Also, she had been seen with Jan, and I hadn't. Still, the interrogations were never easy, and whenever someone had to go, we would send messages through the pipes like "Be strong" and "We'll be praying for you." When they came back it was always, "Are you all right? Did you make it?"

Haaren had been built as a seminary so the rooms were really monks' cells with two bunk beds and a little window up top. I found that if I moved the bunk beds to the door, I could stand on top and sing through the open window to Hetty. We would sing to each other in Dutch, and it sounded like folk songs, but we were actually having little conversations. She told me what she had said to the Germans, and I told her what I had said to them, and we finally came up with a story we could both tell about what we had been doing. One time, though, Hetty looked down from the window and saw a pair of black boots, so we figured they had been listening in all along.

After six months, we were sent to the concentration camp in Vught. There was enough food there, and you could get parcels and so on. But then the Germans sent all the women to Ravensbrück, and the men to Sachsenhausen. Those were bad camps. Ravensbrück was overcrowded, and dirty, and you didn't have enough to eat. The Germans were marching around, well fed, their uniforms new, their boots polished, acting as if the war had already been won. Still, we always thought that the Allies would win the war. Always. It will not take long, we thought. Some weeks. Well, it was many months. But you always believed that in the end the Germans would be defeated, and everything would be all right. We put our doubts and fears into the deep freeze. You couldn't comprehend what was really happening. It was impossible.

While we were in Ravensbrück, a woman came who had been in Auschwitz. She had somehow convinced the Germans that she wasn't Jewish, and they let her transfer. She told us what was happening there, and we couldn't believe it. We gave her extra bread because we felt so sorry for her. Then later the Germans built gas chambers at Ravensbrück, so we saw first-hand.

What I learned in Ravensbrück is that when inhuman conditions go on, day after day, you still can't help but develop some kind of homely routine. And we found that, in spite of everything, cheerfulness would sometimes break through, especially when we sang our little songs to the others.

At first we sang because we were in prison, and didn't have anything else to do. We were alone in our cells, so we sang to amuse ourselves. I had taken classical singing lessons, and I remembered many lieder by Schubert and Schumann. There were two or three other girls who passed through who also had a repertoire, and there was one woman who knew many operettas. So I learned from all of them—we would listen to each other through the walls and halls—and the boys above us knew English songs like "It's a Long Way to Tipperary." Then after a while, Hetty and I started taking some of those melodies and making up our own words to them.

There is one from Vught that we used to sing to the tune of "Anchors Away." It dates back to the time when Hetty and I had to work in a tire factory the Germans converted to manufacture gas masks. We were on an assembly line, and had to glue the nosepieces down. But we tried to botch things up as much as we could.

Come along, mates, to factory Den Bosch
We make the gas masks here
And we don't give a damn
If the Krauts don't like our work
For soon we will be back
In freedom's arms again.

Hours, days, and months,
Creep along so slow
Unglued masks are all around
But on the line that we glue down
Not one nose will stay put
They all will go kaput!

We'll never lose heart
We'll always keep our heads up
They'll never get hold of us
No matter how sly they are

Ahoy, ahoy, striped women
They'll pay for this someday
Ahoy, ahoy, striped women
They'll regret what they have done.

I think that our little songs enabled us to get some perspective on our miseries. We liked making them up, and the other prisoners liked listening to them. They were just silly songs, but they meant a lot to us.

Most of the songs were meant to be rather entertaining, or so we thought. We usually performed them in a humorous, tongue-in-cheek kind of way. It may be difficult to understand how we could still laugh during those times, but somehow we did. A few years ago there was a reunion of women who had been at Ravensbrück. Everyone asked me and Hetty to sing for them, and so we sang once again.

The last song we ever wrote was when we were leaving Ravensbrück. This one is more serious, but still we sang it cheerfully.

It's done; we're finally free
We couldn't believe our ears
When they called us to Appell
Have they more tricks up their sleeve?
We know them all too well.

For years we were held captive
Behind the endless wire
No one lost her faith here, ever
For years we longed for our own homes
Then the white vans of the Red Cross
Came to bring us our salvation
From behind the endless wire.

Captives now, no longer
Behind the endless wire
This is the end of all our longing
Of being hungry, cold, and dirty
For the white vans of the Red Cross
Came to bring us our salvation
From behind the endless wire.

What was life like for you after the war?

My family was very happy to see me, and our friends from the group were happy to find that Hetty and I had survived. They'd never given up hope. In fact, Geert Lubberhuizen had put aside a copy for us of everything the *De Bezige Bij* had published since the day we'd been arrested.

Everyone was eager to get on with their lives, and I soon got married. Ate had spent four years in Buchenwald, Dachau, and some smaller camps. I had known his brother at the university, and I remember the day he told me Ate had been caught. But we didn't meet until 1945, soon after we both had been liberated. He had gone through more or less the same experiences as me, so that was practical—there wasn't much to explain. We fell in love, and that was that.

What are your feelings toward Germans today?

If they are old, you have to wonder what they were doing during the war. But most of the people living today had nothing to do with it.

I've heard that some of the Dutch young people still hate the Germans.

Perhaps they've never known a German.

It's as if the hatred has been passed along to younger generations.

Well, I don't think my children have it.

Did you make a conscious effort to raise them that way?

Well, we tried to teach them to think for themselves. And also to question everything, and not accept oversimplified answers.

Is that what went wrong in Germany?

Well, after the First World War, the Germans were poor and unhappy, and when Hitler came along they thought that here was a strong leader who would make everything all right. If they hadn't been feeling so humiliated from the First World War, perhaps they wouldn't have wanted

Gisela recently. Courtesy of the United States
Memorial Holocaust Museum, Washington, D.C.

a leader like that. Then he gave them jobs, and built up the economy, and directed their eyes to the glistening rainbow of an Aryan utopia.

You know, their national anthem goes "Germany, Germany, über Alles"—Germany above everything. With us here in Holland it was never, "Holland is the best in all the world"—no, not at all. And I think we are not so quick to follow a leader. Hitler convinced the people that he was the superman who was going to make them a superpower. You didn't need to wonder anymore whether something was right or wrong, because the Übermensch was taking care of everything. Hermann Goering, his second in command, used to say, "My conscience is called Adolf Hitler." So a situation arose in Germany where people felt that their leader could do their thinking for them. That's very dangerous.

Do you believe that the Germans still have that tendency?

Oh, no, no . . . Did Hetty tell you that we went to Ravensbrück last year for the fiftieth anniversary of the liberation? I always said that I would never go back. But then we got a very sincere letter from the German government that spoke of forgiveness and conciliation. They said that they knew it would be difficult for us, but that they hoped we would return to Ravensbrück for a special program.

Well, we did. There were many speeches about what Germany has learned from its mistakes, and it was a reunion of sorts with people trying to find each other. There were college students who served as our guides. Such wonderful young people—they became real friends after only three days. On the last day, they took us to Berlin and showed us around. The whole program was excellent.

Do you still see Hetty fairly often?

I go to Amsterdam every three weeks to take a piano lesson, and then we visit together. Sometimes we sing together, too.

Pooh and Piglet, always together . . .

We're fortunate to have had such a long friendship. . . . And Ate and I have been married now for over fifty years, and have three children, and five grandchildren. Sometimes these days when I see a baby, I get a tender feeling, as if I'm yearning to be a great-grandmother.

I hope it happens.

AFTER OUR INTERVIEW, Gisela insisted on walking me back to the bus stop, which was two blocks away. I reluctantly agreed, wishing she would stay inside and keep warm, since it was a cold, blustery day. After we reached the bus stop, she insisted on waiting there with me until the bus came. As an icy wind blew through my jacket, I said, "Gisela, you don't have to do this." Under her breath, she said, "Yes, I do."

At that instant, I felt I had caught a glimpse of the moral discipline that, over fifty years earlier, had compelled her to save Jewish children. Her internal sense of what is right and decent is something she follows regardless of other people's opinions—in this case, mine—or what is comfortable. So we stood there and chatted, and after ten chilly minutes, the bus arrived. After I'd gotten on, and when the bus was already halfway down the block, I looked back and there she was—still standing there, slowly waving goodbye.

five

CLARA DIJKSTRA

Divine Mother

*The whole worth
of a kind act is the love
that inspires it.*

—THE TALMUD

IT WAS A COLD DECEMBER DAY when I knocked on Clara Dijkstra's door. As I stamped my numb feet on her welcome mat, strains of a Beethoven symphony came drifting out to me from inside her apartment. A moment later the door flew open, and Clara, a full-figured matron in a bright red blouse, greeted me with such gusto that I felt more like some long-lost family member than a stranger coming to conduct an interview. Noticing the coldness of my skin during our handshake, she took both my hands in her two palms and rubbed them vigorously. She then led me inside to her kitchen, where she set a kettle to boil for tea, and cut a few slices of lemon.

As I sat in Clara's cozy kitchen, gazing through a corner of the steamed-up window at the street below, I found myself thinking of Lillian, my effusive, Yiddish-speaking paternal grandmother—how she would dash down the hall squealing with excitement whenever we rang her doorbell. It was no coincidence that being in Clara's presence had evoked her memory; Clara had picked up more than a little *Yiddishkeit* from having grown up in what was at one time the quintessential Jewish neighborhood of Amsterdam.

A popular song by Kees Manders captures how the Amsterdammers recall that now-vanished center of Dutch Jewry:

When father looks through his photographs,
we are amazed by the stories he tells
of the Weesperstraat, and the Jodenhoek.
He tells how the day started: the trade and the business,
the humor and the wit that was the source of life.
And if one day you didn't have much luck,
you could go to the Tip Top *in the evening*
and forget all your troubles.
Sometimes, late at night, you could still hear the call:
'lovely onions, pickled onions!'
Amsterdam weeps, where once it laughed.
Amsterdam weeps, it still feels the pain.

As Clara began to recount the destruction of that Jewish community, I was plunged into a world of such sad intensity that, after twenty minutes, I could feel myself going numb. Seeing what was happening, she again took my hand, and, squeezing it warmly, said, "Together we'll get through this."

But Clara also turned out to have an expansive sense of humor, and as she recounted some of her outrageous encounters with the Nazis—so close to being tragic—her laughter proved to be infectious. Like the biblical Sarah, who is said to have laughed when God told her she'd have a child in her old age, and laughed again when she actually did,

Clara was often gleeful about her destiny. She seemed more surprised than anyone that Yad Vashem would give her a medal, and that someone like me would show up at her doorstep more than fifty years later to listen to her stories.

No one hearing her stories would be surprised by Yad Vashem's decision, however; Clara Dijkstra's heart was far too large to be circumscribed by the Nazi agenda or governed by their rules and regulations, and it remains a heart that covers, that shelters, that understands.

I was born in Amsterdam in the middle of the Jewish people. As a little child, I attended a school on Weesperstraat—the old street that led into the Jewish Quarter. There were many Jewish shops all along the way to the school, and the children in the school were all Jewish, except for a few of us. But at that time, you didn't think too much about it. We were all just Dutch.

I got married in 1940, when I was twenty-one. We moved into an apartment house at 210 Oosterpark Street. There was a big Catholic hospital on the next block, but it was still a Jewish neighborhood. And then the Germans invaded in May, and the streets were full of Germans soldiers and their Dutch buddies, the NSB. At first they didn't seem so bad, but I had a couple of run-ins with them early on that showed me what they were really about.

One morning I went out walking with a one-guilder coin on my coat. You see, on our one-guilder coin was an image of the queen. Soon the Germans changed that, but I had taken one such coin and made a pin out of it. As I walked, it caught the eye of a German officer, a stocky man with a barrel chest. "Why do you wear that?" he asked. "Because I want to," I answered. His face got very red and he yelled, "Show me your papers!" I said, "No, I don't have to." It is the law in the Netherlands that you only have to show your papers if you are suspected of having committed a crime. "This is deliberately damaging Dutch money!" he shouted. "What if everyone did this?" I thought he was going to burst the buttons off of his uniform. He took me by the arm, and dragged me into a building full of Nazis. They all screamed at me, and I screamed back at them. After about twenty minutes, they kicked me in the butt and threw me out the door. I was back on the street, but they'd ripped off my pin, and I had a sore butt.

On 29 June it was Prince Bernhard's birthday and I wore a fresh white carnation. All Dutch knew that the prince always wore a white carnation in the buttonhole of his lapel. I was walking near the Muntplein when an ugly man with a bony head stopped me; I think he was a detective for the NSB—he was wearing the wolf trap insignia.

"What a lovely bloom," he said. Then he ripped it off, and stomped on it. He, too, knew about the prince and his white carnation. "Take three steps back," he commanded. He reached into his pocket and took out a gun. My knees started trembling—I didn't know what he was going to do. Just then a big truck full of German soldiers careened around the corner, heading straight for us. I ran, ran for my life! I could run very fast in those days. I ducked under a gate, and then I was safe. But my heart was racing like a runaway train. "I guess I'm not meant to die yet," I thought.

Let me tell you how Nettie came into my life. One spring day in '42, I went to visit some friends, and there was a woman there named Sylvia Bloch. She was very shaken up because early the next morning, she and her husband had to report to the Zentralstelle, the big Nazi office on the Adama van Scheltemaplein, to go to work in Germany. They had been given a chance to dive under, but the people who had offered to hide them wouldn't let them bring their little daughter. "Why don't you give her to me?" I said. "I'll take care of her." She looked at me with red-rimmed eyes. "What can I pay you to do this?" she asked. "Nothing," I said. "Nothing at all."

She'd been almost hysterical, but now she calmed down. She left right away, saying she would bring her child to my place as soon as she could. A little while later she appeared at my front door with two-year-old Nettie. She had brought her stroller and all her clothes. When Sylvia was leaving, the child was crying "Mamma! Mamma!" But after a while she settled down, and took a nap.

When my husband came home, he looked at Nettie asleep in the stroller, and said, "What's this?" "She's ours," I said cheerfully. He was a little shocked, and not very happy about it. I said, "I'll take care of her; I'll handle everything. If the Germans come, just let me do the talking."

My mother wasn't happy either. She said, "Don't do it! Don't do it! You worry me so!" But I told her, "Mother, I love you, but it's already done. We have a child, a Jewish child." Then she said, "Good for you."

Later, when my parents would come and visit, Nettie would call them *Oma* and *Oompa*—Grandma and Grampa. After a couple of weeks, the child started to call *me* Mamma. I let her think of me as her mother because it was a lot safer that way. Young children didn't need to have identity cards, so as long as the Germans thought she was my own child, there would be fewer problems.

A few months later, I was pushing Nettie in her stroller when a German officer stopped me and asked to see my papers. After he inspected them, he looked at Nettie and said in German, "A Jewish child, no?" Nettie looked up at me and, not understanding German, asked, "What did he say, Mamma?" I said to the officer, "See? You're crazy. She's my child." He must have believed me, because I kept on walking, and he didn't come after us.

Before things got really bad, I used to take her everywhere. One spring day we went to Rembrandtsplein to listen to the orchestra play, and have some ice cream and lemonade. Returning home, there was only one trolley back to our neighborhood. A big crowd had gathered, and people started elbowing their way on. Suddenly, a German officer nearby shouted, "Halt!" Everyone froze. In the uneasy silence, he walked right over to Nettie and me. My heart leaped into my mouth; I squeezed her hand, preparing for the worst. He turned to the crowd and said in a shrill voice, "You must board the trolley in an orderly manner." Then he made a little bow in our direction, and, stretching out his arm towards the trolley, said, "Women and children first." I scooped up Nettie, and sauntered very stylishly up the steps.

After a while the Nazis began to make raids—not only to pick up Jews, but to get the Dutch men, too. They picked up my husband, and, later, my younger brother. If you were not Jewish, they would send you to Germany to work in their factories; if you were Jewish—well, you know what happened then.

Once I was coming home from the greengrocer when I got caught in a *razzia*. The SS barricaded the block and moved in from all sides. Sirens wailed, and the sound of Nazis screaming their commands filled the air: *Raus! Schnell!* Dogs were barking, and the children were crying.

Hundreds of people rushed through the streets dodging kicks and blows. While this was happening, I saw the big doors to the hospital open. The hospital offered some safety because the Germans were afraid that if they went inside they would catch typhus or some other disease. Many young men went running towards the hospital trying to escape. Suddenly I saw my husband zigzagging in that direction, but he was seized by a couple of broad-shouldered SS and dragged away. I watched as they used the butts of their rifles to push him into a van.

As the occupation went on, the Germans made life worse and worse for everyone, especially, of course, the Jews. One cold gray dawn the sirens again began to wail, and a black van with a loudspeaker drove through the neighborhood blaring: *All Jewish people must come out of their houses and board the tram. All Jewish people must come out of their houses and board the tram.* In the park were many, many trams that were going to take all the Jewish people away. They pushed them in with everything they had: clothes, jewelry, suitcases.

Late that night, the German police came, looking for Jews who had somehow evaded the transport. We were woken up by their shouts: *"Steh auf!"* They had their green vans parked outside with the motors running, and five or six of them came running up the stairs to demand our papers. Nettie was quiet in her crib, and fortunately they didn't ask about her. Afterwards, they went into other apartments and took more people away. You felt terribly helpless. There was nothing you could do.

The next day a German officer with medals all over his uniform came to my door. "You have Jewish people?" *"Nein."* "Jewish children?" I looked him in the eye: "Definitely not." Then he said, "You have very pretty eyes. I think I'll relax here for a while and then report that I searched and found nothing." I felt nauseous just having him in the apartment, but I fixed him some ersatz coffee and finally he left.

Afterwards, my neighbors were very anxious about my continuing to keep a Jewish child. They were far too nosy. I knew that people sometimes got arrested because their neighbors talked too much, so I just kept repeating, "I do *not* have a Jewish child." I couldn't tell them that she was my child, because they knew she wasn't. So I said, "Her mother is in the hospital, and her father works in Germany."

The worst search came one night when we were awakened by the sound of heavy boots on the stairs. I heard yelling in the hall, and had hardly gotten out of bed before the Germans were kicking the door. *Bam! Bam! Bam!* These men were part of a special death squad that made its own attacks on the Jews. When I opened the door, I had to cover my eyes—the phosphorus lanterns they carried were so bright. One man looked at my papers, while the others stomped through the apartment searching for onderduikers. Nettie had been sleeping, but the noise had woken her up, and now she was crying. I was afraid that these Jew-hunters would see her dark hair and eyes and assume she was a Jew.

One of the men pushed me aside and burst into Nettie's room. I rushed in after him. "When is her birthday?" he asked. "28 December 1939." He held the lantern by her, but, because of the phosphorus, it made her look like a blondie! He stared at me, then back at her, then again at me, and said, "She looks like you." I was thinking, oh thank you, God, thank you. Then he startled me by saying, "She's beautiful." That was it—he left.

As I stood there listening to those brutes go down the stairs, I was laughing and crying at the same time, "It's a miracle. God's miracle. Thank you, God." I went to tuck Nettie in, and she just lay there like an angel—so innocent, so trusting.

The next day, the neighbors couldn't believe their eyes. They thought surely these Jew-hunters had taken Nettie to the *Creche*—that's the building where they put the Jewish children before they were deported. And they wondered how I had managed to not get shot. The ones who helped Jews they would shoot in public to teach a lesson to the neighbors.

Meanwhile, I was in touch with the Resistance a little bit. I taught at the Rosh Pinash Schule—a Jewish day school in the neighborhood where many of the children were refugees from Germany. One day a man asked me if I would take one of the children on my bicycle to a certain address. I knew that it must be the address of a hiding place, but I didn't ask any questions. I did this for about twenty children—one by one I would take them on my bicycle. Sometimes the addresses were far in the south, so I had to stop at a certain point, and hand the child over to someone else. How I hoped things would work out for those children!

Nettie understood very little about the danger both of us were in. I tried as best I could to give her a normal life. Once things got bad, I kept her inside as much as possible. During the war, I would sometimes write to the Blochs at an address I had for them. I would tell them how everything was going, how Nettie was growing up and learning to talk. But I never heard back.

My ration of bread was only half a loaf per week, not enough for both Nettie and me, but I managed to get some more from the baker across the street. He was a Catholic man with eleven children. He had seen me with Nettie and must have known the child was not mine, since when we moved there I had just gotten married, and then, suddenly, I was walking around with a two-year-old. One day as I was passing him in the street, he gave a nod, as if he wanted to talk to me. He knit his bushy brows and whispered, "Tomorrow morning while it's still dark, come around to the back door of the bakery." Oh, what a relief! I knew he was going to give me something. And he was very generous: from then on, every Wednesday morning before dawn he would leave a loaf of bread for me in the milk can by his backdoor. You have to understand: back then, a loaf of freshly baked bread was as close as you could get to heaven.

The last eight months, from September '44 to May '45, were the worst. No coal, no gas, no electricity—which meant no heat and no light. And the food supply was dwindling: everything was ersatz— chicory instead of coffee, sugar beets—which are pig fodder—instead of sugar. And the Germans, who were the cause of it all, threatened us! They said, "If we leave, all you'll have left to eat will be grass."

The child needed food, but I had almost nothing to feed her. So I would leave Nettie with my parents and walk with a cart to where the farms were in the north. Sometimes the weather cooperated and we had some sun and warmth, but when the icy winds came, my feet would turn to wood.

When you finally reached the farmers, they would take your jewelry and linen, and give you beans and vegetables in exchange. They even charged one-and-a-half guilders to spend the night! Where did I sleep? In the barn with the cows. That was not so bad because it was warm. But there was no toilet, nothing. Sometimes a hundred people at a time, staying over on one farm. Then the next morning, we would all have to walk back to Amsterdam.

One day during this "hunger winter" I noticed the date: 5 December 1944. This is Sinterklaas in the Netherlands, when all the children get presents and everything is supposed to be fun. But we were all poor, hungry, and unhappy. No one even remembered that it was Sinterklaas. An icy wind was blowing, but I went out for a walk. I crossed a field where a freight train had stopped. When I looked inside one of the boxcars, what do you think I saw? Apples, potatoes, and onions! I said to myself, "It's Sinterklaas, and the children are going to eat." I stuffed my bag full of produce, and headed for home. It was only three or four in the afternoon, but, because it was winter, the sun was already setting. I'll never forget how happy I felt, walking back under the low hanging clouds. As the sky grew dark, I went around the neighborhood inviting all the children to come with me to a Sinterklaas Party. Twenty-five or thirty of the little waifs crowded into my apartment. I got busy preparing the food. The aroma of the potatoes and onions cooking was like heaven itself!

The neighbor downstairs brought up his accordion, and we all sang Sinterklaas songs. Our other neighbors handed out some white Sinterklaas candy that they had been hoarding somewhere. It was so nice, but the children, oh!, they were so badly off. Their clothes were threadbare and patched, and their legs and arms were so thin. Their shoes were falling apart, and some didn't even *have* shoes.

The food supply didn't start to come back until just before the war ended. My elderly neighbor used to always say, "When the white bread comes, there will be peace." In the Netherlands, white bread is a symbol for peace and happiness; when couples are first married, we call it "the white bread weeks." We couldn't get white bread at all during the war, but shortly before the Allies came, the Red Cross brought in delicious white bread from Sweden. People would stand on line for hours for it. When my neighbor got her slice, she said "There is peace," and then she keeled over and died.

But she was right: on 5 May 1945 the Germans surrendered! Everyone ran out into the street, and we were all hugging and kissing. Flags were everywhere, and the children pinned little strips of orange cloth onto their shirts and blouses. Adults wore orange armbands or ribbons, and we sang the national anthem in public for the first time since the occupation began. I went to Dam Square, which is the place we Dutch like to go to celebrate, and found it a heaving sea of singing, dancing people. You had your arms around people you had never seen before.

I picked a yellow star up off of the ground, and pinned it on Nettie's behind! I wanted everyone to see that she *was* a Jewish child.

But while this was going on, shots rang out, and I heard bullets whiz right over my head. Some drunken German officers were firing into the crowd! People screamed and ran for cover, but some of them were struck down. Suddenly the courtyard had become a place of tragedy. Now, each year, people gather on the Dam to observe a moment of silence in remembrance of the nineteen people who died there that day.

On May 8, Winston Churchill came on the radio and declared V-E Day—Victory in Europe Day. The occupation had lasted almost exactly five years. And the Third Reich that the Germans imagined would rule for a thousand years had been destroyed—or destroyed itself—in barely more than ten.

In the weeks and months that followed, my husband returned, but my younger brother was never seen again. I thought that the Blochs would come right away for Nettie, but I didn't hear anything from them. I remember someone asking my age. I said, "Twenty-one," but then I said, "No, twenty-six." It was as if time had stopped during the war. Nettie was now five-and-a-half; I had loved her as my own child for over three years. But then her parents took her back.

Not such a nice story. Suddenly, one day they appeared and wanted her. Nettie was frightened and didn't want to go with them, because she didn't remember them. She was crying, and saying to me, "Mamma, don't you love me?" I said to Sylvia, "She must make the change slowly. Otherwise it won't be good." But they wanted Nettie back right away. She said, "It's my child, and I want her back." I had become very attached to Nettie, so it was like having my own child ripped away from me. But what could I say? She was the mother, so I gave her back to Sylvia.

As I predicted, it didn't turn out so good. At school, they thought there was something wrong with Nettie; she wasn't able to follow her lessons. When you have a child, you must talk to the child, but the mother was coming to *me* to talk about the child. I told her, "Nettie is not dumb—she is just disturbed because of the change." And every night I went to bed crying for Nettie. For four weeks I stayed in bed at my parents' house crying. I couldn't eat; I could only cry. And to make matters worse, Sylvia acted as if she didn't like me.

Over time Nettie came to love both of us as her mother. She called her Mamma Sylvia, and she called me Mamma Clara.

What was your life like after the war?

I wanted to have children of my own, but for five years I couldn't get pregnant. I went to specialists, but it did no good. Then, when I turned thirty, just for a thrill, I went parachute jumping. Suddenly, I was pregnant! Soon I had my first baby, a girl. A year later, I had a second girl. And then, after that, three boys.

But my husband had started to drink. After work, he would go straight to the bar and wouldn't come home until morning. I stayed with him over the years, but he drank away our earnings so I had to go out at night and work. For fifteen years I worked the night shift at a nursing home. But I started getting excruciating migraines. Finally, we divorced, and after that things were much better. Nettie grew up and moved to Israel. Later she married an Orthodox Jewish man, and now they have two children of their own. They call me Oma Clara.

It was Nettie who nominated you for the Yad Vashem award?

She gave me some forms to fill out, and told me it might take some time, for they have to check everything and find witnesses. In fact, many years went by and I forgot all about it. But then, suddenly, they gave me a medal. I was surprised!

I have taken twelve trips to Israel to visit Nettie, and she has often come here to see me. The first time I went there, Nettie's rabbi came over and hugged my neck. He said, "Whoever saves one life, saves a whole world." I started to cry.

After Nettie had her first baby, she called from Israel to say she was going to come to visit me, and the Blochs. But the day before she was to arrive, Sylvia Bloch called and said, "Nettie won't be coming. You do not keep kosher and her new husband is very strict about the Jewish dietary laws." I cried and cried.

The next day Nettie called to say they were on their way over! She arrived with her husband, and I had plenty of time to cuddle the new baby. They stayed for hours, but when it came time to make dinner, I didn't know what to do. Would he eat my cooking? But he said, "Mrs. Dijkstra, if it wasn't for you, I wouldn't have my wife. I'll gladly eat whatever you put before me." He would have eaten an ox if I cooked it for him!

He spoke truly: if it hadn't been for you, Nettie would most likely have been deported and killed, like most other Jewish children. Why did you help?

It was only human.

But so many other humans did nothing.

Well, you know, the heart has reasons.

In the years since the war, have you ever again had the occasion to help children other than your own?

I have a girl in Sri Lanka, through an organization called Foster Parents. I'll show you her picture. I send forty-five guilders a month to pay for her food and the living expenses. I like to write her letters, and they translate them into Sinhala. And she sends me back little paintings, and I get reports about how she is doing.

Some time ago, I took in a boy through a program that gives disadvantaged children a vacation. I signed up by phone to keep him for a month. When I went to pick the child up, the man led me over to a large boy with a watch and a calculator. My goodness, he's German, I thought. Then I thought, well, maybe I'll be glad it turned out like this; I might even grow to love the child.

It didn't work out so well. All he wanted to eat was fast food; all he wanted to drink was Coca-Cola. When I took him on a vacation to the beach, he spent the whole time buying things. I called the office for the vacation children. The woman said, "You have to understand, some of these children are not physically deprived, but they are in emotional pain." Yah. Well, one day I noticed that all the money was missing from my drawer—about 150 guilders. He said, "Well, I want to buy a very expensive bike." I called the office again, and they said they would take him away the next morning. I realized that all the things he had been buying in Zandvoort had been with my money. When they came to pick him up, my grandson said, "Why don't you search his pockets?" I said, "No." There are so many things in life you just have to put behind you. It was a bad experience, that's all.

Do you feel it's more difficult now for children to grow up in a wholesome way than when you were a child?

When I was fourteen, I used to help take care of the children at the local school. At the end of the school day, I would say to them, "Come on over to my house—you can play there." Now, you can't do that. You have children coming to school with knives, guns—it's meshugah, it's crazy. The children see movies with drugs and violence, and they get the idea that this is exciting. I can cry all day after tuning in to one of those movies. The police pick up young people who use drugs, but the big dealers stay out of range. When they do pick one up, they're afraid to do anything because of his connections with drug cartels. Oy Gevalt! What's the world coming to?

Then, there is that terrible fighting going on in Africa. Brother attacks brother. I can't understand it. Who cares about what is good for the people? The soldiers go and fight, but it's all about what's in the land—oil or uranium. It costs so much money, and all the while the children have nothing to eat. Whenever there's a war, it's always the children who have to suffer.

I believe that most of the strife and wars are all about money, money, money. Switzerland is a nice country, but the Swiss were not nice during the war—not nice. They wanted the valuables of the Jewish people, and they laundered money for the Nazis, money the Nazis had stolen from the Jews. There were

Clara Dijkstra in 1996. Courtesy of Mark Klempner.

many war criminals who had so much money that they could pay off the right people, and live without worry in the Vatican until they could catch a boat to South America. This is how men like Josef Mengele and Adolf Eichmann were able to escape to Argentina or Brazil.

The schools teach the young people about history and current events, but many of them say, "What do I care?" They're more interested in watching TV, and sometimes the parents let them watch anything they want—not good. Many families now eat dinner while sitting in front of the TV set—also not good. With so many mothers and fathers working, the children get out from school and come home to an empty house. Then the parents wonder why their children won't talk to them. As a child, when I came home from school, my mother would be there waiting for us. She had some hot tea and honey wafers set out on the table. With the children today, no one is there for them. Then they become angry and get into trouble.

But where is the love for the children? No, you're working for another car, a better house. . . . You can have your cars and your luxurious homes, or you can have a close, loving relationship with your children. But you can't have it both ways. If children get the love and attention they need, they will have a chance to grow into good people. It's so important. When I look at Nettie, I see that the love that I gave her, she is now giving back to her own children.

Now that you're almost eighty, how do you feel about the way society treats its elders?

It used to be that the mayor of the town would come to see you on your hundredth birthday, but now becoming a hundred years old is not so unusual. I could live that long; but then again, I might die tomorrow. When I die, I want to be buried, not burned. Just put me in the ground with the worms. And no fancy funeral—all I want is one red rose and one white rose from each of the children. Human values, not material things.

All my life I have loved children, wherever they are in the world. Now I have five children, and eight grandchildren, plus Nettie, who I will always love as my first child. On Christmas, they all come over for dinner, and I have to set up this table, and one there, and then a whole table over there. Three tables I have to put up to seat all of them. And the food—I make it all myself. When my children come together like that, sometimes I just ache with love.

◈

WHEN I FIRST HEARD THE STORY of how Mrs. Bloch behaved after the war, I was stunned by her ingratitude to Clara, as well as her insensitivity to her own child. Over time, I've developed a great deal more sympathy for her, having learned about what she must have gone through during and after the war. Truly, as traumatologist Ervin Staub has noted, "extreme and horrible circumstances give rise to extreme and unpredictable emotional reactions."

For those few Dutch Jews who survived the war, the period immediately following was the time when they learned who had been killed among their family members and friends. Those survivors who had suffered heavy losses often felt that their lives no longer had meaning. As Simon Wiesenthal explains, "They had been spared—but they had no one to live for, no place they could go back to, no pieces to pick up." Other survivors were faced with agonizing uncertainty as to the fate of those still missing—would they return, or would their names appear on the death rolls? There are stories of Jews who, for years, met every train that arrived from Poland, hoping to find their missing loved ones.

It's not so hard to understand, then, that Mrs. Bloch, on finding that her only daughter was alive and well, would want her back immediately, and be unable to grasp the effect that might have on the child. Perhaps Mrs. Bloch also feared that Nettie, after having spent her earliest years with Clara, would never really be her daughter again, would never fully see her as her mother.

When the surviving remnant of Dutch Jewry made it back to their homeland, they found, not the stability and comfort for which they had longed, but confusion, disorder, and sometimes callousness. Everyone had their sad stories to tell, and compassion congealed into something like apathy among the Dutch who, for five long years, had watched the Nazis eviscerate their country. Many Dutch coped with the difficult postwar period by refusing any look backward, steeling themselves against what would have been debilitating sorrow. For the returning

Jews, however, the collision between their prewar memories of the place and the postwar realities set off new implosions of grief and anguish.

The larger problem was that Amsterdam—and all of Holland—was like an anthill that had been stomped on for five years. In addition to the hundred thousand people who had been killed because they were Jews, twenty-three thousand civilians had died in air raids, eighteen thousand had starved to death during the "hunger winter," and another five thousand had succumbed in prisons and concentration camps. Another estimated fifty thousand died because of inadequate medical attention owing to the crippled health care system. And what of those five hundred fifty thousand young men who had been taken away to work for the Germans? Thirty thousand of them did not return. Total civilian losses during the war came to 237,300—about three out of every one hundred people in a country of 8.8 million.

And so, although the Dutch wildly celebrated the German surrender of 5 May 1945, with it came psychological license to survey the enormity of the damage the Nazis had inflicted. Though Amsterdam was the only city in which the thrill of liberation was mixed with the shock of additional German aggression, there was no unmitigated joy to be found anywhere in the Netherlands at that time. Yes, the Dutch kicked up their heels in festivity, but in the private spaces of their lives, in the empty beds and silent kitchens, the specter of their missing loved ones continually loomed.

A deeper question remains to be explored about the "hunger winter": how could the Nazis have been so cruel as to intentionally starve their Nordic cousins, the Dutch, especially after the Dutch had fed so many hungry German and Austrian children at the end of the First World War?

Henri van der Zee, a Dutch historian who lived through the "hunger winter," recalls some ironic humor from the time that suggests the Dutch themselves were tormented by this question:

"The German children of 1918 are so grateful for the good food they got in Holland that, in 1945, they give every Dutch child two slices of bread and one potato a day." This bitter allusion to the flood of German and Austrian children who came to Holland after the First World War and enjoyed Dutch hospitality and kindness was one of the jokes that circulated in the Hunger Winter. But just how deep the resentment was, Captain Lipmann Kessel discovered when . . . a visiting nurse remarked that some of those same German children "are now helping to starve out and destroy the provinces in which they were once guests."

Certainly the Nazis were doing all kinds of heinous things in the Netherlands. It can be argued that the "hunger winter" was simply the ultimate example of the same exponential formula of retribution they had demonstrated in 1941 by arresting four hundred young men after the Resistance had wounded a few Nazis. This time, however, the provocation was the Railway Strike of September 1944 in which tens of thousands of Dutch railway workers, taking their cue from the exiled queen, abandoned their posts. (They continued to receive their salaries from the LO, which, by that time, was being funded by the Dutch government in exile.) The idea was to cripple the Nazis' ability to transport military supplies and stop their depredation of the country. However, the Nazis then ran the trains themselves, and, as the Railway Strike continued, they gradually stopped transporting food to the Dutch.

A more far-reaching explanation was presaged by American Quaker humanitarian Clarence Pickett. At an address he gave in Philadelphia in October 1940, four years before the Germans began to starve the Dutch, Pickett suggested that, "the Germany which Britain now faces, and of which she so heartily disapproves, is in no small degree the product of the vicious weapon of blockade used during and following the [First] World War. . . . There is yet to be shown an illustration where the starvation of populations has been proved to be a permanent instrument of peace."

The blockade of World War I may indeed have been a link in the chain that resulted in the Germans starving the Dutch several decades later. Since the time of the Napoleonic Wars, blockades had only been applied to prevent military supplies from entering a country, but in the blockade against Germany during World War I, the Allies also blocked food. The idea was to starve out the enemy and ruin the German economy, and it worked: Germany was forced to surrender. The Allies then presented the defeated country with the Treaty of Versailles, which stated that Germany was fully responsible for the war and must pay all war damages. It also lopped off some of Germany's most valuable territory, reducing it to the size of France, and tightly restricted its military.

The Germans were offended by the allegation that they alone were responsible for the war, as Germany was but one aggressor in "the terrifying momentum of diplomacy" that set World War I in motion. The demand for full reparations was clearly vindictive, for it would weigh the country down with a burden of debt it would never throw off. As early as 1928, historian Sidney Fay, in his classic *The Origins of the World War,* described the Treaty of Versailles as "a dictum exacted by victors from vanquished, under the influence of the blindness, ignorance, hatred, and the propagandist misconceptions to which war had given rise."

When presented with this treaty (after having played no part in its creation), the German representatives objected strenuously to its terms. The Allies, however, had an insidious weapon at their disposal: the blockade. Although Germany was already starving and broke, the Allies kept up the sanctions for seven months after the armistice, until the tattered country finally acquiesced. The result was immediate unrest within its borders: embittered nationalists began incendiary diatribes, resentment escalated into violence, and a revolution that same year toppled the already crumbing monarchy.

The German economy soon spiraled off into a stratospheric inflation—the exchange rate went from 4.2 marks to a dollar in 1914, to 4.2 *trillion* marks to a dollar in 1923. The comic absurdity of this was lost on Germany's working class, many of whom found themselves unable to feed their children. In 1923, the mayor of Berlin decried that one quarter of the children were malnourished, and that even more were unable to do their schoolwork because of bad health. As the German economy collapsed, France occupied the Ruhr, the richest section of the Rhineland, claiming that Germany had reneged on its war debts.

In the political instability that followed, Adolf Hitler and his brown-shirted thugs "rose from the ranks of those whom World War I left disenchanted and alienated, with the war still in their bones." Inge Scholl, who as a college student was part of the White Rose resistance group in Germany, explains, "If a man's bare existence is undermined and his future is nothing but a gray, impenetrable wall, he will listen to promises and temptations and not ask who offers them." Indeed, the discontent of millions of unemployed workers was fertile ground for the Nazi philosophy to take root. When a young Adolf Hitler vowed that under his leadership "the chains of Versailles" would be cast off, the German people listened. Luigi Barzini, a European journalist during the 1930s, recalls that they "honestly hoped Hitler would somehow avenge the honor of their fatherland, restore its pride and dignity and its place in the concert of nations, solve the economic problems, and eventually, one day, unite all Germans under one flag."

Meanwhile, Hitler's brown-shirts were busy smashing the internal opposition, and, in the process, destroying "every institution that under democracy preserved remnants of human spontaneity." Barzini recalls a German cabaret comedian who used to keep silent for a minute or two during his act. He would then say, "Now that we have discussed the political situation, we can talk of something else." He soon was arrested. As early as 1933, it was clear that the German people had turned themselves over to a regime that, to quote historian Gordon Craig, "was as efficient in the techniques of control as it was ruthless and unconstrained by constitutional or moral considerations in its use of force against opponents."

As a way of getting around the military restrictions placed on Germany by the treaty, Hitler formed a plethora of diverse police forces, some indistinguishable from military units. When the Great Depression plunged the country into another financial tailspin, he was able to turn it around by creating a war economy, something he accomplished through remilitarization in open violation of the despised treaty.

During the late 1930s, the Allied powers tried to appease Germany, but by then it was too late. Their new permissiveness, instead of defusing the growing tensions, only gave Hitler the message that he could get away with his plans for expansion, and he cunningly manipulated the Allies using their own belated guilt. One week before attacking Poland, for instance, he wrote to British Prime Minister Neville Chamberlain, "The question of the treatment of European problems on a peaceful basis is not a decision which rests with Germany, but primarily with those who, since the crime committed by the Versailles Diktat, have stubbornly and consistently opposed any peaceful revision."

The arc of this explanation of Clarence Pickett's thesis began with the starvation of Germany by the Allied forces during the First World

War, and ends with the starvation of Holland by the German forces during the Second World War. Clearly, the colossal injustices of the naval blockade and the Versailles Treaty at the end of World War I far outweighed any good the humanitarian programs of that time were able to do for Germany. The efforts of the Dutch to feed hungry German children were too little and too late to prevent the trauma that would later reassert itself when the generation of victims grew up to be the generation of perpetrators. Clarence Pickett was a prophet: starving a population does not lead to peace, but to further starvation.

Much attention has been paid to how a charismatic Hitler took control and mesmerized a malleable German people into following him blindly. By following the chain of causation back, we also see how the Allied nations had some part in the creation of the Nazi nightmare.

six

KEES VEENSTRA

Just the Human Thing to Do

**Should you shield the canyons
from the windstorms, you would never
see the beauty of their carvings.**

—ELISABETH KÜBLER-ROSS

KEES VEENSTRA IS ONE RESCUER whose attempts to save Jews during the Holocaust have remained almost completely unknown. He rarely talks about them and feels strongly that what he undertook at that time was nothing more than the human thing to do. This attitude, combined with his regret over not having done more, leads him to object when someone like myself tries to draw attention to his wartime efforts. "I won't have it," he wrote me recently. "Just because I risked my life a few times does not make me a hero." But isn't that precisely what makes someone a hero?

I first met Kees, a tall man with a frank gaze and a time-weathered face, when I wandered into his little bookshop on Utrechtseestraat in Amsterdam, looking for a Dutch-English dictionary. His friendly manner made me want to chat, and I learned that he had been running the shop for over forty years. When he asked what had brought me to the Netherlands, I explained that I was interviewing people who had rescued Jews during the Nazi occupation. He nodded slightly, but didn't reply. Later, as I was leaving, he suggested hesitantly, "Perhaps you might want to speak with me." For some reason, his desire to go on record for posterity got the better of his usual reticence that day.

A week later, he came to the pied-à-terre where I was staying, ready to be interviewed for the first time. Lowering himself into an armchair, he said, "My, my, I'm to look into the past. Once I start, I do believe I will forget where I am, and it will all come back to me." And that was what happened.

Like other of the rescuers, Kees is still haunted by his encounters with Nazi terror, despite the passage of over half a century. As I watched him grapple with these difficult memories, I thought about the cost of having had a loving, open heart during those horrendous times: where does that pain go after the events have faded into the historical memory?

In Kees' case, nowhere at all. Some survivors find that by telling their stories and giving voice to their feelings, a healing process is set in motion. For most of his life, however, Kees has relied on sailing as a way to free his mind and calm his spirit. He told me he feels the best at the helm of his sailboat, tacking into the spray, enjoying the shimmering brilliance of water, sunlight, and sky.

At the time the Germans overran our country, my father was the managing editor of the largest newspaper in the Netherlands: *Het Volk,* which means "The People." It had its offices here in Amsterdam, and employed about two hundred people. Then, when the Germans came, the editor-in-chief committed suicide. He wasn't

Jewish, but he had always published articles against Hitler, so I guess he couldn't face what was coming. And so my father was made editor-in-chief. The Nazis took control of the paper and my father wanted to resign, but they said to him, "You cannot resign. You must stay at your post." He said, "I'll stay as long as my conscience allows it." But then, in their very first anti-Jewish regulation on 15 May, they dismissed all Jews who worked for the Dutch news agencies. A short time later, they cut off all the pensions of the Jewish people who had worked for the paper—their contracts were declared null and void. My father said, "This is the point where I leave."

Through his connections, he was able to start his own little publishing firm, and he asked me to come work with him. That I did, but because I'd been away working in another place, I didn't realize at first that his entire staff of about twenty people were Jews who had been sacked by the Germans. There was a Mr. Abram who was the bookkeeper, and one day at lunch I asked, "Is Mr. Abram a Jew also?" That got a big laugh. Mr. Abram was a Jew if ever there was one, but I hadn't learned to see it yet. Now, when a Jewish man comes into my bookshop, I immediately think "Oh, a Jew." Formerly I thought, "a human being," but now I think, "a Jew." Which I think is a shame, but it's there now, and it can't be helped.

The Germans were very clever. At first they said to the Jews, "Nothing will happen to you. You need only to register." This didn't seem unreasonable, because non-Jews also had to register. But when you registered, they would stamp a big black **J** on your identification card, and once that was on there, you couldn't possibly get it off.

Here's something remarkable: In my father's publishing firm, there was one young woman who said, "I'm not going to register." Her Jewish coworkers thought that that was very unfair. They said, "We have to stick together; if you are a Jew, you have to have a J." And she said, "Why should I comply with the Germans?" So she never registered; she never got a J, and she never had any trouble! Simply by refusing to take that first step. You see, until you registered, they had no definite way of knowing that you were a Jew. I must say, I know of three other cases like that, but only three. Everyone else thought, well, if that's what we're told to do, then we shall do it.

The Germans came up with more measures, and still more measures, and one day a Dutch Nazi was murdered in the Jewish quarter of

Amsterdam. As a reprisal, the Germans arrested over four hundred young Jewish men and sent them to Mauthausen. After two weeks, you started hearing from people, "Did you know so and so? He was picked up, but now he's died of appendicitis"—or dysentery or sunstroke, or whatever lie they had written on the death notice. After three months, nearly all those boys were dead. Now that should have opened our eyes to what was going to happen. But someone would say, "Well, that's amazing, that they are all dead," and someone else would say, "That's ridiculous. And are they dead? Or is it just—." So we were stupid. We didn't want to face it. We just couldn't believe they were being brutally murdered.

From the age of fourteen, I had been a member of a youth organization called the Nederlandse Jeugdbond voor Natuurstudie. It was a kind of nature club for boys and girls. Some of us were interested in plants; some in insects; some, like myself, in birds. But it had a unique feature: the young people ran it themselves, and when you turned twenty-four you had to leave. I was twenty at the time the war started, so by then I was one of its oldest members.

It was run democratically, and many of the decisions were made by consensus. We would meet in nature spots all over Holland, and go on camping trips, and day hikes, and the like. Thinking back, I realize it really fostered the development of independence and a keen sense of responsibility. And when we turned to hiding our Jewish friends, that all came into play.

I recall a conversation one day between myself and a few of the other boys. It was early in '42, after the Nazis had announced that all Jews had to move into Amsterdam, and we were worried about a boy who hadn't shown up that day. "'Oh, didn't you know, he's Jewish?" "No, I never knew that." "He has to go to Amsterdam, right?" "Yah, but wouldn't it be better if he dived under?" "Yes, perhaps." So we started to think about how we could help him. Han Alta, one of the other senior members of the group, had worked as a typographer, and he wanted to try his hand at falsifying an ID. So he asked one of the non-Jewish boys, "Can you 'lose' your ID?" "Yes, I can 'lose' it." So that gave him something to work with. Later, after he was done altering the ID, the boy it was for—our Jewish friend—said, "Well, now I've got an ID, but we must find out whether it will work." Can you imagine? This young

Jewish boy goes straight to the Gestapo at the Utrecht Central Station to try it out! They didn't bother with him at first, but he loitered around there looking so nervous that in the end they demanded to see it. "Move on," they shouted.

So we were very glad that even the Gestapo at the railway station, strict and exacting, couldn't detect that it was forged. He took a tremendous risk by doing that, and he performed a great service for the Jewish members of the group, because Han then knew he could go ahead and make IDs for them as well.

So Han made many more false IDs, using those that others had "lost." But after a while we had to stop doing that because the Germans caught on. If you said you had lost your ID they would hector you, maybe beat you up. We needed to get them in another way, and the only other way was to steal them. I remember watching a particular boy on the street and thinking: he's about the right age; I must try to get his. I got lucky one night because there was a Christian youth meeting and they all had their coats hanging in the hallway. So, for a short time, anyway, we had a surplus of IDs.

It started out that we only hid members of the nature group, but everyone had a girlfriend, or a sister—or perhaps their whole family wanted to dive under. We wouldn't go around asking, but if someone knew of someone, we would help them. On the other hand, when you were trying to find places for the onderduikers, you had to ask people, or hint somehow. But it wasn't too difficult to perceive who might be willing.

I liked bringing the onderduikers out to the farmers, and I knew quite a few of them because I had gone on many cycling trips into the rural areas. Though there were control posts with guards on the main roads, I would take to the unpaved roads and rutted bicycle paths.

Han, who made the false IDs, lived in a cabin in the woods near Amerongen. It was a quiet, sun-kissed kind of place, nestled away in a vast orchard along the Rhine River. It couldn't be seen from the road, except in winter when all the leaves had fallen from the trees. If people needed an immediate hiding place, I would take them there on my bicycle. It was a long trip—85 kilometers each way from Amsterdam—and sometimes I would have to make it twice a week. When I finally got to the cabin with my "cargo," I'd collapse on my bed like a pile of bricks.

Kees (right), Han, and onderduikers at the secret cabin. Courtesy of Kees Veenstra personal collection.

In the morning, Han would start working on false IDs, and I would tell him any new addresses I had found where the onderduikers could go from there. Actually, very few people could remain anywhere for very long; most had to move four or five times in the course of the war; some lived in dozens of places. When something went wrong, or when conditions became too dangerous, we'd have to find them a new home.

The war was, of course, a terrible thing, but I enjoyed being out there at that cabin. We swam in the Rhine when the weather was nice, and in the fall the trees were ripe with apples and pears. To have something to do, we cultivated tobacco plants—they grew well there, and that brought in some money because tobacco was hard to come by in those days. After dinner, we'd sing and make music. I'd play an oversized ukulele, and Han would toot on his recorder.

On my way back to Amsterdam, if I was nearby one of the girls in hiding, I would stop by and accompany her on a walk. You couldn't do that during the day—it would be too dangerous. But at night you went walking, arm in arm, and if anyone saw you, they thought, "Well, isn't that's a nice couple." I still see one of those ladies occasionally; she's in her eighties now. She says, "I do recall strolling with you along the dike, smelling the fresh air, and looking at the moonlight on the water."

Not all the hiding places were in the country, though. We tried to find places in town, but that was rather difficult, and to hide there was difficult as well. If you were in an apartment building, you couldn't even pull the toilet chain without worrying who might hear it. But sometimes we would find addresses in Utrecht or Zeist, even though that meant the onderduikers would have to remain inside all the time. Of course, if they didn't look Jewish and had good papers, that wouldn't always be necessary.

Once I was biking through Utrecht and I visited a family there, and the father said, "Oh, do meet our niece, Gees Gelok." I said, "How do you do, Gees Gelok." She was a short woman with curly hair. Two months later I was biking somewhere else, and I met a tall woman who said, "I'm Gees Gelok." That's a very uncommon name, so I asked her if she was a relative of the Gees Gelok who lived in Utrecht. She shook her head, but later I learned that the tall one had given her identification card to the short Jewish one. But the curious thing is that I met them both.

I must say, I spent most of the war on my bicycle. It was about 120 kilometers from Amsterdam to Friesland, and I could get five flat tires on one trip. I became very good at fixing them. But at a certain point, the Germans wanted rubber and took away everyone's tires, so I had to ride on the bare rims. I was at home very little, especially towards the end of the war when I had to hide away because the Germans wanted me for slave labor. My father was often away also because they were after him, too—mainly because he had played a role in the Labor Party.

Once, though, when I *was* home, my mother and I took in an onderduiker ourselves—a man who came to us at the time of the Railway Strike. You see, in 1944 the Germans started to plunder Holland on a much larger scale, and they began to completely dismantle Dutch industry. I remember seeing train after train loaded with all kinds of machinery pass through Bussum on its way to Germany. They stole tens of thousands of electric motors, metal-working machines, oil refinery equipment, and other booty. Our government-in-exile, based in London, wanted to put a stop to it, and in September they ordered the Dutch railway workers to strike, which they did. They also hoped that stopping the trains would assist the Allied forces in their bold plan to seize five bridgeheads across the great rivers, including the furthermost one at Arnhem.

Well, the landing in Arnhem was a failure, "one bridge too far," they say, and the strike didn't stop the pillaging either. Participation was punishable by death, so now you had thirty thousand railway workers whose lives were in danger. The Germans themselves took control of the operation of the trains, and the worst consequence was that they stopped transporting food supplies west. That began a period of widespread famine.

There was a raid on our little village of Bussum in autumn of '44, and a section of the town was closed off. But a man came bicycling down our street trying to escape. He rode up to me, panting, "I'm a railway man, and they'll shoot me if they find me." I said, "Come with me." My father and I had dug out a makeshift hiding place beneath the floorboards in the hallway off of our kitchen. There was a big cupboard there, and you had to go through the lower door of the cupboard to get down below. We had sawed the floorboards, so they could be lifted up at that spot.

When we heard the Germans approaching, we opened the cupboard, pulled up the floorboards, and crawled under. Then my mother put the boards back, threw a piece of linoleum over them, and put a vacuum cleaner on top of it all. A few slivers of light came through the slats, but besides that, it was pitch dark. That railway man and I lay beside each other on the clammy ground, listening to the sounds from the street; we could hear German soldiers yelling, and every now and then, a burst of machine gun fire.

Soon the Nazis were at our house, banging on the door with the butts of their rifles. My mother let them in—six or seven soldiers. At that moment, she remembered that there were some illegal newspapers on the dining room table—stupid, for we never left those lying around. The Germans were about to search the house, but my mother said, "Here, let me make you something hot to drink." So she crumpled the illegal papers and lit the wood stove with them. We had no gas anymore, so that was perfectly plausible. Oh, she was clever, and not afraid! Meanwhile, we were lying under there with nothing between us and the jackboots of the Nazis but the floorboards. We listened as the commander questioned my mother.

"Where is your husband?"

"He's been taken already."

Kees (center) riding his bicycle during the war. Courtesy of Kees Veenstra personal collection.

"And your son?"

"He's away in the hinterlands."

"There must be a man in the house, for there is a man's bicycle on the porch."

They fired at the ceiling, hoping to scare anybody who was hiding into coming out. Then they went tromping through the house. When they flung open the door to the cupboard, we held our breath—but they had no idea it was the entrance to a hiding place. And then my mother started talking about our dog: we had a beautiful husky, a dog from Canada, and she said, "Have you ever seen a dog like this? Isn't he a handsome dog?" and they said, "Yah, yah, he sure is." The Nazis loved dogs, so she was able to divert their attention that way. Just then I heard a thumping sound—which startled me terribly until I realized that it was the dog's tail beating against the floorboards, something he always did when he was petted.

All the while, that railway man's heart was pounding like a hammer in his chest—boom, boom, boom. Could they hear it? Thankfully, no. But I must say, my mother was very brave, don't you think? I do believe that she liked to outsmart them—and she did.

. . . .

Six months before the war ended we had the "hunger winter"—oh, that was a wretched time, just trying to get enough to fill your stomach. By November 1944, there was hardly any food left. I remember my mother dividing what little food there was between us, and I had the cheek to say something like, "I think father has more." And then we'd compare our portions again and again. It was all in good humor, of course, but you can't imagine how little we had to get by on in those days.

In Amsterdam, people were starving. Those who were able traveled into the country with handcarts, wheelbarrows, or old bicycles. They would bring their linen, towels, and tablecloths to barter for food. In the beginning they had success, but after a while the farmers had enough of those things and started to make greater and greater demands. There was a farmer named Derk Jan Veldhuis who was so ashamed that his fellow farmers might ask for a golden wedding ring in exchange for food that he gave away his entire potato crop—anyone who was hungry could get ten kilos of potatoes for free.

On one of my bicycle trips into the north country, I passed by the village of Bunschoten where there was a big dairy. That was a very Christian place, and anyone passing by could stop there and have some free soup. Thin soup, just some potatoes and cabbage, but it was hot, and eased the ache in your belly. I stopped there to get my fill, and noticed a young boy, I think about eleven or twelve, sitting there crying his eyes out. Well, there was always something unhappy going on, so I didn't pay much attention. But after I had eaten and rested my bones a little, I went up to him to find out what was the matter.

He told me that his father was doing hard labor in Germany, and that his mother had sent him from Amsterdam to bring back food for her and his two little sisters. She had given him some towels, linen, and a fine tablecloth to barter. He had met a farmer who must have pitied him, for he had given him two pounds of butter—very precious in those days; on the black market it was selling for a hundred times the normal price—and wheat, and oatmeal, and some other things as well. He slept at that farmer's place, and the following morning, when he was traveling back with his two full bags of food, he passed by this dairy and stopped to have some soup. And there he met a woman who said, "If you'll watch my bicycle while I go to eat, then I'll do the same for you."

Kees' friend Derk, who gave away his entire potato crop to feed the hungry. Courtesy of Kees Veenstra personal collection.

So he guarded her bicycle while she went in and had some soup, and when it was his turn, he went in. But when he returned, all his things were gone.

I thought, "This is the limit. This is the absolute limit. He'll never get over it." So I went to the manager of this big dairy and I said, "Look here what I've seen just now." He said, "Don't start— all day long I hear nothing but terrible stories and everybody tries to convince me that their story is the worst." "Yes," I said, "but in this case you *must* help." So I told him what had happened, and he was a very good Christian, that man, but he was swearing— "Godverdomme!" But in the end he gave him butter again, yeh, yeh, and other things as well, and I said to the boy, "Now you go straight home, don't talk to anyone, and try not to stop until you've made it home." Yah, but you have to wonder, what went on in the mind of that woman? Perhaps she had very hungry children at home, and she looked into his bags and saw that there was food. Still, she should have been more—well, I don't know what.

I think more people would have helped the Jews had they known the terrible fate that lay in store for them. Moreover, they were afraid, and I must say, I can understand. The Germans controlled the radio, and they were always broadcasting messages telling people how foolish it was to try to do anything against them. Every week or two death notices would appear: "The German Army announces the death of twenty people, shot for engaging in certain illegal practices." Then they would list their names.

Once, early in the war, I remember talking with Ger Weevers, one of my friends from that nature group, and he asked, "What do you think we can do against the Germans?" I said, "Not very much." He said, "Come visit me in Zwolle, and we'll talk about it." So the next week I took a train to Zwolle, and as soon as I got off, I saw one of those notices and the first name on the list was Ger Weevers. I said to myself, "That can't be correct. I just talked to him last week." I started to walk away, but I went back again to stare at it: yes, there it was: "Ger Weevers, shot while trying to escape." I walked away again, and then turned around—I went back three times to stare at that notice. Even now, I get chills thinking about it. He was no older than me.

Yah, so people were afraid. Still, I came across many people who were willing to help the Jews—often the most simple, modest people. Just an ordinary bridge watcher—a man who would raise the bridge for a boat—he would say, "Well, yes, if that's the problem, I think we must do something." The people who were high up the social ladder were much less willing to get involved. Perhaps they were better able to see the consequences.

I once came to the aid of a Dutch girl who was being harassed and accosted by a few laborers. I took her part, protected her, freed her. And it so happened that her father, Mr. van Eijk, was the head of a big Protestant publishing firm. He wrote me a long letter to thank me and said, "If I can do anything for you, please let me know." So I thought, well, he's got a big publishing firm, and a printing firm in Nijkerk with about eighty workers. Perhaps he would be reliable, and could recommend people to take in onderduikers. So I wrote him a letter that I would like to visit him.

He invited me to dinner at a time when we had very little food, but, as the director of that big printing firm, he had everything. So I went there and had a meal, and at the end of the meal he folded his hands and prayed, "Good Lord," and he had quite a lot of words, and then he intoned, "And I especially ask your attention for all those people who are being persecuted by the Germans." I thought, "Well, I'm sitting in roses, oh, that's good." And so, after dinner, he took me aside and asked, "What can I do for you?" "Well, we are looking for people who will take in Jewish children, Jewish boys—." "How dare you ask me that?" he bristled. "I'm the director of a firm with a lot of responsibilities—how dare you ask me that!" So that was quite different from what I expected. There's theory and there's practice.

How do you think you became a person who was willing to help the Jewish people?

Well, my father was an idealistic man; he always believed that we could build a better world if we all worked together. He was a leftist, a socialist, and a member of the Labor Party. So I grew up hearing "You are your brother's keeper," and "The broadest shoulders carry the heaviest burden." Well, if that's what you believe, you must act on it.

Those sound like religious ideals.

Yah, well, if Jesus was alive today, do you think he'd be a capitalist, preaching that every man should enrich himself to the best of his ability? Socialism raises those same issues of justice that Jesus and the other prophets talked about, but you can be socialist without being religious.

There may be a God, but I have trouble believing in the God that is proclaimed by Christianity. Still, I think that our society here in Holland tends to be a Christian society in the best sense of the word, and perhaps there was some Christian influence in the way I acted.

Did you see those attitudes of "you are your brother's keeper," and "the broadest shoulders carry the heaviest burden" being practiced by your parents when you were growing up?

I must say yes. During the Depression, my father would often help people, though we were rather poor ourselves. My mother was the same way. There was a divorced woman in our neighborhood, and in those days that carried a real stigma. Nobody wanted to have anything to do with her. But my mother befriended her, and came to her aid when she got sick.

How do you look back now at the role you played during the war?

What I did was just the human thing to do. I feel that I did my share— but not enough. But I never believed that all those people being taken away were going to be killed—which I might have realized if I'd thought about those four hundred boys who were sent to Mauthausen. But even late in the war, someone said to me, "Do you know, they're killing people with compressed gas pellets, with prussic acid?" And I

Kees recently on his sailboat. Courtesy of Kees Veenstra personal collection.

said, "That's ridiculous, that can't be—it's just a lurid story made up to scare people." You couldn't believe such things were really happening. When someone I had helped to hide was picked up, I thought, well, they'll be sent to a work camp, and it will be hard, no doubt, but they'll get through it.

I recall one beautiful Jewish girl with dark shining eyes and skin like porcelain: her name was Louisa van Praag. We put her up in Loosdrecht with a baker and his family, and figured she'd be safe there for it was out of the way. However, she had to stay in her room all day long, and it was like solitary confinement for her. At night she could go outside and sit by herself in the garden, but she started to go loopy. We learned of it from the baker, and tried to convince him to let her boyfriend come join her, but being a strict old Calvinist, he wouldn't hear of it. And in the end, she ran out into the heath shouting, "I am a Jew! I am a Jew!" A neighbor called the police, and she was taken away, never to return.

I've known about sixty Jewish people like that, including a girlfriend of mine who was put to death by the so-called medical experiments. And that's what I still feel very sad about.

Although I'm not Jewish, I feel connected with the Jews; my whole life has been bound up with them. I've got quite a few Jewish friends, but we hardly ever speak about the war—that's a subject we do best to avoid. For instance, the brother of that girlfriend of mine survived Auschwitz. I knew him through the nature group; he was fourteen and she was sixteen. Their whole family had planned to dive under—we had found them a perfect place—but they were caught the day before. The mother survived quite well; she was a good seamstress and spent the whole war sewing parachutes for the Germans—in Auschwitz of all places! The father was killed immediately; why, I don't know. As I told you, the girl was used for medical experiments—purposely careless mutilations to test out methods of sterilization—and died three months later.

Over the years, I've seen the brother. During the war, we were friendly with each other, but afterwards there was little left of the old camaraderie. About two years ago, though, he surprised me. We met for coffee, and he said, "Did you know that my sister kept a diary?" I said, "No, how could I?" He said, "She wrote very affectionately about you." He offered to show it to me, but I wasn't very keen on seeing it, knowing how it would affect me. But then, I kept on thinking about it, and several months later I wrote him a letter telling him that I was ready to see it. He wrote back that he never said he would show it to me. He made that quite clear, and we've never talked about it again.

How do you feel about Germans nowadays?

Now when I meet a German, he's a fellow human being. I can even shake hands with him. But the nation as a whole I despise. I'm sorry, but it cannot be helped. Not after what they did.

You know, there was a concentration camp outside Hamburg where twenty-five Jewish children were taken after being plucked from hiding places all over Holland. When they arrived there, one of the German officers went to the camp commander and asked, "What shall I do with the children?" He said, "Kill them. Kill them all." "Shall I shoot them?" the officer asked. "No." he said, "Hang them." There was a deserted school nearby, and inside was a gymnasium with metal stirrups used for gymnastics. So he hanged them from those stirrups, one by one, like rabbits.

After the war, some Dutch people said, "This man must be punished, he must be brought to justice." But no court would take the case because the man had been ordered to do it. And then they said, "Well, then the commander must be brought to trial," and he, indeed, went to trial. They deliberated for less than an hour, and concluded, "Well, he didn't have an order to do that, but he acted according to the guidelines given to him by his superiors." And so that man wasn't punished either. And of that type there are not ten thousand, but a hundred thousand!

I'm wondering if things are ever going to get worked out. Will we ever forgive and forget?

No. No. No. I mean, that girlfriend of mine who was murdered by the "medical experiments"—many of the doctors who did those things were never punished. If we had war criminals like that living in Holland, we would punish them. But in Germany, all those slimy ex-Nazis have lived out their lives, some in prominent positions. No, I cannot forgive. Especially as so many of them have never even admitted their guilt—let alone expressed remorse and asked for forgiveness.

So do you hate all Germans?

Well, look here, if a German comes into my bookshop, he is treated just like anybody else—unless he makes a wrong remark. If he makes a wrong remark, there's a switch, and the old resentment flows through my veins.

And have you met any good Germans?

Why yes; I must say yes. My wife and I went to Peloponnese, that's a peninsula in the southern part of Greece. We were touring around and came upon a certain memorial in the town of Kalávrita for 840 Greek men and boys who had been shot by the Germans. It's a very thinly populated area—there's almost nobody living there—so I was amazed that 840 people had been shot. All the names were listed, and I said to my wife, "Look at this—a twelve-year-old, a thirteen-year-old." Later when we checked into a hotel, there was an old woman behind the counter, and I asked her about it. She told us that some partisans had shot four German soldiers and the German commander had given the order:

"Shoot a thousand Greek men." But they couldn't find a thousand Greek men, so they started taking boys, but even then there were not enough. In the end, the only people left in the town were women.

The next day, we met a German clergyman and his wife who had settled in Kalávrita because they had learned of the massacre and wanted to do something to make amends. They were trying to establish a shelter there for women who were down and out. We invited them to our hotel for dinner, and when they walked into the lobby, you should have seen that old woman behind the counter. She heard them speaking German, and she started crying and yelling, she was pouring out words: "And my sons have been killed, and my nephews have been killed." That German minister was shaking like a leaf. Nevertheless, we had dinner with them, and I talked with him about my war experiences. We were going to meet them again for breakfast the next morning, but his wife came by and said that he was so stricken by what he had heard that he had not slept at all, and didn't feel well. Yah, so he was a good one. Of course there are good Germans.

Why do you think the Holocaust originated in Germany?

The Germans are too good at taking orders, that's why. You know, in Bussum, where I live now, there was a couple who had taken in a four-year-old Jewish girl. One day, two German soldiers arrived, and they said, "You must give the girl to us." Well, they couldn't deny they had the child because the soldiers had seen her playing on the garden swing, but the woman begged, "Can't you just say that you came here, but didn't find her?" "No," they said, "*Befehl ist Befehl*"—an order is an order. Well, the couple offered them money, and tried everything they could to save her little life. But no, they had to take the girl.

You could say that all soldiers are trained to follow orders, but I was in the Dutch army, and I can tell you: we weren't very good at taking orders. And it's the same in civilian life. If the government tells us to do something we say, "Why must I do that?" "Well, I don't like doing that." But in Germany, they would do it. I daresay Hitler wouldn't have made it in Holland. We would have said, "Look at that hysterical little man shouting his big mouth off!" But in Germany they followed him.

One way to prevent this kind of fatal obedience to authority would be to educate the younger ones to be somewhat critical of the leaders;

not to be so quick to believe everything the government tells them. You know, towards the beginning of the war, I went over to the house of a Communist family I knew, and there was a young man sitting there with a black shirt and a skull and crossbones insignia—good God, he was an SS! So I said to the daughter, "What the hell is he doing here?" She said, "We're connected. Hitler has signed a pact with Stalin." Of course, Hitler later broke that pact and attacked Russia, which led to his downfall. But, anyway, I got into a conversation with this fellow.

He was my age, but his mind was so filled with propaganda that it had completely warped him. He started going on about his Führer, and I wanted to say that there have always been tyrants like that, and they always fail—but that would've gotten me arrested. He continued: "We'll win the war, no doubt about it, and the German language will be spoken throughout the world." I had to say something. "Do you think they'll learn German in the United States?" His blue eyes turned icy. "They'll have to. English will be prohibited."

He really thought that the Third Reich was unconquerable and that it would last a millennium. He believed in an absolute order, and the unquestionable right of Hitler as a superman to remake the world however he wished. And that's the way those people were—you couldn't possibly talk with them, because their minds were fixed. They were like automatons—no spontaneity, no thinking for oneself, only the party line. That's what we need to prevent. Once people latch onto some twisted ideology, and reach the point where they are completely convinced that they are right, it's very dangerous.

The war was a terrible time—horrible things happened then. And yet, and yet . . . often I think the war was the best part of my life. You could be useful, you could save people, you could do things. And people were glad with anything they got: food, shelter. And now we are well fed and well housed, and not content. Everybody takes everything they have for granted—even my own children. And I know that life isn't always that way. It can be quite different. Of course, it's ridiculous to say that the war was a great time—I wept during that time—but still . . . something happened. It was quite clear what was good and it was quite clear what was bad. You had to do the good things.

IN THIS CHAPTER, Kees recalled the deportation of over four hundred young men to Mauthausen concentration camp, and his initial reluctance to believe the worst about what might happen to them. However, even if he had been prepared to believe that the men would be intentionally killed by the Nazis, he could not have imagined how gruesomely the murders would be carried out.

Mauthausen, the only concentration camp in Austria, was built in 1938 on land that contained several stone quarries. It was intended to become the source of the large granite blocks that would be used to construct the monumental buildings of the "Führer-Cities" following Germany's victory, starting with nearby Linz, where Hitler had grown up. For the newly arrested young men, however—and for tens of thousands of others—it became the site of a Sisyphean nightmare as they were forced to haul granite slabs up the nearly two hundred stone steps that the SS aptly named "Death's Stairway."

Not one of the young men from that original deportation survived. Hilberg reports: "The 'work' took its toll. Men began to drop from exhaustion, and after a while the Jews joined hands and jumped down, splattering the quarry with bones, brains, and blood." Presser provides an alternate account: "On the third day the guards started machine-gunning the climbers; on the fourth, some ten young Jews linked hands and jumped to a voluntary death."

In Amsterdam, their families were waiting and hoping, unable to believe—this was early in the occupation—that so many young men could be arrested for no reason and detained indefinitely. A few weeks later, when the death notices began arriving, shocked and grief-stricken parents took out obituary ads in the newspapers. This stirred up so much anti-Nazi sentiment that the Nazis prohibited any further ads. At the same time, Presser reports much outright denial among the families of the bereaved, as well as by the general public:

> The Chief Rabbi of The Hague made it known that no one need go into mourning; he had "good" reason to believe that the notifications need not be taken seriously. People went on seeking reassurance, clinging to any straw; for instance, to for-

tune-tellers who "saw" that the victims were still alive, that they had merely been reported dead because the Germans would not publicly admit that the boys had made a successful escape. Some were said to have sent secret messages.

Still, a wave of fear spread, even among those who clung to disbelief. The death reports caused people to dread the thought of being deported to Mauthausen, and the Nazis were quick to exploit the horror the name conjured. An announcement printed on 7 August 1942 in the *Jewish Weekly,* the newspaper of the Jewish Council, warns that all Jews who do not immediately come forward for forced labor in Germany will be deported to Mauthausen. It adds that those who refuse to wear the yellow star, or those who change their place of residence without informing the authorities, even temporarily, will also be deported to Mauthausen. In a cruel irony, the desire to avoid Mauthausen led many Jews to end up in Auschwitz, Sobibór, and other extermination camps.

The German officer most involved in the practical details of implementing the Final Solution in the Netherlands was Ferdinand Hugo Aus der Fünten, acting director of the euphemistically titled General Office for Jewish Emigration. This office worked directly with the Jewish Council, mandating the number of Jews to be called up for deportation on any given week, but leaving it up to the Council to decide who those persons would be.

When Aus der Fünten was initiating the first deportations, he asked the Jewish Council to prepare Jews to form "police-controlled labor contingents." "And why," asked the Council members, "police-controlled?" Aus der Fünten replied that in the camp environment, the police could best look after the safety of the Jews. Through such subterfuge, the Jews were being led into a trap from which few would escape.

Kees's comments about the postwar lives of the Nazi medical doctors are corroborated by renowned psychiatrist Robert Jay Lifton. In his book *The Nazi Doctors* he reports that some of those doctors who had been directly involved in murder returned to their home towns to become "conscientious, much admired physicians." He explains, however, that not all of them got away with their crimes against humanity:

Quite a few killed themselves . . . another group was executed after trials under Allied authority in Nuremberg and elsewhere, and after later trials under German authority. Many served prison sentences, which were, however, generally considered light for the crimes committed. A few, like Mengele, escaped and were never caught. A considerable number returned to medical practice and continued with it until retirement or natural death—or until, as in a few cases, they were discovered to have been criminals and belatedly tried.

seven

JANET KALFF

A Glimpse of Grace

*Dialogue requires an intense faith
in man, faith in his power to make and remake,
to create and recreate, faith in his vocation
to be more fully human.*

—PAULO FREIRE

JANET KALFF AND HER HUSBAND, ANTON, are Quakers from England who originally met at Woodbrook, a Quaker college in Birmingham. In the early 1930s, the Kalffs moved to Apeldoorn, a city in the center of the Netherlands, where they helped to establish the Dutch Society of Friends. During the Nazi occupation, Anton became involved in the LO, helping to locate safe addresses for onderduikers and delivering clandestine funds to the families of striking railway workers. Over the course of the war, the Kalffs took in two Jewish onderduikers: a man named Wolfgang Kotek early on, and later a young woman named Rosa.

My meeting with the Kalffs occurred serendipitously when they graciously offered to act as interpreters for my interview with their neighbor Laura van der Hoek, also a longtime Quaker. Unlike Laura, the Kalffs have not received the Yad Vashem award. However, Wolfgang Kotek honored them directly by planting two trees in Israel, one for each of them, through the Jewish National Fund. My time with the Kalffs was brief—only a shared pot of tea. However, I took from it the following unforgettable story, as told to me by Janet.

We were living in Apeldoorn with our two young daughters when a certain doctor who happened to be in the Resistance asked us if we would take in a Jewish girl named Rosa. Why yes, we would take her, and so she came from Rotterdam—a pretty girl of about twenty. Our neighbors saw her now and then, but we explained to them that a doctor had sent her to Apeldoorn for her health, and we had agreed to rent our spare bedroom to her. Apeldoorn was known for its good climate and greenery, so they believed the story. The children liked her, and we all got along, so everything was fine at first.

But then the Germans moved the entire governmental infrastructure from The Hague to Apeldoorn in order to be further inland and therefore better protected in the event of an Allied invasion. At this time we received a notice asking us to billet our spare bedroom to one of the civil servants who was being relocated. Opposite us was a big building where he was to have his office, and all his underlings would be there as well. Well, we couldn't refuse unless we had a very good reason, and we didn't know anything about this man—he could have been a Dutch Nazi.

So we decided to send Rosa to the boarding house where my mother-in-law Adriana lived. We explained our situation to the woman who ran the place; she was sympathetic because she was up to her neck in the Resistance. But she said, "I'll take her on one condition: if there's ever any trouble, if she's ever questioned, she must say that she was sent here by you."

"Yes, yes, we're prepared to answer for her," I said.

Well, a few weeks later, my husband was arrested. He had a small photograph of the queen on his desk at work, and his boss, an NSBer, reported him. And then Rosa was arrested. She had been told never to go out on the street, but she fell in love with a young man living there, and she wanted to buy him something for his birthday. So she went out one day, and, because she looked Jewish, she was immediately picked up.

It was hard to accept that the Nazis had Anton, and now Rosa, in their clutches, but there was nothing I could do. I also realized that Rosa might give them my name, for she wasn't the type to stand up to a Nazi interrogation, and she'd have to tell them something. I prepared for an interrogation myself but was terribly nervous—if they didn't believe my story, they could have easily executed both my husband and myself. He was in Vught concentration camp by then, and they needed only to send the order.

Well, Rosa *did* tell them my name, but instead of coming to me, they went to my mother-in-law, who was also known as Mrs. Kalff. I'd instructed Adriana, "Remember: if there should ever be any trouble with Rosa, the story is that a doctor sent her here for her health, and we helped her find a place to room. But we never for one moment guessed she was Jewish; if we had known that, we wouldn't have

Adriana Kalff at the time of the war.
Courtesy of Janet Kalff personal collection.

had anything to do with her." Yes, yes, she understood all that. Or so we thought.

When the Nazi interrogators arrived, the proprietor of the boarding house ran up the stairs to my mother-in-law crying "Mrs. Kalff! Mrs. Kalff! Two men are here to question you. *Remember that story!*" But my mother-in-law, who was, of course, an old lady, couldn't remember a word of it. It just flew out of her head. Soon the men entered her room: a German in uniform, and an NSBer. The NSBer did all the questioning—the German just sat there and listened.

Janet Kalff at age ninety-nine.
Courtesy of Mark Klempner.

Adriana was a very religious woman, and while one of them was lighting a cigarette, she said a little prayer: "Dear God, please tell me what I should do!" And, according to her, God told her to tell them the truth. So when the NSBer began to question her, she said, "All of us, myself, my children, my son and his wife, are completely opposed to the way the Jews are being treated, and we feel it our Christian duty to do all that we can to help them. My son and daughter-in-law took in this girl, knowing she was Jewish, because of their strong convictions. And now this has happened."

"Where does your daughter-in-law live?" She gave him my address.

"And where is your son?" Well, his being in Vught wasn't a very good recommendation.

A silence fell in the room after she'd told the whole truth, and she sat there trembling. After a long pause, the NSBer said, very politely, "Madam, I have an old mother, and she thinks just the way you do. You'll hear nothing more about it."

We all went into hiding for a few weeks because we were afraid they would come back after us, but they never did. In fact, Anton was released from Vught a short time later.

❧

I VISITED JANET KALFF AGAIN a couple of years later, and, at the age of ninety-nine, she repeated the story to me in almost the same words. When I asked her what became of Rosa, she gave me a sad look, and took a thin gray sheet of paper out of her drawer—a letter from Rosa that had been written in Apeldoorn prison. She explained that this letter, written just a day before Rosa was deported to Westerbork, was the last anyone had ever heard of her:

> *I believed, but wasn't certain of, my faith in God during difficult moments. But now I realize that every human being has to accept what comes. If God wants the best for me, He will help me, but I must prepare myself for the worst—not the punishments, not even the torture that I expect to endure, but my own self-reproach and regret for my foolishness. And I shiver to think that totally innocent people might now face great difficulties and dangers because of me. So perhaps it is right that I should suffer the same fate that so many others have suffered. Forgive me, dear, dear, people!*
>
> *The little plant that I have in my cell, bought for my sweetheart's birthday, bends over more and more, owing to lack of sunlight. I haven't reached that stage yet. Certainly, I am bowed, but I shall not break. Nothing they can do can really touch me. But thinking things over and remembering the many friends I made, people I loved with all my heart, then . . . no, I will think of them another day. But what if there is not another day?*
>
> *If I should read these pages years from now, I would laugh at their sentimentality. "Last words of a girl in the full bloom of her youth." I will stop now. Who these words are for, I don't know. Someone will read them someday—whoever you are. I hope the Kalffs will read them, and especially the old grandmother, whom I pray for every day. Just one more thanks for all the love and understanding I have been given.*
>
> *Your deeply sad, but grateful,*
>
> *Rosa*

eight

P I E T E R   M E E R B U R G

Mastermind of the Heart

*All human acts and all human creations
constitute a single drama, and in this sense
we are all saved or lost together. Our lives
are essentially universal.*

—MAURICE MERLEAU-PONTY

PIET MEERBURG IS SO EXPRESSIVE That I feel I would be able to understand him even if he barely spoke English—it's as if his spirit leaps ahead of his words. Or perhaps it's that his voice, so vigorous yet nuanced, can pack so much emotion and conviction into a simple phrase.

Piet was born in 1919, but his life as an octogenarian is an unusually active one. When I called recently, he had just gotten back from Boston, having attended an honorary ceremony for a friend; the next time I rang, he was leaving for a fortnight in Italy. But his is not the leisure of retirement. A successful and creative businessman, he usually puts in close to a full day at the office, continuing to work in partnership with his eldest son.

I met with Piet on the fifth of December, which, as Clara Dijkstra explained, is Sinterklaas—the day presaging Christmas in the Dutch calendar on which children customarily receive gifts. Piet's life has been a gift to the hundreds of Dutch children who were rescued by the Amsterdam Student Group: Piet was one of the group's organizers, and, according to those who worked with him, its leader and mastermind.

He welcomed me into his spacious apartment on Beethovenstraat in Amsterdam with a broad smile, his open face, with its generous mouth and bright eyes, crowned with a halo of pure white hair. The subdued afternoon light washed through the sheer curtains as we talked until dusk. Piet's words were equally pellucid: candid, frank, nearly transparent. A dynamic man who clearly possesses a wellspring of *élan vital,* he answered my questions in a direct and sometimes outspoken way, his mind not only making connections between past and present but factoring in the future as well. His level gaze mirrored his conviction that the Holocaust must be looked at squarely; in his steel-blue eyes, I felt his resolve to do what he could to set the historical record straight.

I was very anti-Nazi even before the war. I'm amazed that more people couldn't see what was coming, because it was already clear in '36 and '37. You could read *Mein Kampf,* there were stories in the newspapers. And that's why, as a college student at the University of Amsterdam, I joined a movement called *Eenheid Door Democratie—* Unity Through Democracy. All the political parties except for the fascists were represented in it, and we had a lot of meetings in which people could learn about the dangers of fascism—especially National Socialism as peddled by Hitler.

Then the Germans invaded in May of '40. The first six months they kept a low profile, and were very careful not to provoke anyone. Then in October they made the professors sign a form stating their ethnic origin. A month later all the Jewish professors were forced to resign. We had protests, and some students were arrested. We despised what the Germans were doing, but we didn't realize how dangerous it was to try to resist them.

The anti-Jewish laws that prohibited Jews from going to the shops, or on the train, didn't come all at once, but gradually. Each month, the Nazis would tighten the screws. I remember a turning point: I had a Jewish friend in one of my classes who was called home one day because the Germans were at his house and they wanted to talk to him. He never returned. Ever. So then you say, "This is ridiculous. What am I doing here? Yes, I am studying law, but look what is going on right before my eyes!" Finally you draw the line: "This far, no further."

So in '41 a group of us got together with the aim of resisting in some way. We figured that those who struggle can lose, but those who don't struggle have already lost, so we carried out protests, circulated petitions, did some sabotage . . . And after about six months of this, Jür Haak found his way to one of our secret meetings. He was in contact with the Utrecht Kindercomité, and they were already busy hiding Jewish children. So he said to us, "They're sitting in Utrecht, while you're here in Amsterdam where there are so many Jewish children. Would you like to help them?" And that's how the child rescuing started.

Jür introduced me to Wouter van Zeytveld, a guy just out of high school, who became my partner in the children's work. He was a Marxist, very leftist, and came from a family that was very much that way. And he was in love with Jür Haak's sister, Tineke. So Wouter and me and Jür and Tineke started working together, along with the other members of the group including my girlfriend Hansje van Loghem. By the end of '42, we had gone beyond just helping the Utrecht group; we were carrying out the work ourselves.

By then we were a group of about twelve, mostly guys. That shouldn't surprise you, because doing this work required that you ride on the trains, and in those days that was a very dangerous thing for a young man to do. The Germans needed labor, and might pick you up and make you work for them. Besides, if you were a young man traveling with an infant, it looked suspicious, and you might get questioned. That was a job better done by the girls. So they would ride on the trains and take the children to safe addresses, while Wouter and I stayed in Amsterdam and did the organizing piece.

Of course, it wasn't 100 percent. Geert Lubberhuizen, who started out in that same Utrecht group, made me some wonderful false papers that said I was an inspector for the railway system. Those papers gave me a very protected situation; I could ride on the train, and when the Germans saw I was an inspector, they left me alone.

One of the first things I did was to go to Friesland. I wanted to talk to the ministers there, because most of them could be trusted, and if you found a good one, he knew exactly who was "right" and who was "wrong" in the entire town. So I made contact with some ministers and told them about the razzias taking place in Amsterdam, and how we needed to find places for the Jewish children to hide. And here's the astonishing thing: they didn't believe me. They simply didn't believe the stories I was telling them. Perhaps it was because no one else had told them about it. Being strict Calvinists, they were somewhat isolated and didn't know what was going on in Amsterdam. And also, you have to remember, I was only twenty years old. Perhaps they didn't take me seriously.

But finally I found a blackstocking minister in the town of Sneek who believed me. He was a fantastic man. And then the Resistance there began to spread like wildfire. Within one month, we had set up a network in Sneek, and one in Leeuwarden, another town in the north. And after two months, everyone believed me because they were hearing the same stories from other people. The good thing was, once they knew that I was telling them the truth, they were behind me 100 percent. As Wouter used to say, "Once those fanatical Frisians back you in something, their support is so solid, you can practically build a house on it."

Soon I went down to Tienray, which is in the province of Limburg, another area that was safer than most. I set up another network there, and by the beginning of '43 we had placed about 130 children in the south alone. Later we also found safe addresses in the southernmost part of Limburg, as well as in the town of Joure, which is way up in the north.

The first step was always to get the permission of the parents. At the beginning, a lot of Jewish people thought that they were going to be sent to a work camp—they didn't realize the danger. I'd talk to the parents and they would say, "Well, we'll have to work in Poland and it won't be nice, but we want our children with us." Even later, some of them still thought they could get through it together. The point is: not all the parents wanted our help. And if that was their decision, we didn't argue with them. But if they said yes, we did everything we could to help them.

Following the July razzias of '42, there came a most important development: *De Hollandsche Schouwburg.* Schouwburg means theater, and the Hollandsche Schouwburg had been the place in Amsterdam where people went to hear vaudeville before the war. But the Germans gutted it that summer, and made it into a detention center for Jewish people. It still exists today, and you must see it. It's much more important than the Anne Frank house, because that is the spot where all the misery and death began. When the Nazis picked you up, they brought you to that theater, and after two or three weeks, they would transport you to Westerbork. From Westerbork they would send you east to Auschwitz and the other camps in Poland. And across the street from the theater was the Creche, and that was where they kept the children. The babies were brought there, too—they had some Jewish girls working there to look after them. So what we decided to do was to try to save those infants and children that were being held in the Creche.

Both the Schouwburg and the Creche were supervised by a committee of three men who worked for the Jewish Council: Walter Suskind, Felix Halverstad, and Dr. Bert de Vries Robles. Those were three really good men. The first time I spoke with Walter Suskind, he said, "The reason we're sitting here is to try to sabotage the Germans as much as possible—to use the power they have given us to free as many adults and children as we can." Now that was the right idea! He himself had come from Germany in '38. All three of those guys were Jewish. So we put our heads together to coordinate how to save those children.

The difficulty was that the Germans were very precisely organized. They had a list of everyone who came in, and everyone who went out. If they found out that even one child was missing, the whole thing would have been over. So it was a two-step process: get the child out, and cover your tracks. And that's where Felix came in. Felix developed a system to doctor the books so that there was absolutely no record that the child had even been there. He became an expert at that. But Walter

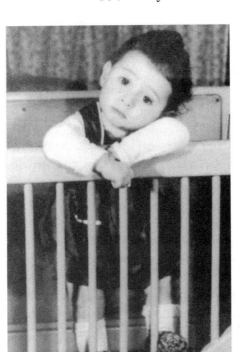

A young Jewish boy in the Creche.
Courtesy of the Netherlands Institute of
War Documentation, Remy van Duinwijck:
Vrij Nederland (18-01-1986) page 5.

Suskind was really the heart and soul of the operation. You see, there was a Gestapo officer named Aus der Fünten whom Walter had known in Germany—they had gone to school together. Aus der Fünten was now the man in charge of carrying out the deportations in the Netherlands, and he was around the theater all the time.

So what did Walter do? He became his drinking buddy. Walter was an actor; he could pull off something like that. In Germany, he used to perform at the theater in Cologne, but it was with Aus der Fünten that he gave his most extraordinary performances. He and Aus der Fünten would go out drinking, and that was how Walter kept him away from the theater and the Creche. And it worked incredibly well. The Germans didn't find out what was going on because the big boss was too busy toasting Walter! And in the meantime, Walter was organizing, planning, talking to all kinds of Resistance people, and talking to us. He would say, "Well, I have so many children of such and such ages. Can you place them?"

So once he and his people got the children out of the Creche, we would take them either north or south. We would talk to our contacts and ask, "Have you got a place for a girl of six, or for a boy of fourteen?" A girl of six would be no problem, but a Jewish-looking boy of fourteen: that would be more difficult. If we talked on the phone, we'd use code: "I have a package of ersatz coffee" would mean, "I have a dark-haired Jewish boy." Him we'd need to send down to Limburg where the people are darker. "A tin of ersatz tea" would mean a Jewish girl who could pass in Friesland, one with lighter features. So we were always in close touch with our contacts in both the north and south. We'd say, "Well, how is it, can you manage it, can you find us something?" And then if it worked out, we'd go back to Walter Suskind and say, "Yes, we can do it." Then he and the girls working at the Creche had all kinds of ways of smuggling them out. Once they were outside, several of the girls from our group would be waiting to take them to the safe addresses.

To get to Friesland, they'd have to go on a ferry from Hoorn to Staveren. And there were always lots of German soldiers on that ferry, and the girls would sit with the children, and talk to the soldiers. Those soldiers had *no idea* they were Jewish children. I mean, the Gestapo would have known, the SS would have known, but not those German recruits. And the girls let them play with the children, because nothing looked better than that.

You know, sometimes it was safest to do things right under the noses of the Nazis. When the house I lived in on Keizersgracht was raided in September '42, I had to escape through the window and run across the roof to keep from being caught. Wouter and I then dived under in the sorority house on Utrechtsestraat where my girlfriend Hansje lived. Two roosters in the henhouse! But the beauty of it was that we were right across the street from the Gestapo headquarters. We could see all their comings and goings, but they never suspected we were there.

Anyway, once the girls arrived at the safe addresses, they would meet the foster families and drop off the children. Some of the children looked very fetching; others were sickly and pale. My cousin Mia Coelingh, who used to accompany Jewish children to safe addresses, tells a wonderful story of the time she dropped off one very beautiful little girl, and all the neighbors came over to admire her. One of them decided on the spot that she would take a child also, so on the next trip Mia brought her a skinny child who looked really pathetic. The woman said, "But I ordered a beautiful child like the other one!" Mia replied, "You don't order anything here! You're supposed to be saving a human being. And this one just had chicken pox!" The woman went ahead and took her, and it all worked out fine.

In general, we didn't follow up much with the children, except to deliver food coupons and supplies. We figured that if the parents dared to take in a Jewish child, they should be able to do it their own way. But if something was wrong, I would hear about it.

Once we placed a fifteen-year old girl with a family, and she told us that the foster father was wanting to have sex with her. We found another place for her immediately, and—guess what?—the exact same thing happened. So I placed her with two old ladies, and that solved the problem.

As for our daily life as rescuers, we never knew what each new day would bring. Wouter and I would talk with the girls in the morning about what was going on, and we would figure out who would do what. Information was coming in all the time about children who needed to be hidden and addresses that were available. And through it all, we worked closely with Walter Suskind, who was coordinating not only with us, but with others groups as well, and not only helping with the children, but also getting many, many, adults out of the theater also.

As the war went on, Wouter and I really began feeling the weight of the responsibility we had taken on. Many children were depending upon us, and we had to be extremely careful. It was frightening. I mean, you realized that if you were caught it could be the end of you. No one is a hero when he's being tortured; you never know how long you'll be able to stand it. But we couldn't think about that. Sometimes at night I'd wake in a cold sweat. But during the day there was too much work to do, and you just threw yourself into it.

The biggest precaution we took was to make sure that no one knew more than one little piece of the puzzle. We told the girls as little as possible because the less you knew, the less you could give away. Wouter and I tried not to write things down, although we had to keep a list of the children and where they were. If there had been one master list and it had gotten into the wrong hands, the results would have been disastrous. So we broke the list into three parts, and kept each part in a different location. Only if the three parts were put together could you find the children, and even then it was in a kind of code.

We had a rule that if you were caught, you needed only to keep your mouth shut for twenty-four hours. After that time, we would have moved your contacts in the group to new addresses and gotten them new names, along with new false identification papers. Another thing: we never let the parents know the address where their children were being hidden. Can you imagine if the parents decided one day that they had to see their child? No, we never gave out the addresses of the children to the parents, or to anyone else.

Once I got a letter from Westerbork from the parents of one of the children we had hidden—it didn't come directly to me, of course, but to my contact address—and they wanted me to bring their daughter to them in Westerbork! That, of course, was out of the question: I go to Westerbork with a Jewish child, and I immediately get arrested. But still, I thought a lot about that letter, and I realized that even if I could have been invisible, I wouldn't have done it, because it would have endangered the child.

The parents had given us their children to save, so now we had to do our job and save them. We didn't realize at the time what an unbelievable thing it was that these parents had been forced by circumstances to give their children away to young people who were themselves barely adults. I think that one of the reasons we were able to do the work was because we were not yet parents—we couldn't fully understand what it was like for them. But, despite that blind spot on our part, I must say that once those parents turned their children over to us, we assumed responsibility for those children, and we took that responsibility very seriously.

For instance, the LO wanted to give us food coupons for the children in hiding, but they insisted on knowing their addresses. I said, "If that's what you require, we don't want your food coupons." Instead we got food coupons from one of our contacts in Friesland. They were doing all kinds of things up there, like stealing coupons from the city hall. So we had no problem getting enough coupons, and we never had to give out any of our addresses. I think this was one of the reasons why not a single one of our children or rescue workers was ever caught, although we had a few close calls. It's always 80 percent luck that you survived, isn't it?

My near brush with death occurred when I had to rendezvous with Krijn van den Helm in August 1944. Krijn was the head of the

Resistance in Friesland, a wonderful man, and absolutely a very dear friend. But towards the end of the war, someone had talked in Friesland, and all the Resistance people in the north were on the run. Krijn called me from a pay phone, and told me he had left Friesland and was hiding in Amersfoort, in the middle of the country. He said he needed to see me. So I met him in Amersfoort and he said, "I need a new false ID. But it must be a real one, not a copy. Can you do it?" I said, "Give me your photo, and I'll take care of it. I'll have it for you in a week." The real IDs were the ones that were filched from the municipal offices. I had contact with some people who could take care of that, so I went to them and I got him a real ID, with his photo attached.

A week later I was to meet him at six o'clock in the evening at a certain address. He might have been the man the Germans were most after in the entire country, so I had to be very careful. I said to my wife, Hansje, "I have the feeling I mustn't go alone." Why? Because this was a very important mission, and I couldn't afford to get stopped on the way. I still had my papers that said I was a train inspector, but on that day I didn't trust them for some reason—I had the feeling that something might go wrong. Since riding on the train was not a danger for a woman, I said to Hansje, "Darling, please come with me. It's too important—we must go together. You carry Krijn's ID. Even if they pick me up, they won't search you."

So she came with me, but when we got to the station the strap of her shoe broke and it slowed us down. We missed the train by a few seconds, and I got very angry. I prowled around the station for a few minutes, and then sat down with her and waited. After a long hour, we caught the next train, but when I finally reached Krijn's address, a woman hissed at me, "Beat it!" so I left immediately.

Later I learned what had happened. That afternoon, some men from the SD had tracked Krijn down and surrounded the house. They wanted to get some information out of him before they arrested him, so they had an operative in plain clothes knock on the door who pretended to have a message from Esmée van Eeghen—a woman Krijn worked very closely with in the Resistance. Krijn came down, but he knew right away that something was wrong. Looking out the window, he saw that he was trapped. He reached for his pistol, but the other man shot him instantly. The SD later punished that man for they had wanted to get Krijn alive.

Whenever the SD arrested someone at a house, they would remain for twenty-four hours to catch anyone else who might show up. In this case, perhaps because Krijn had been killed and needed to be removed, they only stayed until 6 P.M.—the exact time of my meeting with him. If the strap of Hansje's shoe hadn't broken, I wouldn't be sitting here. That's the kind of luck you need. But you must listen to your intuition. Your intuition is what will save you.

How did the SD find out where Krijn was? Someone must have told them, but it wasn't Esmée, as some people claimed. True, Esmée played a singularly tragic role in the Dutch Resistance: she was considered Krijn's "right hand," and because she spoke perfect German and had the looks to match, Krijn had asked her to do a little spying, to try to infiltrate a certain Nazi social circle. When she fell in love with a German officer, many people died as a result, including herself—but she never betrayed her friends in the Resistance. Let's not go into that story, though . . . it's too emotional for me. I'd rather remember Krijn: he was a fantastic man.

You know, for most of the war, Hansje and I were engaged, but one day we said, "Let's get married." There was a great sense of danger at that time: when you said to your friends in the Resistance, "See you later," you couldn't be sure that you really *would* see them later. We didn't know how the war would turn out, we didn't know if we'd live to see the end of it, but we wanted to be man and wife. So we made our wedding plans and tied the knot right in the thick of our Resistance work. It was the only time during the occupation that all the members of the Amsterdam Student Group and the Utrecht Kindercomité were in the same room together, except for Hetty and Gisela, who had already been arrested.

We wanted so much for Krijn to be there too, but it was too dangerous for him to come. And then just a few months later he was killed—on the very day of our meeting. After the war, Hansje and I named our first child after him. That's my eldest son, the one I still work with today.

· · · ·

Wedding of Pieter and Hansje. Their wedding was the only time during the war
that the members of the Utrecht Kindercomité and the Amsterdam Student Group were together
in the same room—except for Hetty and Gisela, who had just been arrested.
Courtesy of Pieter Meerburg personal collection.

*You originally approached ministers in Friesland to get support. How involved
did Holland's churches become in your rescue network?*

The churches played a big part in it, because the pastors urged the people to participate. In Sneek, there was a committee that included a Mennonite minister, a Dutch Reformed assistant minister, and a Roman Catholic priest. That was unheard of at the time, because Protestants and Catholics didn't have anything to do with each other. And on top of that, the Dutch Reformed assistant minister was a woman. But for this they came together, and they did a wonderful job—although, after one year, the Catholic Church moved the priest to another town.

Could it have been that the Catholic Church didn't want him to help with that cause?

Absolutely not. I have no religion, so I can speak impartially: The Catholic Church in Holland did a wonderful job during the war. I once saw a letter that Archbishop de Jong of Utrecht had sent to the bishops in Holland. I can't believe this man wasn't immediately arrested because here was a letter with his official seal asking them to take up a collection to help the Jews. If even *one* person had given that letter to the Germans, that would have been the end of Archbishop de Jong.

Another reason I can say that the Catholic Church did such a good job is because they didn't baptize the Jewish children or try to convert them. You know how it is—there's always someone overanxious to win another soul. My present wife is a Jewish woman who, as a young girl, was hidden for awhile by a Catholic family. She went along with their religious practices, and it would have been very easy for her to take on that religion. You see, if a Jewish child didn't look Jewish, the host families could make up a story; they could say it was a cousin who had been bombed out of Rotterdam, or something like that. Then that child could do everything with the family, and there was no need to hide. But it also meant going to church with them, because otherwise it looked suspicious. And, anyway, the child wanted to go. After all, it's quite a show, the Catholic Church, eh?

But the churches didn't try to baptize the children—the Archbishop had told them not to. I think that was very, very decent of him. On the other hand, I think that the Pope, in general, behaved very badly during the war. He was one of the few who could have really done something, but he didn't speak out. But the churches in Holland, both Catholic and Protestant, were absolutely against the Germans, against the occupation, and very much in favor of trying to protect the Jews from persecution.

You know, one of the things I'd really like to see happen is for Yad Vashem to start honoring the *Jewish* people who helped in the Resistance. Many people think the Jews went to their deaths like sheep to the slaughter, and that's not true—it's absolutely not true. I worked closely with many Jewish people in the Resistance, and I can tell you, they took much greater risks than I did. People like Walter Suskind and Felix Halverstad really behaved very bravely, and with a double risk: they were Jewish *and* in the Resistance.

Pieter Meerburg in 1996.
Courtesy of Mark Klempner.

Felix survived the war, and he remained one of my closest friends until his death a few years ago. Walter Suskind, until the end, kept on trying to save people. And what about my friend Max Dikker, who, even though he looked very Jewish, went all over Amsterdam trying to hide children, and doing all kinds of things? I think it's completely wrong that Yad Vashem only honors non-Jewish people. I hope they will change their minds on that, because the world really needs to know that the Jewish people *did* resist. Of course, there was not a mass, open resistance in Holland. That wouldn't have worked. But if some of the stories of what the Jews did to save themselves and others during the war became known, I think that many people would be astonished.

On the other hand, the Jewish Council—with the exception of men like Walter Suskind and Felix Halverstad—was the biggest mistake that the Jewish people in Holland ever made. Absolutely. And that we can say now, now that we know everything. I mean, it's easy to say they made a mistake; most of them agree they made a mistake.

The Jewish Council did their work with the assumption that if they could keep things in their own hands, it would be better than if the Germans were doing it. But that was not the case, because if the Jewish Council said, "Report to Westerbork," it was worse than if the Germans said "Report to Westerbork." Though the Germans had all the power, and were, you could say, holding a gun to their back, they could still have found ways to resist, or at least purposely done a bad job. I mean, after the war, Eichmann said about the Netherlands: "There, the transports ran so smoothly that it was a joy to watch them." Those transports all operated in coordination with the Jewish Council—every person on them was selected by the Jewish Council. Instead of being an institution that subverted the plans the Nazis had made to deport the Jews, it helped to get them into the concentration camps as quickly as possible. Now, that was completely the wrong approach. In the face of unjust authority, they should have been saboteurs, not servants.

The two men at the top were David Cohen and Abraham Asscher. Cohen had been a professor of classics—he was a pipe-smoking intellectual type—and the other was a businessman, a diamond merchant. The professor wielded more power, because the other guy really looked up to him. And I can tell you something that is unbelievable: the one non-Nazi who really threatened me during the three years that I was in the Resistance was David Cohen. When he learned I had taken a certain child from the Creche, he said, "If you don't bring him back, I'll turn you in." I don't usually talk about this in the Netherlands because I'm very close to his daughter, Virrie. She's a wonderful woman, everything her father wasn't—she was a childcare worker at the Creche, and helped to smuggle out the children. We're such good friends, but in my opinion, one of the things that must really be looked at in the coming years is the terrible role played by the Jewish Council.

Let me say this: when it started out it was all right—Asscher and Cohen had determined never to do things that were "contrary to Jewish honor." Some say they bent so that they would not break. But it came down to self-preservation: if you worked for the Jewish Council, you and your family were exempt from deportation. So they did what the Germans wanted in order to hold onto their deferments. But that, of course, turned out to be a ruse: toward the end of the war, nothing could save you. Once the people on the Jewish Council had served their purpose, they, too, were sent to the camps—including Cohen and Asscher.

There were so many children who needed to be saved, but we could only save a few of them—we knew that. By the end of the war, about 350 children had passed through our hands, and several other groups were able to rescue about the same number, bringing the total up to about eleven hundred children. But what's that out of one hundred forty thousand people? It's infinitesimal; it's not enough. One of the things that I regret very much is that we couldn't do more. I mean, we really worked very hard at it, as hard as we could—it was all we did for three years. But still, I think it's such a tragedy that so few people helped. It's a shame for humankind. Half of the children should have been saved, or, if not that, at least a third of them.

But one of the things I'm absolutely sure about is this: the people who were rich, the ones with many assets, didn't want to take a chance, didn't want to participate in the Resistance. I know of only one man, Dr. Wetzlar, who was an exception. He was a multimillionaire who had come from Germany. He always said he was one-eighth Jewish but, to be honest, I think he was at least half. But he didn't consider himself a Jew, and he never wore the yellow star.

The man did everything, he did *everything*; he put his whole fortune on the line. Not only did he give money, but he had warehouses that were packed with arms for the Resistance—the man really did everything. But he was the only one like that who did it. He survived the war, and we became great friends. He was a wonderful man.

Why didn't more people help? Well, in the case of the people who had money, I think it was greed: they didn't want to lose their money. But people had other reasons, too—they were very afraid, and they had all kinds of reasons. But one thing I know for certain is that you could find far more addresses among the common people.

We would go to these large families in the north who had very little, and they would say, "Oh well, one or two more children won't make any difference. Just send them along." My present wife lived with one of these families; as a child, she was hidden with one of the *poorest* families of Friesland, really one of the poorest families. I went over there for dinner a few times, and all they had to eat was a kind of soup with some potatoes in it. This is before the "hunger winter," but still, they kept her for six months. Those are the kind of people who were really wonderful. But the ones with money didn't want to take the risk.

Do you think many people regret that they didn't do more to try to help the Jews?

There are a few people who feel ashamed, but I think, in general, if you didn't care during the war, you're not going to care after the war. I wish I could give you a different answer.

Cornelis Suijk of the Anne Frank Center tells a story about Karl Silberbauer, the policeman who arrested the Frank family. About thirty years after the war, Suijk located him in Vienna and found that he was employed by the police force there. When asked about the Frank family, he remembered the arrest but seemed to have no pangs of conscience. He'd even purchased the diary of Anne Frank but dismissed it as "kid stuff."

Well, you know, the majority of the police collaborated with the Germans during the war, and they were never punished. The courts went after the big war criminals, but some people were never . . . I mean, in this very building a Jewish man was killed by the man who was hiding him. He hired a boat to try to dump the body in the river, but the Dutch police intercepted him. Years after the war, he was brought to trial. The man he killed was very wealthy, and he was accused of killing him for his money. What he said—and no one believed him—was that the man had threatened to betray him, and that he had been given permission to kill him by the Resistance. But he couldn't name a single living Resistance person that he had talked to about it. Half of the people who know him don't speak to him anymore. I don't speak to him anymore.

I've heard that after the war people from the Resistance sometimes took vengeance on those who had collaborated with the Germans—humiliating them, beating them, sometimes even killing them.

Yah, but don't forget there were many different kinds of people in the Resistance. There was a paramilitary part that we had no connection with—people with bayonets and so on. I didn't like those people at all. And there were the "September Resisters" who jumped on the Resistance bandwagon around September '44, when Maastricht was liberated, and the Germans fled the country (but later came back again). They had the biggest mouths, but they did very little, and they were the ones who shouted the loudest against the NSBers after the war was over. But we didn't. We had a humanitarian Resistance.

Are you a pacifist?

I don't deny that sometimes armies are necessary. But I would never go into the active military service. I couldn't—it's not in my nature. I think the humanitarian side is far more important.

After the war ended, what happened to all the children that you had helped to save?

Many of them, of course, had become orphans. The *Commissie voor Oorlogspleegkinderen* was set up by the Dutch government to figure out what to do. I worked with them for a few months because I felt a need to finish what I had started. I knew things that very few others knew. But I didn't want to stay there because I could see what was coming: a big fight over the orphaned children. Should they stay with the foster families, or be raised by relatives? And if there were no relatives, should they stay here, or be sent to Israel to be raised by Jewish people? Let's say there is an eight-year-old boy who has been hidden by a certain family since the time he was five. The parents don't return, but instead you have a seventy-year-old uncle who comes and asks for him. What do you do? The liberal Jews felt that in certain cases it would be better for the child to remain with the foster parents; the Orthodox Jews felt that every child had to be placed in a Jewish home. Everyone had a different idea about what should be done. Who was I to be involved in such decisions? The war was over; there was no danger anymore. I had given it three years, and I felt that was enough.

My plan was to finish my education. But for three years I'd been independent of my parents, and I'd grown up a lot during that time. I didn't want to return to my parents asking for money, or to depend on a government loan. So I had the idea of starting a business with my friends from the Resistance to help us pay our way through the university. And what I wanted to do was to open a cinema.

During the war, the Nazis had made everyone feel so strictly defined; even as students, you were in this group or that group, this box or that box. I wanted to create a space where we could get out of our boxes, and the idea of a cooperatively run art cinema seemed perfect. That it had never been done before didn't daunt us; we went looking for a good building, and, ironically, found a theater that had been used by the Nazis to show propaganda films. We got money from all kinds of people to "liberate" it—that multimillionaire, Dr. Wetzlar, paid for more than half of it, and a lot of other people were willing to be sponsors. Felix Halverstad was our treasurer for thirty years. So that's one business that came straight out of the Resistance—yah, we all came together again to run the cinema.

I continued to run it all the way through law school, and that's how I got into the business of managing theaters and, later, distributing films. And that's the way it's been all my life—I'm always working three jobs at the same time. But that first theater, the *Kriterion*, is still open today, and it continues to be cooperatively owned and run. Later, we took over another theater, the *Uitkijk*, and I'm proud that those two theaters together currently employ about fifty students.

Any ideas as to how we prevent a situation like the one that happened in Germany from recurring?

Information and education. That's the only way. In the years leading up to the war, the people in Germany weren't well informed. They didn't have a free press. Albert Speer, Hitler's armaments minister, later testified that through mass media propaganda eighty million Germans were subjected to the will of one man. And that's what you always find in a dictatorship: independent thinking is stifled because all the information from the outside gets closed off. The German people only heard what the government wanted them to hear, and they went along with it. You find people like that everywhere—there are as many here in Holland as there are in Germany.

What I mean is that what happened in Germany could have happened in Holland, too. And though the Germans were somewhat responsible, the Dutch were also responsible for allowing so many Jews to be deported. We had exactly the same responsibility, yet we didn't do anything. So who are we to look upon the Germans as the contemptible people of Europe? That's ridiculous. We need to look at ourselves.

Why do you think the Holocaust originated in Germany?

I've never had an explanation for that. Germany was at the vanguard of theater, film, literature, and music and was also producing the greatest scientists—men like Einstein and Planck. The Germans were the most sophisticated, intelligent, intellectual people of Europe—unbelievable!

You know, after the war I met a Dr. Hüneke, who had been a doctor in the German army. He was one of the greatest men of conscience I have ever met. He took the entire weight of what happened onto his shoulders, and he atoned for it all his life. He really took responsibility

for all that his country had done, and he worked on restitution, reparations, and so on. By the way, he had nothing to do with the medical experiments, but that was partly what he was so distressed about. He was
acutely aware that members of his profession—perhaps his fellow classmates—had done those terrible things.

But the point is that this doctor was better than 99 percent of the
Dutch people. In recent years I have met other very sincere German in-
tellectuals. Some of them still suffer over what happened during the
war. These are wonderful people, much more wonderful than 80 or 90
percent of the Dutch people of that generation who all say they were
in the Resistance when very few of them actually were. So what's it all
about? German or Dutch, there's always a big mass of people who follow the crowd, and only a small number who really think about what's
going on and take responsibility. It has nothing to do with being
German, Dutch, or French.

The French! Look at what's going on in France at the moment.
Fifteen percent for Mr. Le Pen! That's far too much—I mean, he is
absolutely a fascist. His National Front Party wants to drive all the immigrants out of the country. And in Germany—maybe a fraction of a
percent are in the extreme right. They have laws to prevent radical
splinter groups from gaining seats in their parliament. So what have the
French to boast about? They are the ones we have to watch out for
these days. I lived in the south of France for fifteen years, and I can tell
you, half the people there are for Le Pen—maybe even a majority. It's a
beautiful country, I like it, but I see a danger in the French mentality. A
people as nationalistic as the French are already dangerous.

So that's why I can't stand to hear people vilify the Germans.
Because who are they to talk? The young people today had nothing to
do with the war. They can't help it if their parents or grandparents did
the wrong thing. Right now, I think Germany is the most democratic
country in Europe.

So it seems clear that your negative feelings toward Germany are all in the past.
Yah, but I admit, I won't take a vacation in Germany.

The past associations are too strong?
Yah, and I *won't* buy a German car. Which is emotional, not reasonable.

It seems like your mind is in one place and your heart is in another.
Isn't it so with everyone?

Looking back, do you see things differently than you did at the time of the war?
You know, there was only one good thing about the war: everything was black and white. You absolutely knew you stood on the right side—there was no question about it. That has never again happened in my life.

PIET'S BLUNT CRITICISMS OF THE JEWISH COUNCIL have come to be shared by many historians. It seems that, from its inception, the Jewish Council functioned as a kind of ventriloquist act in which the Germans would talk and the words would come out of the mouths of the Council staff. Even during the war, some of the Jews called it the *Joodse Verraad*—Jewish Betrayal—instead of *Joodse Raad*—Jewish Council.

The role of the Jewish Council, especially that of its leadership, has been the subject of heated controversy in the post–World War II Netherlands. At the height of its operations, as many as 17,500 Jews were on the Council Staff, and each of them received an exemption. Regarding these exemptions, A. J. Herzberg, commented, "At best, they gave the odd fugitive time to go underground; at worst, they lulled many people into a false sense of security and prevented them from deserting their posts." He knows of what he speaks: Herzberg resigned early on from the editorial board of the Council's weekly newspaper. Many did not have the moral strength to make such choices, including the diarist Etty Hillesum, who accepted a position at the Council but likened it to "crowding on to a small piece of wood adrift on an endless ocean after a shipwreck, and then saving oneself by pushing others into the water and watching them drown."

The Nazis created such Jewish Councils not only in the Netherlands but throughout occupied Europe. Their strategy to subvert Jewish leadership in this way was far from original—Jewish history is mottled with other such instances. During the time of Jesus, all the high priests who served the Jewish community—including Caiphas, who presided over the Sanhedrin—were appointed by the Romans and beholden to Roman interests, lest they lose their positions and, possibly, their lives. But never before had Jewish leadership been employed in a plan to obliterate the entire Jewish people. This strategy was in keeping with the overall Nazi aim to make the Jews accomplices in their own annihilation and thus destroy them spiritually as well as physically.

Every opportunity was taken in the councils and concentration camps to pit Jew against Jew, typically by granting special privileges to a few. By manipulating their victims' instinct for self-preservation, the Nazis sought to eliminate any possibility that the Jews might rise up as a united force to resist them. Guided by their notions of eugenics and social Darwinism, their plan was to create a competition in which the weak lost out to the strong. Once the losers had been done away with, they would then take special care to eliminate the winners, because, to quote Reinhardt Heydrich, these survivors "will represent a natural selection and in the event of release would be the germ cell for the resuscitation of Judaism."

As the Jewish renewal that the Nazis so much wanted to obviate has arisen in the world, younger generations of Jews must take a hard look at the choices some of their grandparents and great-grandparents made in connection with such institutions as the Jewish councils. Though it can be argued that they made these choices because, as Browning puts it, "they couldn't even conceive of the program of systematic mass extermination awaiting them," the realization that some Jews were involved in the destruction of their own people remains deeply disturbing. It is not "blaming the victim" to take from this disastrous chapter in Jewish history an indelible lesson about the perils of placing personal privilege over the collective good.

By the end of 1942, Walter Suskind had become an expert at rescuing Jews, not only by sneaking children out of the Creche and adults out of the Schouwburg detention center but through a number of other dicey stunts. When someone discovered that the key to the men's locker room in an Amsterdam bathhouse fit the padlocks being used on the railway cars to Westerbork, Suskind and his associates showed up when a train stopped in the freightyards of the Polderweg and freed its occupants. Back at the Schouwburg, he destroyed all records about the passengers so that, on paper, they ceased to exist.

Walter Suskind with his young daughter.
Courtesy of the Ghetto Fighters' House
(Beit Lohamei HaGetaot).

He would also randomly slip yellow armbands to people during deportations from the Schouwburg, instructing them to put the armbands on during the ride to the transfer point and then to ask the conductor to be released. Since the armbands showed that the deportees were on the staff of the Jewish Council, their arrests would appear to have been a mistake, and the conductor would dutifully let them go.

The reader may wonder what happened to Walter Suskind—a sad story, but one worth telling. On the eve of Rosh Hashanah, 29 September 1943, the last razzia was carried out in the Netherlands, resulting in the arrest of thousands of people. Among them were the remaining staff of the Jewish Council, including Asscher and Cohen, who were taken to Westerbork and informed that their services would no longer be needed. Suskind managed to evade arrest, but his wife and daughter, as well as his mother and mother-in-law, did not.

Piet begged Suskind to dive under and try to help his family from the outside, but Walter thought that he could be more effective from within. Even as the Nazis had established the Jewish Council in Amsterdam to carry out their commands, in Westerbork, also, a handful of Jews presided over a cruel semblance of self-government. Suskind hoped that, in collusion with these Nazi-appointed Jewish administrators, most of whom were also German, he could save not only his own family, but many other Jews as well.

Unfortunately, after Suskind reported to Westerbork, that did not turn out to be the case. Piet recalls, "Over there, he wanted to do what he did in the theater: play around with the index cards, and allow people to escape. However, those in charge did not dare."

Suskind was able to talk his way out of Westerbork using his connections, but he could not get his family released. He returned to Amsterdam and continued his rescue activities, somehow managing from a distance to get other people released through the manipulation of official records. He was also able to delay the deportation of his family for a full year. Before they boarded what turned out to be the last transport ever to leave Westerbork, he returned to the camp to go with them. They all died shortly afterwards.

nine

MIEKE VERMEER

Staring Truth in the Face

*If things are ever to move upward,
someone must take the first step and
assume the risk of it.*

—WILLIAM JAMES

OF THE HANDFUL OF KNOWN RESISTANCE GROUPS dedicated to help-ing Jewish children, several had their origins in the Calvinist Church. Mieke Vermeer, while only a teen herself, became involved in the main one, named, with a touch of irony, the *Naamloze Venootschap*—"Limited Liability Company."

The seeds for the Naamloze Venootschap, commonly known as the NV, were planted by Rev. Constant Kikkel in Amsterdam at the time when two teenagers of Austrian-Jewish background in his congregation, Marianne and Leo Braun, were called up for deportation. The following Sunday he preached a sermon in which he guardedly brought up their dilemma, and two young men came forward after the service, brothers Jaap and Gerard Musch, to say they would try to find hiding places for them. Together with a friend named Dick Groenewegen van Wijk, the three began their search, not only to help the Brauns, but to find hiding places for other Jewish children as well.

Success came when they followed up on Rev. Kikkel's suggestion to talk to Reverend Pontier in the southern province of Limburg. Pontier recognized the importance of their mission and promised to talk to families he felt would be receptive; he soon reported back that there were a number of households standing by to help. Meanwhile, additional people were joining the cause in Amsterdam, including Joop Woortman, a former waiter and owner of a taxi business, who was known and trusted by many people within the Jewish sections of Amsterdam.

Soon the NV was funneling a steady stream of Jewish children from Amsterdam to Limburg to be placed by Rev. Pontier into Christian homes. Though most of his contacts were Protestant, Catholics predominate in the south, and he soon began approaching Catholic families to meet the increasing demand for safe addresses. Many Catholics opened their hearts and homes, and members of both branches of Christianity pulled together to help save lives.

Mieke Vermeer, in her direct yet soft-spoken way, could be the Dutch counterpart of the wandering monk in the *Autobiography of a Yogi* who describes himself as having "long exercised an honest introspection, the exquisitely painful approach to wisdom." After asserting that true self-examination leads to the perception of "a unity in all human minds— the stalwart kinship of selfish motive," the saddhu adds, "an aghast humility follows this leveling discovery," one that "ripens into compassion."

In Mieke, that compassion has fully matured, but that doesn't mean she has mellowed. She does not flinch from looking at the world as it is, nor does she hesitate to turn the searchlight of impartial analysis onto herself. Though she can seem pessimistic about what she sees, she is clearly more interested in healing the world than in despairing of it.

"I'm willing to talk to you, but first may I ask *you* a question?"

"Sure."

"You don't mind if I'm very blunt?"

"No, go ahead."

"What gives you the right to do this?"

"To interview you?"

"Me and the others. To collect our memories. To look into our lives."

"I *don't* have the right, unless you give me the right. Your stories belong to you—it's just that if you don't tell me, I'll never know. Not firsthand."

"You came all this way to hear firsthand?"

"I wrote you that my father and his family made it out of Poland by the skin of their teeth. Nearly all the relatives left behind were killed. I guess I desperately want there to have been a different ending to the Holocaust—a happier ending. That, of course, is impossible, but if I can meet someone like you, if I can look into your eyes and listen to your stories, then I know that, yes, there was some goodness, there was some decency. Otherwise, it's just too depressing."

"Where do you think God was during the Holocaust?"

"I think He was in people like you."

Mieke looked at me hard. "If that's true, then God became very small. Very small indeed."

I asked, "Where do *you* think God was?"

She paused, and then answered ruefully, "I think He was weeping because of all the terrible things people were doing to each other."

At the start of the Nazi occupation, I was a young teenager living here in the south with my family—one of seven girls in a family of eleven. One day, a young man named Gerard Musch came to our door, wanting to know if we would consider taking in Jewish children.

It was my mother who first made the decision to help. I don't know what she was feeling, but if she was afraid, she didn't show it. She said to Gerard, "It's fine with me. When my husband gets home, I'll talk with him about it." She believed she had a duty to care for not only her own children, but other people's children, too, if they were in danger. When my father came home, he said it was all right. Soon our homestead became one of the main safe addresses in Limburg. We took in as many as fifteen Jewish children at a time, many of them having been smuggled out of the Creche in Amsterdam. When you added the eleven of us, that made twenty-six in all. Gerard would come every couple of weeks with food coupons, money, clothes, and other supplies. We didn't have time to think about the risk—it was as if we were running a summer camp.

I have happy memories of those days. We had never known anyone Jewish before, but we liked the new children very much, and they quickly became like part of the family. They were free to run around outside, and, because of our location in the south, we didn't have the food shortage. We had fun together playing and singing. My mother sang also, and if you were feeling down, she would sing you a happy song to cheer you up.

Meanwhile, what was happening in Amsterdam was very exciting. Joop Woortman, who by that time was in charge there, made contact with Walter Suskind, and together they came up with all kinds of ways of getting Jewish children out of the Creche. Lisette Lamon, who worked at the Creche, told us that the children were smuggled out in laundry bags, rucksacks, crates, bread baskets, burlap bags, or held under a coat. One newborn even passed through a cordon of SS men in a cake box!

Just before the Creche was shut down in September '43, there was a tremendous push to get as many children out of there as possible. Jaap, Gerard, and Dick went to the Creche themselves, and, in a daring operation, left with fourteen children. When Gerard arrived to drop some of them off at our house, I begged him to let me join the group. Though I was only sixteen, he saw that there was no stopping me. When I turned seventeen, I took over his route, delivering whatever was needed to about fifty families who were hiding Jewish children. I bicycled all over the countryside, visiting the foster parents and checking up on the children.

At first, my parents objected, because it was so dangerous, but later they became very supportive. Gerard and I fell in love during those months and we even got engaged, but our happiness was cut short when he was arrested in May '44 and sent to the concentration camp in Vught. Dick Groenewegan was also arrested, but he managed to escape, and made his way back to our house to

Wartime portrait of Gerard Musch.
Courtesy of Mieke Vermeer
personal collection.

hide. Naturally, I was terribly worried about Gerard, but my mother would say, "Mieke, just take one day at a time." She really lived by that and convinced me to live by it also.

As far as our own safety and the safety of our young charges, we were fortunate to have a contact in the police department who would warn us when there might be a raid. Then we would hide our Jewish friends in the bathhouse, in the cellar, and some we'd put in the church behind the big pipe organ or up in the belfry. The Germans never caught any of the children at our house, and only two of the children hidden by the NV ever fell into the German hands. In all, we were able to save about 250 of them.

Sometimes I think my war started after the war was over. Gerard had suffered so much in the concentration camps, and when he came back, he was a changed man. We learned that Jaap had been executed by firing squad after having been tortured very badly, and that Joop Woortman had been killed as well. They had even arrested and tortured Rev. Pontier, although after six months they let him go.

So what did we do? We tried to move forward. Gerard began to work and to study as hard as he could. We got married and had our children, but there was a lot under the surface. It's hard to explain—we'd made it through so much, but it was only after the war that we began to feel its full effects.

Before long Gerard started drinking. When he eventually sought treatment, they tried to get him to talk about what happened to him in the camps, but he'd blocked it all out. He had spent the last year of the war in Sachsenhausen where men were strapped to blocks and whipped, or put in straitjackets and starved. How can you put that behind you without talking about it? Instead he became an alcoholic.

He was a good husband in many ways, but finally I had to choose between what was best for the children—we had seven of them by then, including one who is deaf—and his continuing to live here with us. I have no doubt as to the origin of his problems.

The older I get, the more I think about those war years. They never leave you.

Why do you think so few people helped?

For the same reason that there would be so few today. Nothing has changed. And the same kind of men continue to stoke the machinery of war. Sometimes there's a sort of rage within me. I want to shout: "It's ridiculous what you're doing! Why do you use people as soldiers to kill other people!"

You say nothing has changed, but we don't have German soldiers outside ready to shoot Jewish people.

Ah, well, give the German a rifle and he will shoot. And perhaps you could say, "Give the French," or "Give the Dutch." It depends on how you get them behind your bad ideas, you know? The masses are easily manipulated, and so are their violent urges. . . . Is this too depressing for you?

No.

People say "Never again," but just because they say that doesn't mean that they're any more aware than the Germans were when Hitler was making his debut. How many people who read the newspaper can tell the difference between propaganda and fact? How many can see through the bad politicians? There's such a lot of dirty politics.

So you're saying we mustn't underestimate our capacity to be misled . . .

Yes, or to do the wrong thing when we think we're doing the right thing. We have it good here in Holland, and we are proud. But in many ways we shouldn't be, we shouldn't be . . . especially if you look into our history. I recently read a book about the slavery in South Africa at the time it was a Dutch colony. It makes you feel really ashamed to be Dutch. And if we have done many bad things in the past, why should we think that we are so much better now? You see what is happening with people who come here from Africa because their lives were in danger in their own country. Some Dutch complain about the social assistance these people are getting, as if it is being taken out of their own pocket. They might not say directly to you, "I hate blacks." But you feel in the way they talk about them that if they had a chance, they would drive them out. Sometimes people, like cab drivers, will call them racist names. They fall silent when I say, "I have a black son-in-law." I tell them, "There's no *us* and *them*—we're all part of the same human family!"

We have to watch the way we think. I sometimes find myself stereotyping people—it's a startling discovery to make about oneself. When you have had several bad experiences with people of a certain type, you must be very careful to not begin thinking about all of them like that. My husband suffered terribly at the hands of the Germans, but he didn't hate all of them—he hated the people who had caused the suffering.

When we educate our children about the Holocaust, it's not enough to tell them about the horrors—we have to tell them that it should not happen that way again. That hate doesn't bring peace, and that violence doesn't bring peace, and that you need to be strong in mind and think things over before you get a weapon to use against the one you call your enemy.

It sounds like you believe in nonviolence.

Well, that's simply the message of Jesus: love your neighbor—even love your enemies. His words are more real to me than the things of this world. Yet I have many doubts. Very many. I read in my Bible every

Mieke Vermeer in 1996.
Courtesy of Mark Klempner.

night, and as I read I have the feeling that I know very little. Jesus came to bring peace, yet there is still so much bloodshed in the world. Every time I turn on my TV, I see that we are a violent, killer people. The more we hate, the more we become what we hate.

I am troubled by the misguided, sometimes terrible, things that are done in the name of God, or Jesus. Often it seems that people are practicing tribalism, not religion. Then there are those who think they must fight falsehood with their truth, but they don't want to fight the falsehood *within* their truth. They are pristine, while the others are evil. But the devil is no respecter of religion or nationality. As Solzhenitsyn has written, the line separating good and evil doesn't move along national borders, or between political parties, or social classes. It passes through every human heart—through all human hearts.

In prewar Germany, there were those who opposed Hitler. Some stayed and tried to alter the fate of their country; others fled before the gathering threat. I remember immigrants to Holland who were good Germans and aghast at what was happening to their homeland.

It's always a fight trying to uphold the truth, but truth is not the sole possession of any one person or group. I really don't understand the fanatic Christians and the fanatic Jews who are so sure about what they think is the right thing. And also the Muslims. And I don't understand how you can fight for a religion with weapons.

And then the victims just hate you and your religion more. When my father was growing up in Glowaczow, a little town about fifty miles from Warsaw, churchgoing peasants would assault Jews on Christmas and Easter. He had to stay indoors to keep from getting beaten up by these so-called Christians. Now, when he sees a crucifix, it nauseates him, because to him it's a symbol of hate, not of love.

Hmm . . . I wonder what he would think about you talking to me—someone who has come to believe in Christ, and yet who helped rescue Jewish people.

I think he would consider you an exception; someone who wouldn't have taunted him when he was a child.

God forbid. [*deep sigh*]

Do you have any advice for younger generations as to how we can prevent something as terrible as the Holocaust from recurring?

Do what you can, where you are, with what you've got. There are many little holocausts going on in the world, and all around us. Step in wherever and whenever you can.

What do you mean "little holocausts"?

I'll tell you about one I once heard about from a social worker: A nine-year-old girl was kept locked up in a closet by her legal guardians, who were crack cocaine addicts. When the social worker opened the door, she found the girl lying there half-starved. Her clothes were soiled, there were lice in her hair, and she had cigarette burns on her body. That little girl was trapped in a little holocaust. If my friend hadn't stepped in, I don't know what would have happened to her.

Some might think that it cheapens the Holocaust to compare the children of crack cocaine addicts with Jewish children during the occupation. But what could be cheaper than the Holocaust? If you were the wrong religion at that time, or if you were a gypsy, or gay, or disabled, your life had no value. I believe the best way we can honor the memory of those who died during the Holocaust is to try to alleviate the suffering of innocent people now. Especially children.

During the Nazi years, people didn't always want to know about the harm being done to children. They would turn away because they dreaded what might happen to them if they tried to do something. But today, there's no excuse. There are many people, very well off, who don't want to be bothered. That's why I believe in comforting the afflicted, and afflicting the comfortable.

What do we do about people's cynicism? Joni Mitchell asks in one of her songs, "Is justice just ice? Governed by greed and lust? Just the strong doing what they can. And the weak suffering what they must?"

We lived through that. It was very frightening, but we weren't cynical about it—we took action. And action is still needed today. The prophet Amos says, "Let justice roll down like waters," but that isn't something God can do alone. He needs our help.

Where do we start? Besides the "little holocausts" you speak of, there are un-precedented global problems such as the widespread destruction of the environment, and so-called free trade agreements that devastate the poor.

Each generation has to face a new set of problems, but God also gives you the power to solve them. Think of what a terrible problem Nazism was in my day. Now it's history.

How did Yad Vashem come to honor the members of the NV?

A group of the "hidden children" went to them, including Ed van Thijn, who had become mayor of Amsterdam. We told him that we didn't want any special recognition—that we were more than rewarded by the fact that he and the others had survived and found their way in the world. But they were insistent and filled out a lot of paperwork testifying to what we had done. In the end, all twenty members of the NV were honored by Yad Vashem.

Do you remain in touch with the "hidden children"?

Oh, yes. Now they live in many different places: Israel, Canada, America, South America. Every year, we have a reunion of the people we hid and their helpers. Not all of them can make it, of course, but there are always some who are able to come. They bring their children, and sometimes their grandchildren. We bill and coo over the new babies, and have a grand old time.

Onderduikers playing at the Vermeer homestead.
Mieke's younger sister is on the far right. Courtesy of the collection of the
Jewish Historical Museum, Amsterdam.

I AM OCCASIONALLY ASKED why I didn't meet with the Polish rescuers. For years I said it was because there were so many Yad Vashem honorees in Holland, and, besides, the Dutch speak English well, and I would not have to become fluent in a new language. But there was a hidden reason, so visceral that not until my wife Sophia spoke it—and I felt the accompanying jolt of recognition—did I realize that it had been there all the time.

"It would have been too close to home," is what she said. Indeed, to return to the place where, even before the war, my father and his family were taunted by anti-Semites; the place from which they barely escaped; the place where my remaining relatives all perished; the place where the crematoria of Auschwitz roared late into the night spewing human ash into a strangely mute world—no, it would have been too much for me.

While hundreds of thousands of people travel to Poland each year to visit Auschwitz, Treblinka, and Maidanek, I haven't even been able to

set foot in the United States Holocaust Memorial Museum until recently. The Holocaust figured too frightfully in my imagination for me
to seek it out in that way, and I already had enough inner demons to
wrestle without needing to invite more. To give one early example:
when I was twelve, an educator at my synagogue showed the members
of my bar mitzvah class footage from the concentration camps. That
night, the horrific images kept tumbling through my mind. I remembered, in particular, emaciated corpses—or were they still alive?—being
pushed down a chute. For me, this was the start of a recurring nightmare
in which a Nazi stabbed me in the back with his bayonet. I'll never forget the horror of seeing its blade come out the front of my chest.

If the subject of the Holocaust is so distressing to me, why did I un-
dertake this project at all? Like a moth to a flame, I have been drawn to
the Holocaust, and the idea of going to Amsterdam and meeting with
the Dutch rescuers seemed like a scenario I could flit in and out of un-
singed. I didn't expect a healing, but as my relationship with the rescuers
developed, my relationship to the Holocaust shifted—some psychic
valve opened, much of the fear siphoned away, and I can now confront
the historical realities with the calmness of someone who has at least
partly come to terms with the catastrophe.

When Hetty Voûte told me how she had made it through
Ravensbrück with a smile and a song (many songs, actually, and a special friend), her words were like sunbeams pouring into a certain dark
corner of my mind. When Clara Dijkstra reached across the table, took
my hand, and said, "Together we'll get through this," I felt some ancient
miasma melt away. Ted Leenders, profiled in the next chapter, had me
chuckling about the same kind of Nazi who used to terrorize my
dreams. The sum total of my meetings with the rescuers left me overwhelmed by their warm assurances that, yes, it was terrible, but yes, we
remained human beings, and, yes, we would have taken in you, too, had
you come to our door during those years.

T H E O   L E E N D E R S

Laughing It All Away

*It's easy to say "It's not my child, not
my community, not my world, not my problem."
Then there are those who see the need and respond.
I consider those people my heroes.*

—FRED ROGERS

EVEN THE SHORTEST CONVERSATION with Ted Leenders is punctuated
by his relaxed chuckle, gentle and continuous, as if he's constantly de-
riving mirth from the circumstances of life. Laughter comes to Ted as
easily as breath.

He met me at the platform of Heerlen station in the province of
Limburg, his wiry frame exuding an unmistakable energy, as did his eyes

and voice. I'd intended to first take a taxi to interview Mieke Vermeer, but Ted insisted on picking me up at the train station and driving me around, first to her apartment, and then to his.

"Later you will meet my wife, Tilla," he said, as we got into his old but well-maintained Volvo. "We've been married for over fifty years." After I congratulated him on his lifelong partnership, he proceeded to tell me the secret of marriage: "Never bring your troubles home to your wife."

"Isn't your wife supposed to be your best friend?" I countered. "If you can't share your troubles with her—."

"Of course you want to confide in your wife. But sometimes the husband will come home and dump all the problems of the day onto his wife. I never let myself do that."

Not wanting him to share more of his life philosophy without the tape recorder rolling, I changed the subject by asking him if he'd been interviewed before. "No, but just last week some woman named Doris tried. She and her crew came to my apartment with cameras and lights. And then she starts asking me questions, and I'm trying to tell her what I remember, but she says she wants to know the first and last names of people, and all the things more, and I felt like my memory was on trial. Some I didn't remember, or maybe the person is living, and might not want me to say. When I complained, you know what she answered? 'What I ask—you tell!' I said, 'Go to hell,' and threw her out of my apartment!"

"Ted, I know her!" I exclaimed. Just two weeks earlier, I'd been looking for an interpreter in Amsterdam to help me interview several rescuers who couldn't speak any English, and an archivist at the Jewish Museum had suggested that I call Doris, since her project made use of many interpreters. After I had explained my situation to her on the phone, she replied, "Who do you think I am? Do you think I can give you interpreters out of a tin?" I felt as though I'd been punched in the stomach; now it turned out that Ted had been mistreated by the very same woman! I told him my story and we laughed over our respective encounters with the disagreeable Doris.

My spirits were up as we climbed the concrete steps to his modest apartment. Tilla opened the door, and, with smiles all around, Ted introduced us. An earth grandmother with ruddy cheeks and an apron, Tilla's sedate hospitality made Ted's jauntiness stand out even more.

There's something playful about this man. He sits you down on the sofa as if he expects to have a lot of fun with you. Even his stories of the Nazis were sprinkled with moments of grace or good fortune that drew forth his contagious chuckles. Still, there was a pedal tone of sadness that often sounded below Ted's good cheer—one that even his invincible laughter couldn't drown out.

I was born in Nymegen, in Gelderland, in 1915. My father was from a well-to-do family, but he lost all his money playing cards. Ha, ha, not really, but almost—he bought a lot of German marks the year before I was born, thinking that after the war they would be worth lots more. But the German economy collapsed, and the currency became completely worthless. So he had to go to work.

He didn't loaf around; he came down to this mining town where nobody knew him, and he got a job scrubbing floors. He was the lowest paid man, but he worked to support us. I was three years old when we came here to the southern part.

I'm a duplicate of my father. You don't realize that when you're young, but when I look back at the way he was, and how I am now, then I see him sitting in this chair here. He was a very religious man. My mother would talk about something bad that had happened and he would say, "Cora, that is all God's will."

He was a very humble man—he had to be humble because he had nothing. So we grew up poor because my father had no trade. And after everything I've been through, I thank God that I have been poor also. I'm not ashamed to say that. Because I can understand the poor man, you know? People in need. I can bring my whole heart to the case. When I was a boy, the other kids had a ball to play with and I didn't have one. And the other kids had candy and I didn't have any. But I am grateful to God that He put me through that, because I know what it means to have nothing.

Now, my father was a quiet man, but my mother, she liked to laugh. She would make all of us laugh. She had tremendous nerves—nothing could throw her. She never complained about having to do without—she knew that we had a lot of love in our family, and that

that was what mattered. She used to say, "Some people are so poor that all they have is money."

When the Germans occupied our country, we started taking down the names of Dutch people who were helping them, so that after the war we could do something about it. But as the war continued, Tilla and I decided to skip that and spend our time helping the Jewish people. I met a man named Siem de Vries who was already helping Jewish people and we started to work together. Jewish children were being held in a certain building, and the German soldiers guarding the place were willing to sell the children for a handful of silver—not to help the children, just for some pocket money to buy drinks. Aach, you could bribe anybody. But those children, they were lucky to get out.

Siem de Vries would come to me and say, "Here are some people who need to be brought somewhere," and all the things more. And so we did it. Our little house given to us by the mining company became a place where people could hide. At first we only took them for a few days, until they could go somewhere else.

You should have seen those people when I told them they had to move again—they would shrink, get smaller. Their faces would become like ash. I always felt like some kind of a bastard when I had to tell them that. We didn't know where they would be going either, or who they would be staying with, so we couldn't promise them anything.

During this time, I was working in the nationalized coal mines. I had no education beyond grade school, but the mine offered a course of study in engineering, which I completed. So around that time they made me a geological engineer. This meant that the entire site was my place of work, and I was free to walk anywhere in those mines. This allowed me to be in secret contact with Siem de Vries. He was the man representing the labor union in the mine, so he was able to walk all over too. We became very good friends. Every day, I had to write down in a log where I was going to be. When Siem needed to talk, he would look in that log, and come and find me. Outside of the mine, we didn't associate with each other. Everyone knew that he was a big socialist and that I was a Catholic. It would have looked suspicious.

I had no telephone in my house, but Siem de Vries had one because he was with the labor union. And he was in contact with a big man in the Resistance named Gill. Gill would phone Siem from Amsterdam, and Siem would come to me and say, "We need to hide so and so." The job Tilla and I spent the most time on was hiding people. This also meant looking for addresses where people who were on the run could stay.

I would go to someone who already had an onderduiker and say, "Do you know someone else who might help?" And if he said that he knew someone, then *he* would go and talk to that person. If that worked out, he would give me an address, and I would say, "Tell them that I will come tomorrow night with the onderduikers."

I found out that those people I had in my hands had tremendous endurance. They went through so much. I knew a man who lived for two years in an attic. The couple who hid him had four children of their own, but the man had nowhere else to go, and they wanted to save him. So they kept him up there, and he couldn't come down. If the family downstairs had company, he couldn't even flush the toilet. In the wintertime he was there, too: no heating, no light—nothing. Two times I went to him and sat with him and held him. I had to hold him. When I came into that attic, it was freezing cold. Terrible—nothing but a bed. Not even a chair to sit on. He lay there all day in that bed, pale and cold. Every time I looked into his eyes I thought, My God—what these people are going through! And that man, he survived the war.

Once, three of us from the Resistance had to meet a certain Jewish family at the train station. I was to take the child. The station was very crowded because the buses weren't running. And then they arrived, those people, and we walked over to them. I went in between, and took the child from the mother, and walked away with him. And that child, four or five years old, never cried for his father or mother, as small as he was. He just walked away with me, a total stranger, and left his parents.

I tell you, that was the hardest damn thing I ever did, handling those children. I can't explain it to you, but I still feel it. The woman went one way, the father another, and I walked off with the child. For four months, those parents didn't know where the child was—and I couldn't tell them, because I didn't know where *they* were. When I found out, I took the child to see his parents, despite the risk. I felt I had to do that.

I believe more people would have helped, but they were too scared. In the beginning the Germans didn't talk about the Jews, but in 1941, they started putting notices up on the shop windows, and in the newspapers, saying that anyone who helped the Jews would be arrested. At first they didn't say they would kill you. But after a while, you knew that if they came for you, you would never return.

Yah, so it was just fear. People lived close to each other, and not everyone could be trusted. There were some people who disliked the Jews, even though they had never known any Jewish people. And don't forget that in some churches they were saying that the Jews killed Jesus. There was always something against the Jews. Then there were the Dutch people who were collaborating with the Germans. Those were not just a few. I mean, one third of the mayors had joined the NSB.

In 1942 the raids began. One day a policeman came to our door and told Tilla that the Germans were coming to our street. He was a good man; he went to each house to warn everyone. Tilla got a message to me at the mine and I came home right away. We were hiding a Jewish family in our house—a couple with a young boy. The boy was supposed to move somewhere else, but he hadn't gone yet because he had pneumonia.

Tilla started to put away all their things. She sandwiched their clothes between our clothes in the drawers. She hid their personal items. But in the cellar was a cache of about forty weapons that had been left by the policeman who used to live in the house. He wanted me to get them to the Dutch Resistance, but I hadn't had time to move them. And now, the Gestapo were coming, and I had a cellar full of weapons. What to do? I had an idea: we had an old vacuum cleaner that used a canvas bag to collect the dirt. I attached the dirt bag to the air intake. Then I brought it to the top of the cellar stairs and turned it on. You should have seen the dust! After it had settled, it made it look as though no one had been down there for years.

We'd already gotten false papers for the people we were hiding so that they could not be identified as Jewish. We gave the boy a note and sent him to stay with someone we knew on another street. It was summer, but because he was sick he was wearing a winter coat and scarf. The mother worked as a nurse at the tuberculosis sanitarium, and she could stay overnight there for a week. But the father refused to go with her. "It's a false alarm," he said. "They wouldn't come here." We tried to reason with him, but our time was running out. Finally, Tilla said, "If you won't leave, then I'm leaving." And the man was barely one hundred yards out the door when the Gestapo arrived.

Ten, fifteen Nazis surrounded the house shouting "*Sie! Komm her!*" and all the things more. They came in fairly rude and rough, and started searching. They didn't ask where, what, or how. And then the man in charge, Commandant Müller, stomped in.

We were lucky in many ways. To validate the ration coupons you needed to paste a small stamp on them—without that stamp, you couldn't get food. So I had some rolls of those stamps sitting in the cupboard. We'd forgotten about them, but I had always told Tilla, "*Never clean in there.*" So when the man who was searching picked up a cup and saw that it was dusty, he turned to Tilla and gave her a look, like, "What a bad housekeeper you are." Then he walked away in disgust. But two of those cups were full of validation stamps. They had been issued by the government, but we had stolen them. If he'd found them, we would've been finished. I wouldn't be sitting here now.

So they're asking me this and that, and accusing us of *everything*. And I kept on saying, "I don't know what you're talking about. We've lived here many years. I work in the mines." They said, "Yah, we know where *you're* working."

They treated Tilla very rough. She was scared, and I was too. I thought it might be the end for us, that they would shoot us before they left. Then Müller started interrogating us. The questions he asked would make you so confused that you didn't know what to say anymore. But Tilla was very brave.

I knew that they would go down in the cellar. But I acted first, to turn it to our advantage. I said, "Herr Müller, you haven't been to the cellar. Let me take you down there." He glared at me. I went on, "Müller, you are accusing me of all kinds of things, but I am going to show you I have nothing to hide. Follow me down to the cellar." The SS hated to be told what to do by a civilian. He looked at the dust on the stairs and didn't want to bother. He shined his flashlight and said, "Aach, there's nothing there." Then he shouted to his men to clear out. But just as he was going, he grabbed me by my hair, and pulled my head back. "I'm going to get you someday. I'll get you while you're sleeping," and *crack!*—he slapped me in the face.

After he left, Tilla, who we didn't even know was pregnant, started to bleed very heavily. Then everything came out, and the doctor who examined her told us that she'd had a miscarriage. He said, "You will never have children." And that is the price we paid—she and I.

Let me tell you about what happened on 20 April 1944—I remember the date well, because it was Hitler's birthday and the Germans were celebrating all over. It was on that day that we went down to the cellar and dug out the rifles and pistols; there were about forty of them. Some men from the Resistance came with a truck, and in ten minutes we had them all out of there.

But just as we were crossing some railroad tracks, the truck shook, rocked, and then stopped. What was worse: four German soldiers came walking by. "*Was ist das?*" they demanded. "Well, we work at the mine in Heerlen, and we had to go to another mine to get some spare parts for the mineshaft. And now our truck has stalled. But I must congratulate you because today is Hitler's birthday!" We had two bottles of genever with us—that's a Dutch gin, popular with miners—so I said to the soldiers, "Let's drink to your Führer's good health." So the six of us polished off two bottles of genever. And you know what? They helped us push the truck!

I was starting to get used to this mixture of pathos, excitement, and gallows humor that made up our conversation. Ted broke into hearty laughter, and I found myself thinking that perhaps this was how he got through the war. I asked him if he laughed back then, also.

You must never forget that, even in misery, there can still be a lot of fun. Of course I laughed. And if you sat with the Jewish people who, you know, were really in trouble, they always tried to find a way to laugh. They told jokes, all kinds, especially jokes making fun of the Germans. Let me see if I can remember any . . .

One of the songs the German army sang was "*Wir Fahren Gegen Engeland*"—"We're on Our Way to England." So once a troop was singing that song as they goosestepped down our street in Heerlen, and the Jewish man here in the house sang, "*Plons, plons*" at the end of each line. "Splash, splash." You know, like they were going to march straight into the North Sea. Ha, ha. Just remember: life is too serious to be taken seriously.

Tell me about some of the people you hid.

Our favorite was a child named Michael—we kept him here at the house. Michael was a good boy who enjoyed playing with the little wooden figures that I carved for him. After we'd been looking after him for a few months, I asked him, "Michael, what is the difference between our house and the other houses where you were hidden?" And he said, "You and Tilla have given me love all over the place."

We had young, old, rich, poor—you name it. One fellow, Mr. Engel, had such good false papers that he was able to get a job in the coal mine. And his wife worked at the hospital. Just out in the open. Nothing could happen to those people. As far as anyone could tell, they were not Jewish.

Mrs. Engel had blue eyes, but to be on the safe side, Tilla would bleach her dark hair blond with peroxide. Mr. Engel didn't look Jewish at all, but when he got his job in the mine, he came to me and said "Ted, but, uh, I am circumcised." He was worried about the big shower area that all the miners had to walk through to get cleaned up. I said to him, "Man, don't you worry about it—there are plenty of guys like that in the mine." [*laughs*]

The craziest time was when "The Singer" came to live with us. I'd never seen anything like this girl. One day Gill phoned Siem, and Siem came to me and said, "We have a German-Jewish girl we don't know what to do with. We have the biggest problem with this girl because we can't get her to stay inside. Ted, you are the only one who can handle her." I said, "No, man. I don't want to do that." But after thinking it over, it seemed to me that we had to help the girl. So they brought her here by train from Amsterdam.

The first thing she did was to tell me she was a singer. "But you're not going to sing in this house," I told her. "We can't have that." All the houses on the street were close together, and when the windows were open, anyone walking by could hear everything. So I said, "You can do whatever you want but not *that*. And don't go outside, either, because I can tell you are a girl who likes to go outside."

She'd been with us for about a week when one night we heard the Germans marching into town—they had hobnailed boots so you could hear them coming from far away. It was late in the evening, and we heard the clackety-clack-clack. Whenever they marched through, we always got scared, Tilla and I. We never talked about it; we just listened as they went passing by. But that night there came a knock on the door.

That German girl ran out of her room, and—can you believe it?—*she opened the door.* Standing there was a German soldier. Just a common foot soldier, thank God, who didn't know the road. So she calls out, "He needs directions." I went outside with him; he was only about eighteen years old—you know, an innocent boy. We walked down the road together, and I showed him where he needed to go.

But when I came back in I said to that girl, "Look: I don't know your name, and I don't want to know your name, *but you are going to leave this house.*" She stamped her foot and said, "If you mess with me, you'll be sorry." I said "Calm down, everything will be all right." So I went to Siem, and Siem phoned Gill.

Gill said we should take her to the train station and buy her a one-way ticket to Amsterdam. Siem asked him what he was going to do when she got there and he said, "Nothing." Just leave her there. But Tilla, God bless her, said, "Ted, you can't do that. That poor girl, all alone in Amsterdam, a Jewish girl," and all the things more. So we gave her money—about fifty guilders, which was a lot in those days. And then we put her on the train. Once again there was peace in the house.

Two days later there came a knock on the door. I opened the door and there she stood: The Singer. She remembered the way back, the name of the street, the number of the house. She was not stupid, that girl. She said, "You put me on the train to Amsterdam, and nobody came for me. I hid in the railroad station for two days. Now I've come back, and good luck getting rid of me this time." So I went to Siem; Siem called Gill. Gill asked, "How is it possible that she found her way back to you?" Well, Siem told him that I had given the girl more than a one-way ticket.

Gill came up with another plan, quite complicated. He asked me to go with the girl on the train to Amsterdam, and meet him in Amsterdam. So we got to the Amsterdam station, and he was there waiting for us. The three of us went across the street to a quiet café, you know, not many people, and he explained the false identity he'd concocted for her. He gave her the best false identification papers I'd ever seen, including papers for France, Germany, and all the things more.

Then the two of us got on the train with her to France, because that's where she wanted to go. But two other men from the Dutch Resistance got on the same train—that was Gill's plan. When the train stopped in Gare du Nord, Gill and I stepped off the train with the girl. Those two friends of Gill's pretended to be operatives working for the Germans. They walked up from behind and shouted, "Halt! Gestapo!" And that girl didn't ask who, what, where—she ran!

That was the idea: that she would run away and never come back. She would figure that if we had been arrested, it wouldn't be safe to ever return. So we never saw her again.

But about six months later, I was talking to Siem, and I asked, "Whatever happened to The Singer?" I wondered if he had heard anything. He said to me, "Ted, you won't believe it." I asked, "What's she done now?" He said, "She's singing in a cabaret in Paris. She performs there every night, and is a big hit. Even the German officers like her."

Ted broke into long laughter, and I joined him, but there was a disturbing undercurrent in his tale. How could this ambitious young singer have been so oblivious to the war's implications for her own people? I shook my head incredulously, and asked him if anyone ever figured out that she was Jewish.

I don't think so. We gave her such good papers that she could travel the whole world, you know? So you had good things and bad things. Have you ever heard a story like that? Well, we lived it. I was so happy that the girl was gone, but I was even happier when I learned how well she was doing in Paris. So I think that she survived the war. But I tell you once more: that girl was not stupid.

Less that a year before the end of the war, Vos was captured. Vos was a Jewish man we should never forget: he was one of the brains behind the entire Resistance here. Because of him we had all those false papers, and those papers were very important, you know. If you didn't have them you were nowhere—you couldn't get food, and all the things more. Before Vos figured out how to counterfeit them, we used to have to rob the town halls where they were being stored. We stole many thousands of those papers, not in one place only but in different town halls all over Holland.

This could only be done with help from the inside. You would break in, and the man inside would show you where the papers were.

After that, you would tie him up, so that when the Germans came, he could say he was overpowered. The police were good; they worked with us. They had to patrol the building at night, and so, after we left, they would open the door and go inside, and would find the man who was all tied up. And then they would make a hell of a noise until the Germans came.

Once Vos took me to Delft and introduced me to a girl who worked in the town hall there. He said to her, "If this man comes to you, give him whatever he needs." So later I went over there and said to her, "I need papers for a man, woman, and child." She said, "What are their ages?" I told her, and she said, "Come back tomorrow."

During that time she went into the files of the deceased, looking for people had been born in those same years. She removed them from the "deceased" file and put them into the file of living persons. And when I returned, she gave me the papers for each person, and told me everything I needed to know about them: who their brothers and sisters were, and their mother and father, and all the things more. Then she would ask, "Where are they going to live?" I would tell her, and then she'd send the files to the town hall there. After two days, that Jewish man would come to the town hall to get those papers. They'd add the photo and fingerprints. And after that, that family was safe—there was no way you could trace them. Of course, we had to be careful not to send them to a place where they would run into the relatives of the dead people!

We took care of many Jewish people in that way. It gave them the best situation. Others you just had to keep hidden. I had about fifteen people that I hid away in my house. Nothing ever happened to any of them—they all came out all right.

Around the beginning of 1943, we learned that the Germans were designing a new distribution card that would be very hard to counterfeit. But Vos, unbelievably, got his hands on one of them, and even before the new cards had been issued, he had printed perfect counterfeits. When people started using them, no one could tell the difference. That was the level of skill he had.

Vos was a very tight, closed man. He didn't say much. We traveled together once from Heerlen to Amsterdam. I always stayed a few yards behind him. In Amsterdam he got off the train and was stopped by the

Gestapo. He had papers saying he was a real estate agent, but he wasn't doing no real estate, I can tell you that.

I went to the telephone at the station and immediately called Sonia. Sonia was the Jewish girl who worked very closely with him. She knew exactly what he was doing all the time. So I called Sonia and told her they had stopped Vos. "Hold on," I said. And I waited to see what would happen. Two minutes passed, and I said, "They've released him." I had to call her right away because if something happened to Vos, the whole Resistance in the southern part of Holland would go to pieces. But he had such good papers that no one could touch him.

Around that time, the Germans killed a man who was at the top of the Resistance. That was a shock for all of us. Vos went into hiding, and Sonia was the only one who knew where he was. We had contact with Sonia, and we'd ask her this and that, and she would say, "Well, I can't give you that because I'm out of contact with Vos." If we pressed her, she would say, "It's too dangerous. Leave him alone." After three weeks, our whole operation came to a halt; we couldn't help anyone anymore. So we went to Sonia and said, "Look, you've got to go to Vos. Tell him he has to come back." And so she did, and he listened to her.

Then in the summer of '44, after the Allies had landed in Normandy, and our hopes were up that soon we'd be liberated, Vos was arrested in Amsterdam.

A big meeting of the Resistance was being planned in the south. The Germans had found out about it, but they didn't know the location. After Vos was arrested, they began to torture him very badly to tell them where it would be. Nothing worked; his mouth was shut like a steel trap. But then they brought a Jewish baby before him, and said, "If you don't tell us where the meeting is, you won't like to see what we do to this baby." He still wouldn't tell them, and then they broke one of the baby's legs. Then he kind of collapsed.

After that he was like putty in their hands. They got the meeting place out of him: a certain monastery in Weert, which is here in Limburg. When the day came, they got him drunk and took him with them. They arrested about a dozen people in that raid, including some monks and priests. There was only one man who escaped by hiding behind some curtains.

We continued to hide Jewish people even though the war was almost over, and guess who came back to pay me a visit? That fall, when the Battle of Arnhem was being fought in the north, and the Allied forces were fast approaching from the south, I was sitting at my kitchen table with my back to the window, and Tilla was sitting right across from me. A canvas-covered truck pulled up in front. Tilla said, "Ted, there he is." I didn't ask who-what-where, didn't even look—I ran out the back door. By the tone of her voice I knew that it was Müller.

He chased me into a field, but what he didn't know was that there was a knokploeg that had been following him. They had been planning to ambush his truck and free the Jews and political prisoners that he was taking to Germany. And so these men from the knokploeg ran out there too, and shot him right there in the field. He was coming to get me, but they got *him*. We opened the back of that truck, and helped all those people down. Now they could all go home again.

That was a sign of things to come. The war ended a short time later.

What was your life like after the war?

Well, the exiled government came back, and most of the Resistance people were shunted aside while bureaucrats who had been lockstep with the Germans were kept on in their positions. I returned to the mines and worked as chief geological engineer. Then one day I opened the paper and read that Vos had been arrested as a collaborator and sentenced to two years in prison! I saw his picture and almost fainted. That one man who had escaped the raid on the monastery had reported that Vos had been there with the Germans, drinking and carrying on with them. The verdict was appealed, and his case was eventually sent to the highest court in The Hague. I was called up as a character witness, and for the first time, I learned the full story of what had happened to him, and what his real name was: Daniël Jesse, or Bob Jesse.

For a lot of the trial, he wasn't present. Then finally he came in—he had his arms around the shoulders of the two guards because he could barely walk. The judge said, "You can't stand up, Mr. Jesse?" He shook his head no. "What happened to you?" He said, "Well, I have been in a Dutch jail for six months." They had beaten the hell out of him in that jail. The prosecutor said, "Because of him, eleven people were betrayed. And he only served half a year in jail." "Yes," the defense attorney said, "but he saved the lives of hundreds." In the end he was acquitted, and the judge ordered that he be set free immediately.

After the verdict was delivered, he remained in the dock, and I went over and sat down next to him. "Hell, man, look at how you've been treated." "I understand why they have done this to me," he said. "But you must understand, too, why I did the things I did." I put my hand on his shoulder and said, "Don't you worry. I'll always remember you. Compared with what you did for the Resistance, this is nothing." He said, "During the war, the Nazis treated all Jewish people like this. So now I have been treated like this, too—by men who hate the Nazis and thought I was one of them." And that is the price he paid.

We had paid a price too, Tilla and I. We were still reeling from what the Germans had done, and disillusioned with Dutch society as well. We wanted to start a family, but we couldn't. And the trial of Vos . . . well, I've never been so upset by anything in my life. When I saw in the paper that the Liberian Mining Company of Bomi Hills was looking for a geological engineer, I applied for the position. At that time, there was nothing I wanted more than to leave the Netherlands.

You wouldn't believe all the killing that is going on in Liberia now—streets strewn with bodies, a brutal civil war. But they're such easygoing people that it's hard for me to understand what it's all about. When we moved there in 1947, it was a time of great peace, and the people were famous for their hospitality. They would help you; they would do anything for you.

When you walked into a village, the first person you met would give you a big greeting and take you straight to the town chief. The chief would sit you down in the shade, and bring you some cold water. He'd offer you a banana or an avocado and tell you how honored he was that you had come to his village. And if you needed a place to stay, he would give you the best hut. He'd move out the people who lived there for a few days, but *you* had the good hut.

In Holland, Tilla and I had been living comfortably. When we got to Liberia there was no running water and no indoor light—except for kerosene lamps. The weather was hot, with heavy rains in the summer, and dry dusty Sahara winds in the winter. Our cabin was in a dense tropical forest. So we realized immediately that this would be a completely different life. But it was a healing place for us, a place where people really understood how to work together in harmony.

We spent twenty-five busy, productive years there. In addition to being in charge of civil engineering and exploration at the mine, they made me head of a sawmill, quarry, panel factory, and carpenter shop. That enabled me to help the Liberians with all kind of projects: we built a railroad from scratch—that was a hell of a job—and a bridge over the Maher River. I also helped them to build churches, all kinds of churches: Catholic, Protestant, you name it. I gave them plans, construction materials, labor, and all the things more.

Tilla volunteered at the local hospital, and she started a project to teach the local women how to sew. The Red Cross gave her a donation of ten sewing machines, and later she was able to get fifteen more. The Catholic women used to all come to Tilla for communion dresses for their young girls, because whenever we went to Holland on vacation, she would bring back as many used dresses as she could round up from family and friends. She became like a mother to all the children in our corner of Nimba County, but we longed for a child of our own.

Then one day we came home to find a little nappy-headed boy sitting on our stoop. He said his parents had left him there. We talked with the family, and they said they would like us to adopt him because they didn't have enough money to provide for him. To us, it was an answer to our prayers.

John was a good boy, and he came to live with us. We took care of him and started him in school, but we always encouraged him to visit his family during school vacations, and to keep his family name and the religion he'd been taught. We raised him in Liberia and then sent him to medical school in the United States. Now he's a physician in Kansas City with a wife and family of his own. He calls us every Sunday.

We've also remained close with Michael, the boy we hid in our house during the war. He went to college and studied chemistry, and later he became a headmaster at a polytechnic institute. He lives nearby with his wife, and we see a lot of him, especially now that his own parents have passed away.

So we have children, two children, and even some grandchildren. We returned to the Netherlands after John had grown up, and I had retired from my last position as vice-president of the mining company.

There's so much fighting in the world over religion. "How we hate one another for the love of God," Cardinal Newman said. But when you sit down together, you find that we're all praying to the same One. So all the fighting is just foolishness, isn't it? I see every person I meet as a child of God. You know, during the war we once had a very bad fire in the mine. Six people were killed. The next day the priest came to me and asked, "Ted, are any of them *ours?*" I looked him in the eye and said, "Father, they're *all* ours." Should I care about someone less because they're not Catholic? No, to me, the religion doesn't matter; the pigmentation of the skin doesn't matter. And if someone does something to me, I pray to God to forgive me my sins—

—as you forgive those who sin against you?
Yah. If someone does something to me, I never get mad.

Unless it's Doris.
Well, that was something else, and I forgave her. I was very mad at her, but I wrote her a letter saying, "I forgive you, and if there's anything I can do for you, just call me." Because I wouldn't have been able to live with myself if I didn't do that. Whenever I have a problem with someone in my life, I fix it in that way.

I had trouble with a man not so long ago, a close friend of ours. His wife was good friends with Tilla, and we knew him very well. One day, after his wife died, he started to raise hell with us. Two weeks later he phoned me and said, "I'm very sorry about the way I acted." I said, "Forget it. Do you want to come for lunch on Saturday?" And you know what? He comes here every Saturday, and Tilla likes to cook for him. We just handled it as if nothing had happened.

What about the Germans? Have you forgiven the Germans?
I have nothing against the younger Germans, for they weren't there. The ones who did the terrible things are nearly all gone now. But even in that older generation, not every German was a Nazi. Tilla's family

Ted Leenders in his later years.
Courtesy of Ted Leenders personal collection.

was German. They were treated very rough because they wouldn't join the Nazi party. It's easy to lump people together, and then be prejudiced against them, but it's better to treat each individual as a separate case.

Some years ago, we had a wave of foreigners come from all different countries to work here in the mines. In the beginning, everyone kept to themselves, so they didn't get to know each other. You have to watch out for that, because when people don't know each other, mis-understandings occur, and prejudices grow. But one day someone on the town council said, "Can't we have a mixer to bring everybody together?" So we planned a big community feast with food and music from all these different countries. It was a great success, and got people talking to each other. And that led to meetings, and committees, and all the things more.

Later I helped build a community center that is used now by all the different groups. And now they all march together on the Queen's Birthday. You should see it when all those people with their different flags go marching down the main street singing, "Hail to the queen!" There you have it.

I asked Ted if I could see his Yad Vashem medal. He opened a cabinet and took out a box containing not only the Yad Vashem award, but many other honors as well. Lifting the gleaming disc from the pile, he placed it in my hand.

Yah, so this is what Yad Vashem gave to us. They also made us honorary citizens of Israel. We've been back there many times. And here is the cross I was given for having been a member of the Dutch Resistance. This is something you get, but what do you do with it? Nobody wears it—if you did, maybe you'd get shot. [*chuckles*] And this ribbon is from Queen Beatrix when she made me a Knight in the Order of Orange Nassau Royal Family for what I did for the churches in Liberia. And I got this insignia from President Tubman of Liberia when he made me a Great Commander of the Order of the African Star. And here, you can see, Pope Paul VI also commended me for what I did in Liberia by making me a Grand Commander Gregorius the Great.

As a Catholic, that was a great honor, but whenever I get up there— I hope I do—but even if I make it to heaven, I wonder how many popes I'll meet. You know, at the end of the eleventh century, Pope Urban II spearheaded the First Crusade. He incited the Christians to storm Jerusalem, and that was the beginning of a centuries-long bloodbath. And later they canonized him. I tell you, there are not many true saints.

I'm going to make a statement that I've never made to anybody before: We say the Germans killed the Jews, but it was the Christians who killed the Jews. All those Nazis, you know, and the NSBers who collaborated with them here in Holland, were Christians. They were baptized as Catholics and Protestants.

Pope Pius XII didn't talk about what was going on. He reigned from 1939 to 1958, and before that he was the papal nuncio in, of all places, Germany. He knew very well what was brewing in Germany. If he had opened his mouth and said, "Anyone who lays a finger on a Jewish person will be excommunicated," that would have been a great help to us. But he kept his mouth shut. As a result, many people joined the Nazis, especially in the occupied countries, and some of them became more dangerous than the German Nazis.

At this point Ted said that he had something personal to ask me. I asked him if he would like me to turn off the tape recorder, and he gave a slight nod.

Mark, do you forgive me for what my people have done to your people?

A single tear traced its way down his wrinkled cheek as I sat there, awestruck. He was asking my forgiveness for something he had had no part in, something he had put his life on the line to resist. I could see he was in earnest, and I didn't know what to say. I thought of Primo Levi, who, having survived Auschwitz, was haunted by the reality of what human beings are capable of doing to one another. Levi felt implicated and ashamed, just by being a member of the human race, despite the fact that he had been a victim, not a perpetrator. Perhaps Ted had some of these same feelings. Though a maverick, he was

*also a devout Catholic. He had to live with the knowledge that others profess-
ing his faith had acted as they did.*

*I looked at him, fragile and drawn, hanging on the air for my response. Who
was I to forgive anti-Semitism in the Roman Catholic Church? That would be
up to the victims. But in Ted's presence, it was easy to act from the heart. "Of
course," I said. "I forgive you, Ted." He put his shaking hand on mine, and his
face broke out in a lucent smile. Everything felt lighter as we sank back into our
armchairs. Turning the tape recorder back on, I reminded him that he had just
said that it was the Christians who killed the Jews.*

That's a hard statement I made. If you publish it, maybe they're going
to kill *me* now. [*chuckles*] So you see, Pius XII's sin of omission played a
big part in it, you know? But don't think that because he stood silently
by, those under him did also. Here in Limburg, Bishop Lemmens helped
the Resistance to save Jewish people. And many monks and nuns took
their Jewish brothers and sisters into the monasteries and convents—
wherever they could hide them, they did.

The pope that we have now, John Paul II, has apologized to the
Jewish people—he has said, "You are our brothers, because all of us have
come out of the Jewish people." Even the previous Pius, Pius XI, made
a beautiful statement in 1938, a year before he left office: "Anti-
semitism is not permitted; we are spiritually Jews through Christ, and
in Christ, we are all the children of Abraham."

*Do you have any ideas as to how peace can be achieved between Jews and Arabs
in the Middle East?*

The Jews and Arabs need to look at one another as human beings. More
than that, they need to look at each other as family, for they too go all the
way back to Abraham. How do you bring about peace? Not by violence!
The Arab extremists need to realize that they will not get what they want
by blowing themselves up. But the Jews must understand that roadblocks
and razor wire can never keep them safe in the long run. What we need
to do is build goodwill and trust. How do you start? By talking to your
brother, and trying to understand him, by putting yourself in his place.
This will not weaken or endanger you—it is the way *out* of danger.

*Seeing that Israel rose from the ashes of the Holocaust, it might be hard to get
Israeli leadership to take this approach.*

You've heard the quote by Santayana that those who do not remember the past may be doomed to repeat it. That's true. But we must not be prejudiced by the past. Sometimes it can be good to put aside the past if it doesn't help us solve the problems of today. Sometimes we need a fresh approach.

Take our situation here in Europe. There's no question that the guilt of Germany in the twentieth century can never be erased. But some people dig their heels into the past just so they can keep feeling angry. In that case, I say, put an end to it! You know, now we are working on coming together with the Germans. Close to the Dutch-German border, we have towns on both sides of the line pursuing joint ventures. We have to get beyond the old ways of thinking. Because if we don't, that's just stupid.

The war was already a stupid thing. You send your son to get killed because of the madness of some fanatical leader. To reheat the old hate is not going to get us anywhere. We who remember the Nazi occupation have to master the feelings of resentment and humiliation that those memories stir up in us. Then we'll be able to move forward into a brighter future.

Our leaders, especially, need to be motivated by love, not hate. And I don't mean love of money. They should take to heart Gandhi's advice: he said to recall the face of the poorest and most helpless person you've ever met, and then ask yourself if the step you are contemplating will be of any use to him. When we visited John in Kansas City and went driving around, I was amazed to see so many beggars, poor people without homes, scavenging in the garbage on the side streets. In such a rich country! You don't see that here in Holland, and I don't think we would accept it. We would feel ashamed—I would feel ashamed, and if I were an American, I wouldn't stand for it.

Now that you're in your eighties, how do you feel about the way elders are treated?

I told you before about Africa. That is where we really saw respect for the elders. In Liberia, when the people were going to eat and an old man was sitting there, nobody would eat, nobody would touch the food, until the old man had eaten. When I was growing up in Holland, we respected old people. We'd go out of our way to help them. You don't see much of that nowadays.

As for me, I accept life as I have it now. I live very modestly; you can see that for yourself. I have money in the bank, but I don't need it. They're studying me at the hospital down the street to see why I am so healthy for a man my age.

After all you've been through, are you surprised that you've lasted this long?

Well, you know, there have been eight times in my life when I absolutely could have been dead. I told you about that fire in the coal mine? Well, that was one of them. Each day I had to write down in a log where I would be. So one morning I put down where I was going, and I went back to my desk to get something. I turned to leave, but decided to stay and do office work. An hour later an alarm went off, and it made a hell of a sound. I ran outside because I was part of the rescue squad. My boss shouted, "Let's go. A mineshaft is on fire." I said, "Which one?" It was the place I had just written down in the log.

Another time—this is after the war—I had to catch a plane, but I got a flat tire on the way to the airport. I arrived at the gate just in time to see the plane flying away. That flight crashed, and everybody on it was killed. So nowadays, when I miss a train or a bus, I never feel bad about it. There was a reason I missed it. I've come to believe that nothing happens in this world by chance. There's something deeper behind it.

God's will being done?

Yes, I am sure of that now, but don't take it away from me. I always wonder whether one day I will meet someone who will make me doubt my beliefs. So I pray to God every night that He keeps things the way they are.

Why did God allow the Holocaust?

That is what I don't understand. I've struggled with it for many years, but I've never gotten anywhere. I've said to Him, "All right, you've given us free will, even to be monsters. But what about the free will of the victims? What about their will to live, to love, to love You?" I've cried to Him about it, raised the devil with Him, too. But I don't have an answer for you on that one.

It sounds like your relationship to God is sometimes stormy.

He's the only one I can swear at and nothing happens.

Ted, hearing himself, shook his head and smiled.

He's a very dear friend. I feel Him all the time. He's with us right now.

He paused, and took a worn card out of his breast pocket.

Let me share with you something I always keep with me. It's what I've lived by for many, many years.

He read aloud this short paragraph by Etienne DeGrellet as though he were reciting the happy ending to a story.

> I know I shall pass this way but once. If there is any kindness I can show, or any good thing I can do, let me do it now. Let me not defer it or neglect it, for I shall not pass this way again.

eleven

THE HEART HAS REASONS

&

A history is required that leads to action:
not to confirm, but to change the world.

—PAUL THOMPSON

JEWISH TRADITION HOLDS that a small number of truly righteous people are born in each generation. Though unknown to the world, they are the ones who ensure its stability and even its continuation. This is the way I think of the rescuers: though few in number, their existence changes everything. Had there been more of them—one hundred thousand or perhaps one million—there might never have been a Holocaust.

But who *are* the rescuers? How did these common citizens rise above the typical human responses of fear and passivity to express the "better angels" of our nature, the ones they hint at when they say, "It was just the human thing to do"?

Karl Popper, a philosopher of science, has written that if you observe one thousand white seagulls, you can't conclude all seagulls are white, since you haven't seen every seagull in the world. However, if you see one black seagull, you *can* conclude that not all seagulls are white. Likewise, it's difficult to generalize about altruism in human nature, but the existence of even a single rescuer enables us to draw one very hopeful conclusion: at a crossroads where ethical action and rational self-interest lay in opposite directions, not everyone chose to look out for themselves. Scholars have speculated about the rescuers in an intellectual way, but the impetus behind the rescuers' behavior often transcended the rational. As one rescuer remarked, "the hand of compassion was faster than the calculus of reason." Though the world's great spiritual teachers and traditions have called us to it, how many people are prepared to lay down their lives for others? Can we fully understand such people with the intellect? To borrow from Saint-Exupéry, what is essential about these people is invisible to the eyes; it must be looked at with the heart.

In fact, what I discovered about the rescuers is that they seemed to rely on a fundamental intuition, and tended to act without much deliberation. Often they told me that if they had thought too much about what they were doing, they might have talked themselves out of it. Not that reasoned determination didn't sometimes play a part, but so did sheer courage—and even blind impulse. Their high purpose tended to keep fear at bay, but even when it didn't, they wouldn't let fear stop them. Some said they were too busy to have had time to be afraid. But the long hours of the night would have paralyzed less robust individuals. The positive, often gutsy, attitude of the rescuers seemed to be what enabled them to carry on; it was an attitude that didn't allow for much pondering of what might await them if they were arrested.

Empathy was also a key ingredient. Where did the rescuers develop "moral imagination," something Bill Moyers describes as "the ability to feel life as others live it"? All of the rescuers told me they grew up around someone who went out of his or her way to help people. A surprising number had parents who had taken in malnourished Germans and Austrian children at the end of the First World War. So part of the answer to the question of how the rescuers became who they are is simply that they learned altruism at home. Many even had parents or siblings who were rescuers.

Did growing up in such families mean that the decision to rescue made itself? No, it still took initiative. Mieke Vermeer's parents, though they were saving dozens of Jewish children, objected when their teenage daughter wanted to take on some serious responsibility in the NV group. Hetty Voûte, who came from a "Resistance family" if ever there was one, quoted her father as having said, "If I had known what you were doing, I would have locked you in your room!" Many children didn't know about the rescue activities of their parents, and many siblings kept what they were doing secret. Usually, it was only *after* an individual became involved in helping Jews that he or she came in contact with other people who were also taking action. Such a decision often had to be made without a word of advice from family or friends.

Those who looked outward for a clue as to how they should respond to the Nazis' treatment of the Jews would have thought that everyone seemed to be minding their own business—if not collaborating with the Germans. The instinct to conform would have led them to do the same. Everything depended on one's ability to disregard the apparent ways of the world and move forward independently.

Rescuer Catherine Klumper was ninety-eight when I met with her. When I asked her to tell me about the war, she asked, "Which one?" for she was already a teenager during the First World War. She recalled the lively discussions her family had around the dinner table while she was growing up during that first decade of the twentieth century; each family member would argue his or her own point with guests who had come for dinner—people she characterized as "Marxists, artists, philosophers, and an occasional anarchist." She explained, "That taught me to make up my own mind, and stand on my own two feet." When World War II came along, Mrs. Klumper helped to hide the children of her Jewish neighbor, and later, through her contact with Piet Meerburg, many other Jewish children.

What motivated the rescuers to do what they did? Only Piet seemed primarily motivated by political convictions; his early understanding of the Nazi ideology led him to steadfastly oppose it, which he did by forming the Amsterdam Student Group with the aim of resisting Nazi policies. His group soon gravitated towards saving Jewish children after Piet came in contact with members of the Utrecht Kindercomité.

The Utrecht Kindercomité, on the other hand, was formed in the wake of the July '42 razzia in Amsterdam when many Jewish parents were torn away from their children. Seeing these orphaned Jewish children wandering the streets, one young woman hastened to help them, and soon she and her friends were having a political as well as humanitarian impact.

Before she began to rescue Jewish children, Hetty Voûte took every opportunity to defy the Nazis; her daredevil personality was well suited for the Resistance. However, she explained her efforts as a member of the Utrecht Kindercomité by saying: "You just did it for the children. You can't let children be taken away." When people such as Hetty came into direct contact with the victims and began to take action, their concern over the plight of those victims became a more powerful driving force than even their most deeply felt political convictions. In that moment when Hetty held a child's life in her hands, political abstractions gave way to humanitarian exigencies.

Overall, the rescuers rarely framed what they did in political terms. Does this mean they acted with no thought to the political implications? Far from it. They realized, to varying degrees, that by saving Jews they were directly opposing and subverting the racial imperialist agenda of the Nazis.

All of the people I interviewed are what I would call *spiritual*, but this adjective often tends to resist specific definition. One broad quality I associate with spirituality is love for humanity, and this I witnessed in abundance among the rescuers. Put simply: to them, people are the most important thing. From this core value emerges a feeling of responsibility for the welfare of others, including that of strangers. As Hetty said, "You can't let people be treated in an inhuman way around you."

This love of humanity extends beyond any abstract principle, as was easy to see from the photographs they have around their homes—not only of the people they rescued, but of the children and grandchildren of those people. The many affectionate anecdotes they told me about the people they helped, and, undeniably, the way the rescuers treated me personally, left me with the overwhelming impression that the ethos of these people is their love of people. Ted Leenders even seemed to have a warm spot in his heart for the impetuous young singer, who, after he had risked his life to hide her, threatened to report him to the authorities!

The rescuers' insistence on putting people first leads them naturally to turn away from materialism and consumerism. "Human values, not material things," as Clara Dijkstra said. They don't measure their worth or that of others by possessions or social status and are content to live simply, finding satisfaction in their relations with family and friends and through their "loving and creative participation in life."

Most of the rescuers I interviewed are religious, and they felt challenged by the occupation to put their faith into action. Certainly, the ideal of resisting tyranny lies deep within the Calvinist heritage to which many of the Protestant rescuers trace their roots. Two of the most religious rescuers, Heiltje Kooistra, a Calvinist, and Ted Leenders, a Catholic, believed that God had guided them in their rescue activities, and Heiltje even felt that God said or did things through her at critical junctures. The faith of these transcendentalist rescuers seemed to be more a personal matter than one connected with church affiliation. Each of them could be quite critical of their church, a further indication that they are capable of standing apart from the group and thinking for themselves.

The nonreligious rescuers are a colorful bunch, some of whom yet have a touch of the mystic. Catherine Klumper has believed in reincarnation since she was a child, and she mentioned having had prescient dreams and telepathic experiences. Kees Veenstra quipped that he is a "nonpracticing agnostic," but added that he believes in God when he listens to Bach's *St. Matthew's Passion.* Henk Pelser distances himself from conventional religious beliefs but articulated a highly developed life philosophy "just a shade different from that of Spinoza."

Piet Meerburg feels no need to speculate about a supernatural authority or the existence of a hereafter, as he believes that humans must take full responsibility for themselves, and that the good we do here on earth is its own reward. (Interestingly, his present wife, who lived as a hidden child during the war, is now an energy healer with an international practice.) Rut Matthijsen shares Piet's humanistic approach, believing that each individual must develop his or her talents to the utmost, for "each life is a unique event in the evolution of the world." Some of the rescuers, like Gisela Söhnlein, aren't much interested in religion and philosophy and seemed to have simply acted from the heart in a way consonant with their personal values. Certainly moral and caring behavior need not be coupled with any theistic belief, and these rescuers amply demonstrate this. The cooperation between the secular and religious rescuers also demonstrates that there need not be conflict and polarization between secular humanists and "true believers" in pursuing a shared humanitarian goal.

Some of the rescuers I met had a special feeling for Jews, either through personal contact with Jewish people or because they had developed, through their study of the Bible, a regard for Jews as "the chosen people." However, helping Jews only because they were Jews was not given as a reason by anyone I interviewed, and several made the point that, whatever their special feelings for the Jews, they would have done the same for another group in need of help. (Of course, for those who had Jewish friends from before the war, the transition into rescuing was a natural outcome of the caring and friendship that had already developed.)

Were the rescuers sure they were doing the right thing? They said yes. However, the knowledge that they were subjecting not only themselves but their loved ones to great danger was a tremendous burden. Those rescuers with families who took Jewish children into their homes often struggled with the question of whether it was right for them to put the lives of their own children at risk. And even if all went well, hiding Jews involved hardship and sacrifice; could they justify putting their loved ones through all that? Those who made the decision to go ahead in spite of it all seemed to feel that the need was so great that they simply could not turn away. As Catherine Klumper said, "I had to do it. I couldn't bear to witness the pain and sorrow of the Jewish people." Once involved in rescuing, they accepted the consequences these activities had on their families as part of the price they had to pay to do what they felt they must do. Several expressed that the example they set for their children had a moral value that was commensurate with the risks.

Both love and duty played out in the drama of saving Jewish children during the Holocaust, and continue to be expressed in their lives today. When I visited Jo Habers-Vinke, she told me about the elderly Jewish woman whom her family had hidden in the attic of her childhood home, and then, during a break in the interview, she and her husband took me outside to see their garden. When we walked by their garage, I saw that it was filled to the ceiling with garbage bags. "These are clothes that we've just finished collecting from all over our province," Jo remarked. "Next week we'll be sending them to Romania, where they will be distributed to people who don't have enough warm things for the winter." Though now in their seventies, eighties, and nineties, most of the rescuers still do what they can to help people who are suffering. And not only people: it is in the same spirit that, with her children, Hetty Voûte runs her foundation to promote the humane treatment of Icelandic horses.

Another of the rescuers, Laura van der Hoek, is a Quaker who, before the war, was part of the American Friends Service Committee (AFSC) network that helped to get Jewish children out of Europe to safety. She says her best Christmas ever was in 1942, when all her house-guests sang together and then shook hands. Why was this so memo-rable? Because her "houseguests" consisted of two Jews, a German army deserter, and a member of the Dutch Resistance—all of whom Laura was hiding in her attic.

When I asked if she had helped any groups of people since the war, she told me of how she had once become friends with a neighbor who, she later learned, worked as a prostitute in Amsterdam's red-light dis-trict. When her neighbor contracted syphilis, her blotchy complexion and oozing sores caused her to lose all her clients. Left with no income and rapidly deteriorating health, she turned to Laura, who took her in, and cared for her. Laura later became involved in health education out-reach to prevent other prostitutes from suffering a similar fate. This re-sponse of Laura van der Hoek illuminates another characteristic of the rescuers: a nonjudgmental attitude. They may be righteous, but they're not self-righteous. They seem much more interested in understanding people than in condemning them.

Often this generosity of spirit extends to those who had been by-standers during the war. This surprised me, for the rescuers, more than any other group, would seem to have a right to criticize such people. I suspect that their refraining from judgment is rooted in their under-standing of the great difficulties everyone struggled with during those years. They realize that many people who did not take in Jewish chil-dren were only trying to protect their *own* children. Also, I doubt that the rescuers demand of others as much as they demand of themselves.

Some of the rescuers even expressed the view that the behavior of their bystander neighbors possessed some merit. They explained that if someone suspected that you were harboring Jews and yet did not in-form the Nazis, that person was, in a way, helping with the Resistance. Why would the rescuers give bystanders so much credit? Perhaps they can never forget how much such silence was worth. The rescuers would also point out the people who helped in little ways. There was the baker who gave extra bread to Clara Dijkstra, and the policeman who noti-fied the Vermeers when there might be a raid. Here again, the rescuers gratefully remember how much they once depended on such people.

Though the rescuers generally demur from condemning their by-stander neighbors, the cruelty of the Nazi perpetrators—including the

NSBers—still evokes strong emotions, even after six decades. The rescuers cannot forget the terrifying disregard for human life and human rights they once witnessed. Rage, fear, and grief arise unexpectedly when events trigger old and painful memories.

Kees Veenstra tells a story of going with his nephew to visit a military museum near Arnhem. After viewing dioramas depicting maneuvers involving Canadians, Americans, and Poles during World War II, he turned a corner and there stood a formation of mannequins in black SS uniforms. "You have no idea the impact that seeing that had on me," Kees exclaimed. "I started swearing, and got all worked up. My nephew said, 'But uncle, they're just dummies!'" Kees' visceral, instantaneous reaction testifies to the depth of the trauma he once experienced. The rescuers have had to learn to live with such residual distress, as have their loved ones, but the pain still cuts to the bone.

And yet, despite all the anguish that the Nazis inflicted as a group, the rescuers seem ready to acknowledge any particle of goodness that particular individuals had manifested. They often made a distinction between the hard-core Nazis and the German soldiers, many of whom were teenagers who had been forced to serve in the army. Even Kees, though he spoke more strongly than did any of the other rescuers of continuing to feel outrage toward the perpetrators, acknowledged these differences. He told me the following story about a time when he was biking towards Friesland with a Jewish boy on his handlebars:

I thought, I'll never get there in time for the curfew. Well, I'll just see whether I can find someplace for us to stay for the night. And there was a man in his shirtsleeves standing by a little gate in front of his house and I said, "Hello there, I'm here with an onderduiker, and we have to be in by eight o'clock. Do you think you could put us up for the night?" He just stood there and looked at us. "We'd be satisfied to sleep on the floor, if it comes to that." Finally he said, "I can't help you." "Why can't you help us?" He gave a crooked smile and answered, "Because I'm a Nazi." What could I say? Stupid. I biked on, and kept looking over my shoulder, but he was still standing there in his shirtsleeves. I even got off my bike, as if to fix my chain, just to see what he was doing, but it didn't look like he was going to phone anybody. He was "wrong," but not so terribly wrong. He was what you would call a faulty one, but not of the worst type. Yah, such people there were also, of course.

By refusing to generalize about the Nazis, the rescuers practice a principle they spoke about often: the importance of not stereotyping people. That is what Hitler did to the Jews, they would explain, and that was how he got people to hate them. Miep Gies reports that Otto Frank, father of Anne Frank, survivor of Auschwitz, and founder of the Anne Frank Foundation, was adamant on this point:

> All people make their own decision, Otto used to say. Even parents and children do not always think and act in the same way. He felt very strongly that we should not make the same mistake millions of Germans once made. German children were never told that each person is an individual, free to make his or her own decision, free to take a personal stand in matters of human rights. Therefore Hitler had an easy go in Germany.... And so, Otto Frank insisted that we should stop talking about the Jews, the Arabs, the Asians, the Germans, or whatever. Lumping people together is racism, Otto said. And it leads to the Holocaust, and still destroys countless lives today, like, for instance, in Rwanda, Bosnia, and many other places.

Through witnessing the Nazi propaganda campaign against the Jews, the rescuers saw firsthand the destructive effects of negative stereotyping. Gisela Söhnlein recalls that "during the war, there were people who had never known a Jew, yet they believed that the Jews killed Christian babies, and all the other terrible lies the Germans were telling them." And so, the rescuers are highly sensitized to the need to see each person, not as a stereotype, but as an individual.

The Nazi interrogator in Janet Kalff's story about her mother-in-law is the ultimate demonstration of this principle. When Mrs. Kalff told him the truth about her rescue activities and those of her children, he replied, "Madam, I have an old mother, and she thinks just the way you do. You'll hear nothing more about it." Such responses were, of course, rare, but they did occur within the Nazi ranks and at times made the difference between life and death. One of the most striking examples occurred in Le Chambon, France, where the successful rescue of hundreds of Jewish children by the residents of that pastoral French hamlet would not have been possible without the purposeful inattention of the chief Nazi officer responsible for overseeing the region. Those perpetrators who acted in this way removed themselves from the killing machine, even though tremendous pressure was being exerted on them to function as its cogs.

Browning comments that many of the qualities I have been discussing—moral and social autonomy, empathy, habits of caring, rejection of stereotypical thinking—were as absent in the perpetrators as they were present in the rescuers. His observations on how ordinary men were able to commit unspeakable crimes parallel to some extent the process by which other ordinary people, the rescuers, were able to rise to extraordinary moral heights:

> Few among the perpetrators held firm political convictions that shaped their decision to become killers, but once the initial direction had been taken, subsequent behavior deepened commitment. Ideology was shaped by what they were doing, and, in the case of the killers, they internalized and adopted as their own the political doctrines of the regime that legitimized their actions.

Considering the moral impoverishment of perpetrators and the strong social and political forces sanctioning their criminal behavior, for a perpetrator to *not* do his job was perhaps as much of an ethical achievement as for a bystander to become a rescuer. How then can we justify encouraging the exercise of conscience in bystanders without doing the same for perpetrators?

Through my contact with the rescuers, I have come to believe that we must stop thinking of perpetrators as two-dimensional figures, figures we could never become. We all have the capacity for evil, and all of our institutions and social structures are capable of being perverted to serve the wrong ends. Those institutions and social structures, in turn, are capable of socializing people to do the wrong things. Our sense of what to guard against may be informed by the past, but evil is nothing if not protean. Even the vigilant could end up as perpetrators of something that is not recognized until later to have been a moral disaster. It is critical to ask, then, how does evil become transformed?

One answer is that it may be transformed through a genuine encounter in which people step out of their set roles and relate as one human being to another. I believe this was a factor in the outcome between Mrs. Kalff and her Nazi interrogator, who, for all we know, had never responded in such a way before. This cannot happen when either party insists on viewing the other as less than human: a mere statistic or a generic representative of a category. Nor can it happen when the human element is foreclosed by distance and technology, as when a missile is launched from hundreds of miles away by a technician who will never know whom he is killing, let alone see their faces and hear their screams. In contrast, consider the "truth-in-reconciliation" hearings in South Africa in which enemies encounter each other, albeit after the damage has been done, in a setting carefully structured to promote mutual understanding and effect "restorative justice." Sometimes dramatically effective, these hearings can result in repentance on the part of the perpetrator and forgiveness on the part of the victim.

I often asked the rescuers about their current feelings towards Germans. I was interested in how their love of people had played out over time towards those who had caused them and others so much agony. In answer to this question, the rescuers tended, overall, to be forgiving, even as they reported that younger generations, perhaps their own grandchildren, are carrying on the old hatreds. Several Dutch young people told me the same urban legend about a Dutch boy who goes to Germany on holiday and, after lingering in a store for a while, is asked by the impatient shopkeeper if he's going to buy anything. "First give me back my grandmother's bicycle," sneers the Dutch boy. This may get a chuckle from Dutch youth, but the rescuers do not join in. They seem to be struggling with the paradox that while those who forget the past may be condemned to repeat it, dwelling on the past can sometimes perpetuate hate and prejudice. The solution that some of them have pointed towards is for the lessons of the past to be remembered well, but not interpreted narrowly. Instead of drawing literal conclusions from history, we must recognize those principles and patterns that *will* recur, though under different and most likely unexpected circumstances.

Indeed, even those who know their history will probably misread current events if they are not prepared to broadly interpret the lessons of the past and to expect the unexpected. When the rescuers' generation was facing a possible Second World War, the Netherlands had historically been a neutral country—how did it serve the Dutch to remember that? Never before had genocide occurred on the scale of the Holocaust—what use was their knowledge of history in facing it? Furthermore, they had been raised to mistrust the fabricated atrocity tales of the First World War—how did that help them to recognize the real horrors of the Second?

The Nazi occupation required the Dutch to find their bearings on a new set of historical coordinates, and most were not up to the task. Faced with uncertainty, they did their jobs and kept on in other ways as before, clinging to the familiar and trying ineffectually to maintain some semblance of a normal life. To some of these people, Nazism had an appeal, for it offered definite answers and a master plan in which the Dutch, as "Aryans," came out on top.

The rescuers' approach was dynamic, even creative: they were able to think outside the historical box, as well as the Nazi propaganda box. Underlying this was the ability to *see* the reality unfolding before them. Though one might think that such awareness would come easily to all Dutch under Nazi occupation, it did not.

Many were too preoccupied with their own problems to notice what was being done to others more vulnerable than themselves. Many decided, consciously or unconsciously, *not* to see, for seeing would necessitate action. Then there were those who were trying to be optimistic, but their optimism blocked their view of reality. Those who did act were able to admit what was going on without being overtaken by a need to believe that "things can't really be that bad."

Initially, I was dazzled by the extraordinary positive thinking of people like Gisela and Hetty, whose buoyant attitudes enabled them to cheer up others, even after they were in a concentration camp. Gradually, however, I became aware of another, subtler, aspect to the rescuers' narratives: that while hoping for the best, they were often, as William Sloane Coffin puts it, "taking a long, full, look at the worst."

Human beings will often substitute illusion and rationalization for the simple awareness of a painful truth. In occupied Holland, such tendencies were intensified by the sheer enormity of the Nazi crimes, and the smokescreen of prevarication behind which they were taking place. To see the painful truth, one had to want to look. Even then, it was more a matter of intuition than reason, for few solid facts were available.

Unlike the naïve optimism of those who were ready to believe that the Germans were resettling Jews or sending them to labor camps, the hardheaded optimism of the rescuers allowed for the possibility that the Jews were being destroyed. But even as the rescuers considered this painful truth, they were also looking beyond it. Hoping against hope, they would imagine an eventual victory, a restoration of justice, a return to freedom. It was on that nexus of optimistic and realistic thinking that the rescuers rode out the war.

Many of the rescuers' core values are conveyed through their statements about our present society, and some of those values were no doubt shaped during the difficult Nazi years. When my discussion with Clara Dijkstra led into the subject of parenting, she had some strong words:

> With so many mothers and fathers working, the children get out from school and come home to an empty house . . . no one is there for them, and then they become angry and get into trouble. But where is the love for the children? No, you're working for another car, a better house. . . . You can have your cars and your luxurious homes, or you have a close, loving re-lationship with your children. But you can't have it both ways.

Clara places an either/or choice squarely before today's upwardly mobile parents. Her penetrating recognition that one cannot "have it all" echoes the unflinching way that she observed the world around her during the Nazi occupation. And if you think back to what Piet Meerburg and Kees Veenstra said regarding those who helped—that people with assets and position didn't want to take the risk, while com-mon people were more likely to say yes— it can be heard as a variation on the same theme. When asked, "Would you be willing to take in a Jewish child?" a hard choice had to be made. *They* could not have it both ways. Those who said yes took a leap into radical altruism, and perhaps the kind of people they would become was determined at that decisive moment. As the occupation continued and they daily risked everything to save the lives of others, those altruistic values grew deeper and stronger, like roots that take hold in ravaged soil.

In contrast to the untested idealism that many of us have as young people, including that expressed by Anne Frank in her famous saying about people really being good at heart, the idealism of the rescuers has been forged in the crucible of their confrontation with evil and tempered over a lifetime of righteous living. It's a moral achievement that, sad to say, Anne Frank never had the opportunity to reach. Inured to evil, the rescuers yet affirm the good.

When I asked Ted Leenders how we can educate our children to keep something like the Holocaust from recurring, he replied, "First, we should teach them how bad people can be. Don't fool them into believing that everybody is nice. The evil in people is awful. It's tremendous. But, also, we must teach them to be the best, most active citizens around. Don't wait for someone else to do it—you be the leader!" Ted's prescription is also a description of the rescuers: people able to face the worst about the world while laboring to repair it.

Do the rescuers have any regrets? They regret the pain, suffering, and, sometimes, the loss of their friends and loved ones. They regret that the lives of more people were not saved. They regret that they couldn't have done more, despite the fact that they were the ones who did the most. There is a vulnerable quality about the rescuers that caused me to go beyond seeing them only as objects of admiration. Over time, I came to realize the obvious: that their choices to help were in no way inevitable, that their burdens could have been made immeasurably lighter had more people pitched in, and that they still regret that more people didn't.

We have seen how the vast majority of human beings at that time played it safe and didn't want to involve themselves with other people's problems. We can join with the rescuers in not condemning them for that, and, while we're at it, in not condemning ourselves, if we suspect that we would have acted the same way. However, the inaction of the bystanders resulted in tremendous suffering. Can we really let them—and ourselves—off the hook so easily?

The rescuers' generous attitude says more about who *they* are than about those they have forgiven. And, ultimately, what's past is past, and it is up to us today to show by our actions who *we* are. I have seen people fret about what they would have done during World War II had they been, say, "Aryan" in a Nazi-occupied country. After spending time with the rescuers, I realize that the really relevant and vital question is "What am I doing now?" While many of us are content to visit a Holocaust museum and pick up a "Never Again" button, the rescuers would have us take up their mission, and carry it on.

Indeed, most of the rescuers continue to help victims of injustice and urge others to do the same. Mieke Vermeer is active in Amnesty International, especially the Freedom Writers Network, through which she writes letters on behalf of people who have been unjustly imprisoned and sometimes tortured because of their political or religious beliefs. She explained to me that such letters can lead to the prisoner receiving better treatment and even to his or her release. "It's better to light a candle than curse the darkness," she said, quoting an Amnesty slogan. Rescuer Cornelis Termaat said, "We've tried to support groups that take care of victims all over the world, like Doctors Without Borders and Christian Solidarity International." His wife Dory added, "We are also involved with Greenpeace and Partners in Health, and sometimes the campaign to free Tibet. And through our church, we've been part of the sanctuary movement, helping to resettle people who fled political persecution in the Congo. . . . In a way it's a continuation of what we did during the war, but without the risk."

We are all, in one way or another, in a position to continue the work of the rescuers, and what a privilege to be able to do so without putting oneself in mortal danger. It's an opportunity we can't afford to pass up, for to be content to admire the rescuers from a geographical and historical distance puts us in *moral* danger of being passive in our own life and times. Miep Gies declares, "we cannot wait for our leaders to make this world a better place," but that we must take action in our own sphere of influence. In the United States, such diverse voices as Jimmy Carter, Marian Wright Edelman, and Michael Lerner have put out the call for citizen leaders willing to respond to the suffering of groups toward whom society is indifferent. While government may be encumbered with bureaucracy and politicians constrained by their need to get reelected, there is nothing to stop such self-appointed citizen leaders from fully expressing their highest altruistic impulses. And, as the example of the rescuers has shown us, being responsive to the plight of others in times of peace increases the likelihood that one will act heroically in times of danger.

How, though, does one keep from falling into despair? Seemingly insurmountable obstacles stand in the way of anyone who dares try to stand up for the dispossessed or in other ways right society's wrongs. The rescuers, too, felt helpless and overwhelmed when confronted with the enormity of what they were up against. Yet they did what they could, and later they looked back at the war as a special, almost halcyon period. As Kees Veenstra put it, "Often I think the war was the best part of my life. You could be useful, you could save people, you could do things." Like us, they doubted whether an individual could make a difference, but we, looking back at them, can see that the answer is yes.

twelve

R E F L E C T I O N S

&

*To write history is not merely to
recover the lost content of the past; it is to perform
metaphorically a work of personal restoration.*

—JOHN PAUL EAKIN

WHAT IS THE POINT of trying to do good at all? That was the question
that haunted me after hearing Ted's tale of Vos, the man who had been
broken by the Nazis, attacked by the Resistance people he'd made
great sacrifices to help, and then brutalized by Dutch prison guards. I
knew, of course, that heroes aren't indestructible and that good deeds
often go unrecognized, but I guess that somewhere in my mind the
comic book heroes and fairy-tale endings I'd absorbed in childhood—
the ones I had relied on to assuage my Holocaust fears—were still ex-
erting their influence. Or perhaps I was still in L.A. mode, thinking that
everything you do, even if it appears to be for others, should finally
yield some personal reward.

The rescuers, however, never thought about personal rewards. They
simply recognized a desperate need and took action. It's a bit like the
Talmudic tale of how the Jews came to be the "chosen people": every
other nation was offered the responsibility, but only the Jews accepted.
And like the Israelites at Mt. Sinai, the rescuers accepted first and only
later fully understood what would be involved. On the other hand,
by doing what they deeply believed to be right and just, there *was* a reward, one that blurs the distinction between the "altruistic" and the
"selfish" gesture: by acting on behalf of others, they were safeguarding
their own humanity.

Hearing how the rescuers became involved in their Resistance activities had a particular resonance for me because when I first went to the

Netherlands I was trying to figure out what to do with my life. Joseph Campbell's exhortation "follow your bliss" sounded good, but what could constitute bliss? It wasn't until I met Gisela and Hetty that I realized it might mean a state of contentment and self-respect that has nothing to do with outer circumstances—a sense of satisfaction at having done the right thing, at having stood up for what one believes, at enjoying a good reputation with the people who most matter, especially oneself.

During those months in Holland of getting up early every morning, taking the train, and ringing the doorbell, something passed between me and those who welcomed me into their homes that was more than just words. William James may have described it best when he wrote about "those invisible, molecular moral forces that work from individual to individual." The love that permeated my time with the rescuers made it clear to me that the path they have taken is far superior to the crowded superhighways of ambition and consumption that many people in the United States imagine will make them happy. Though most of them live modestly, the rescuers are rich in *chesed*, a Hebrew word meaning lovingkindness. That quality of *chesed*, so tangible in their presence, convinced me that *this* is what life is all about.

Later, after returning home, I discovered that part of me was still gazing at the vistas that had opened under the rescuers' expansive influence. As I traveled on a Trailways bus from New York City to Ithaca in December 1996, I tried to hold on to my memories of them, even as the sight of acres of cars parked in front of huge shopping malls reminded me of a life I knew well, but no longer wanted.

It was my last semester at Cornell, but suddenly the emphasis on achievement and grades seemed out of balance. I knew that I was in the midst of a moral and vocational sea change, but with graduation fast approaching I felt pressured to quickly decide my next move, so as not to be left behind in the "real world" I would soon re-enter.

And yet the rescuers' choices—both during and after the war—suggested that finding one's way in life is not so much about using the will as it is about willingness; not so much about setting goals and pursuing them as it is about being open to life and able to respond to it: responseability. After all, most of the rescuers had had educational and professional goals before the Nazis invaded; if they'd held to their plans, they might have graduated on time, but they would have missed the opportunity to save the lives of hundreds of children. I decided to do less planning and calculating about my future, and more listening and responding. I also did some volunteer work at a hospice and, later, at a homeless shelter. In short, I aspired to be a bit like the rescuers. Looking back now, ten years later, I see that by moving through the world in this way, my calling has taken care of itself.

I learned some practical things from the rescuers, which can be summed up in a few sentences: Spend less than you earn. Save some money. Give some money away. When I visited one of the rescuers recently, he had a six-inch stack of letters on his dining room table. As we sat down and he moved them out of the way to make more room, he mentioned that they were fund-raising letters from various charities. He lets the letters build up and then, once a year, goes through them and writes checks to the worthiest causes. But he feels bad for the other organizations, so he writes little checks to many of them also. "Even a small donation can give a lot of encouragement to people doing good work," he explained.

What a nice way to spend an afternoon. Beats trying to figure out what's going on with the plastic in your wallet. When I lived in Los Angeles, I rarely gave away money, but I must have had a dozen charge cards. I was always trying to keep track of them, and I often spent too much. Now I have one. Life is good.

However, after being around the rescuers, it is difficult to conceive of my life as merely a personal journey, disconnected from civic and political responsibilities. Through their influence, I became aware of the tremendous opportunities that exist to join with others who also want to spend not only their money but their time to help build a more just and compassionate society. I have discovered that there are a mind-boggling array of good causes out there, and that the people championing them typically believe, as do the rescuers, that it's better to care about others than to watch out for yourself; that if you care about others, things will work out; and even if they don't, you won't regret it. As I've gotten involved with some of these causes, my sense of connection to others has been restored, and I now think of myself as a part of a caring community striving to effect positive social change all over the world.

. . . .

As for my own personal debt to the rescuers, there is a deeper layer still, for they have revivified my relationship with Judaism. Many of the rescuers told me that they hadn't registered a difference between Jews and non-Jews before the war, but that Hitler changed all that and there was no going back. As the Nazis imposed their divisive way of seeing humanity onto the entire Dutch population, it became impossible not to see Jews as Jews; instead of ostracizing them, however, the rescuers came to their aid. This often brought them into close contact with strong Jewish individuals and a rich Jewish culture, even as that culture was being eradicated before their eyes.

When I met with the rescuers, I sometimes sensed that they were looking at me as a child or grandchild of someone they had rescued. They definitely saw me as Jewish, and that in itself had a profound impact. Why? Because being Jewish meant something different to them than it did to me.

I had been brought up with "Judaism lite"—the half-hearted observance of certain customs, rituals, and cultural traditions—superimposed on a mostly unspoken family history of trauma and dislocation. In contrast, the rescuers had had a tremendously powerful experience of Judaism. They associated it not only with the incredible endurance that Jews demonstrated during the occupation, but also with a vibrant canvas of culture and religion that had enlivened all of Amsterdam before the war. They saw all this as my inheritance and thought I was helping to carry it on. They didn't go out of their way to affirm my heritage, and yet, by seeing me in that continuum, they did just that. Ironically, it took people who were not Jewish to introduce me to a Jewishness I had never before encountered.

After I returned home to the United States, this new way of seeing Judaism stuck. Suddenly, its interweaving of social justice with spirituality seemed incredibly advanced and potent. Certainly the rescuers embody many of the ideals of Judaism. To know that, I needed only to remember some of the Torah I had read as a young person, passages such as Deuteronomy 10:17–19: "For the Lord your God . . . upholds the cause of the fatherless and the widow, and befriends the stranger, providing him with food and clothing. You too must befriend the stranger, for you were strangers in the land of Egypt."

However, as a young person, I never saw that commandment—repeated thirty-six times in the Torah—being fulfilled in any earnest way by the people around me or the larger society, except at the nearby suicide prevention and crisis service, which provided runaways with free counseling and set them up with a place to stay. I discovered that by running away myself when I was about fifteen, running from an emptiness so profound that to be with the caring volunteers at the crisis service felt like an emotional step up.

I've gradually come to realize, though, that the spiritual and emotional vacuum in which I was raised was yet another part of the legacy of having been born in the shadow of the Holocaust. My father, having lost faith in any God that could have allowed the death of six million innocent people, tried to escape his sense of fear and rootlessness by fixating on material security. His childhood experiences of anti-Semitism caused him to dig in his heels against a threatening world, and this meant armoring himself against any emotion that might make him vulnerable, including the whisper of his own spirit.

As a young person, I tried to kick a hole in that emptiness, which often meant rebelling against Judaism itself. I realize now that I was flailing against a post-Holocaust Judaism that had yet to recover its shining heart—a Judaism that had grown rich materially, due to the affluence of Jews in the United States, but one that had remained spiritually bereft, even as my father had remained spiritually bereft. In the presence of the rescuers, I was finally able to break through that shell to breathe the fresh, heady air of a life lived on the other side of fear and trauma.

This was no small thing. Unresolved fear and trauma are more than old wounds that have not healed: they shape the present and determine the future. Mistrust generates mistrust; abuse generates abuse. This is bad enough within a family, but when it happens within a community, or an entire society, the negative synergy can be deadly—as we see in Israel/Palestine today. Violence breeds fear; fear breeds violence. How to break the endless cycle?

There must be many ways, but I suspect it mostly happens one by one by one. I am grateful, in my own case, to have had the help of the rescuers. They present a crucial testimony to the Jewish community that the Jews were not entirely alone in the world during the

Holocaust. The solace of that truth may be seen as a last parting gift from the rescuers to the Jewish people.

In contemporary Jewish circles, there is an oft-repeated folktale of how the saintly Baal Shem Tov, a great zaddik who lived in eighteenth-century Poland, used to go to a certain spot in the forest where he would light a fire, meditate, and say a special prayer on behalf of the Jewish people. Years later, one of his disciples went to that same place in the forest but didn't know how to light the fire. Nevertheless, he meditated and said the prayer. Still later, another disciple came along who knew neither how to light the fire nor say the prayer, but he was still able to meditate at the place in the forest, and that was sufficient. But finally, there came a disciple who said, "I am unable to light the fire. I do not know how to meditate or say the prayer. I can't even find the place in the forest. All I can do is tell the story, and that must be sufficient." And it was sufficient, so we are told.

I believe that this tale obliquely expresses the sense of loss that Jews felt, and continue to feel, in the wake of the near-destruction of Jewish life and culture in Europe. To be sure, it ends with a message of comfort: the suggestion that remembering what was lost is sufficient. But Judaism can't subsist on memories of a time when Jews lived full and vibrant spiritual lives, any more than the rescuers can subsist on memories of what they once did during the war. Though this book is full of the rescuers' stories, the rescuers did more than tell me their stories. By possessing a spirituality that was strengthened rather than shattered by the Holocaust, and by being powerful embodiments of the lovingkindness through which, the Jewish sages tell us, the world is sustained, they were able to offer me a new vision of my heritage, one infused with *chaim*—life. In the course of being swept away by the immensity of their faith, I found myself carried back to my own.

ENDINGS

&

For righteousness shall lead
to peace; it shall bring quietness
and confidence forever.

—ISAIAH 32:17

THE CURTAIN IS QUICKLY COMING DOWN on bystanders, rescuers, perpetrators, and survivors alike. Soon the Holocaust will be but a memory of a memory. My father, *alav ha'shalom,* died in January 2004, shortly before this book found a publisher. I had hoped that all the rescuers would live to see their words inspire younger generations, but that was not to be. Of those profiled, Hetty Voûte, Heiltje Kooistra, Janet Kalff, Mieke Vermeer, and Theo Leenders have passed away. It has been my great honor to share the stories and wisdom that they and the others entrusted to me.

I continue to keep in touch with Rut Matthijsen, Gisela Söhnlein, Clara Dijkstra, Kees Veenstra, and Pieter Meerburg. Since 11 September 2001, I have heard them decry both the subsequent hostile backlash against Arabs and "the new anti-Semitism" toward Jews. I have shared their dismay over the unfolding tragedy of the war in Iraq—especially troubling to the rescuers because it was started by the trusted nation that once liberated them from oppression and starvation under Hitler. Though George W. Bush has on several occasions drawn a parallel between the war on terrorism and the fight against the Nazis, the rescuers do not buy it. They, along with most Europeans, tend to distrust his motives and means, and know that terrorists and terrorist groups cannot be defeated in the direct military way by which the Allies once defeated Nazi Germany.

My wife and I had a son in June 2005, and Kees Veenstra called to offer his benediction: "I hope he grows up to be one of those people who bring some light into this troubled world." That, of course, is as good a description of the rescuers as any I could come up with. Although the historical context in which they made their courageous choices is increasingly distant, their witness continues to shine. Against the seemingly limitless void of the Holocaust, the rescuers have revealed to us nothing less than the ultimate power of the individual, when surrounded by hate and fear, to act with love and compassion.

COMMENTS
AND
ACKNOWLEDGMENTS

﹩

IN CRAFTING THE PROFILES of the rescuers, I used my initial interviews as a starting point but over time incorporated material from our further conversations, as well as correspondence via letter, e-mail, and fax. I also occasionally included information supplied by other sources, such as the rescuers' spouses, their children, or the children they rescued. Along the way, I shared the work-in-progress with my subjects and made changes based on their comments. Thus, over the course of nine years, what began as oral history interviews evolved into literary narratives, or something approximating "as told to" memoirs. An additional layer to the rescuers' stories became available when I gained partial access to the transcripts of interviews that Dr. Bert Jan Flim conducted during the 1980s with some of the same individuals. With his kind permission, I have included a small amount of his interview material.

In order to avoid provoking "Sylvia Bloch" (chapter 5) and "Doris" (chapter 10), I gave them false names. All the other names are factual. On a more scholarly note, in referring to what happened to the Jews during the Nazi years, I prefer to use the word *holocaust* rather than *shoah*, or the lesser-known *hurban*. Some object to *holocaust* because its original meaning in Greek traces back to "burnt offering," and such a connotation is deeply troubling. They prefer *shoah*, because, as James Carroll points out, when the genocide is referred to by this Hebrew word meaning "catastrophe," "a wall is being erected against the consolations and insults of a redemptive, sacrificial theology of salvation." However, Amos Oz cautions, "I never use the word *shoah* when I want to refer to the murder of the Jews of Europe. The word *shoah* falsifies the true nature of what happened. A *shoah* is a natural event, an outbreak of forces beyond human control. The murder of the European Jews was no *shoah*." In the end, I chose to use the word *holocaust*, simply because that's what I grew up with, and, for me, it holds the appropriate resonance of terror.

In composing this work, I have relied on several historians (see page 235), especially the aforementioned Bert Jan Flim at Friesland College in Leeuwarden, whose Ph.D. dissertation documents four rescue networks that saved Jewish children. The dissertation was published in Holland with the title *Omdat Hun Hart Sprak*. A condensation of that tome has recently appeared in English with the title *Saving the Children*.

In writing the historical introduction, as well as in the conclusion and elsewhere in the text, I have relied on several major Dutch historians of the previous generation, especially Louis de Jong, who has been studying World War II since the time he lived through it, and whose works on the subject could fill a small library, and Jacob Presser, a Jewish survivor of the Holocaust in the Netherlands who devoted fifteen years to his poignant masterwork *Ondergang*. De Jong's most accessible book is *The Netherlands and Nazi Germany*, based on a lecture series he gave at Harvard, and Presser's *Ondergang* is available in English as *Ashes in the Wind*.

Another valuable resource has been the work of British historian Bob Moore, who is generally recognized as the outside expert on the Netherlands during the occupation. His book *Victims and Survivors* authoritatively explains why the Jewish survival rate in the Netherlands was so low, despite the country's history of tolerance, and the pro-Semitic attitudes held by most of its population.

Finally, I owe a great professional debt to U.S. historian Christopher R. Browning, whose book *Ordinary Men* explores the chilling parallel universe of the perpetrators, and whose most recent book *The Origins of the Final Solution* has been hailed as a definitive volume by scholars worldwide. In writing my book, I have been most fortunate to have Dr. Browning as a historical consultant. The responsibility for any errors in the text, however, rests entirely with me.

. . . .

It takes a village to write a book, at least in my case. For my initial research undertaken as an undergraduate at Cornell University, I am thankful for the help and support provided by Steven T. Katz, Alison Lurie, Susan Tarrow, and the staff of the Institute for European Studies. In addition, I will always remember the good cheer and confidence in my work that the late Robert Farrell extended to me. In the Netherlands, Anne Dunkelgrun, Director of Cultural Affairs at the Israeli Embassy, was a great help, as were Monique and Rob van der Wel, Taas van Santan, and Minka and Jörn Bos. When I returned to Cornell and began to work with the interview material, Ann Boehm, Jennifer Krier, Helena Viramontes, and, later, James R. McConkey helped me to formulate my thinking and direction. As I continued this process in graduate school at the University of North Carolina at Chapel Hill, I was aided and abetted by Jacquelyn Dowd Hall, Glenn Hinson, Patricia Sawin, Bland Simpson, and Terry Zug. My fellow grad students also provided vital support and encouragement and Kathryn Walbert offered many great ideas and suggestions. An angel appeared at this time in the form of Barbara Jacobson, who volunteered to transcribe my interview tapes and went on to help in other valuable ways with the project.

When I returned to Ithaca, New York, to begin work on the book, Jim and Gladys McConkey stepped into their full role as archangels of the project. Thanks are also due to Ellen McHale at the New York Folklore Society and to my supporters at Kendall of Ithaca, especially W. Jack Lewis and Roy Unger. Jack was a great champion of the project from the get-go, and I will always be grateful to him for that and so much more.

Several people were kind enough to help me with translation, especially Martinja Briggs at Cornell University, who gave generously of her time and expertise. A big thanks also to Ingrid Blom and Galit Smilansky. A number of Holocaust institutions helped me as well: Yad Vashem, the Ghetto Fighters' House, the Netherlands Institute for War Documentation, and the United States Holocaust Memorial Museum. Thanks also to the libraries and CIT departments of Amherst College, Cornell University, Smith College, Springfield Technical Community College, and the University of North Carolina at Chapel Hill. The reference desk at the Jones Library in Amherst, Massachusetts, also was a great help.

I started to show the nascent manuscript to friends and colleagues and benefited from the comments of Gary Cartwright, Craig Comstock, Annie Corbett, Mike DeHeer, Amy Denham, Rob Early, Stephen Fantina, Deb Fitzpatrick, Tess and Paul Frost, Kevin Ginsberg, Julie Heath, Lamar Herrin, Edward Hower, Brian Muszynski, Jan Nigro, Rabbi Jonathan Rubenstein, Joy Salyers, Albrecht Strauss, Maurice van der Pol, and Mark I. Wallace. I also brought onboard Alice Truax, who fully upheld her reputation as being one of the best freelance editors in New York. Thanks also to Duncan Murrell, whose editorial expertise helped bring clarity to my analytical chapter. Other publishing professionals who offered valuable advice and suggestions include Matthew Carnicelli, Donald Cutler, and especially Renee Sedliar, whom I count as another true angel of the project. Special thanks also to Jane Gelfman for taking the project into her heart and trying to find a home for it in the world.

During the final stage between completed manuscript and published book, the Pilgrim team stepped in and offered their enthusiastic support and expertise: thanks especially to Ulrike Guthrie, Aimée Jannsohn, Pamela Johnson, Michael Lawrence, and my publisher Timothy Staveteig. A big thanks also to Paul Rogat Loeb for being the matchmaker and overall source of encouragement, and to Shira Dicker, Carol Fass, and Gail Leondar for helping to get the word out. Thanks also to Kristin Firth for her diligent copy editing and Rick Porter for the artful design. Other people who have provided valuable advice, support, and assistance include Lynne Abel, David Cecelski, Ron Coleman, Janet Ellis, William Ferris, Bert Jan Flim, George Gibian, Phyllis Janowitz, Rabbi Harold Kushner, Julius Lester, Theresa Maitland, Daniel Mendelsohn, Elizabeth Salon, Pete Seeger, Tzvetan Todorov, and Hans de Vries. Thanks also to the rescuers' families and friends, especially Anneke Burke-Kooistra, Rietje de Haan-Kooistra, Liesbeth Hes, Aad Kuenen-Dutilh, and Michael Schlejen.

And through it all, my lovely and wonderful wife Sophia was plugging for me and kept things together when they surely would have come apart. I thank her for this and all the other blessings she brings to my life. A special thanks also to my mother, Miriam, for doing all that she could to help me. Finally, thanks to the rescuers one and all, for making this book possible, and for performing those deeds that keep the world turning.

ENDNOTES

❧

BEGINNINGS

xvi *Hitler took them all* Readers may hear my grandmother tell stories and sing snippets of Yiddish songs from pre-WWII Poland in the documentary *Image Before My Eyes* (New York: YIVO Institute/Axon Video Corp., 1981).

xvi *"a strange interweaving"* Daniel Mendelsohn, "What Happened to Uncle Shmiel?" *New York Times Magazine,* 14 July 2002.

xvi *"hinge generation"* This expression is used by Eva Hoffman in *After Such Knowledge* (New York: Public Affairs, 2004).

xvi *"wound without memory"* Nadine Fresco uses this expression in "Remembering the Unknown," *International Review of Psychoanalysis* 11/4 (1984): 418–19, 421.

xvii *different estimates by historians* Compare: Presser, 539; J. C. H. Blom, "The Persecution of the Jews in the Netherlands in a Comparative International Perspective," *Dutch Jewish History 2,* ed. Jozeph Michman (Jerusalem: Graf-Chen Press, 1989), 273; B. A. Sies, "Several Observations Concerning the Position of the Jews in Occupied Holland during World War II," *Rescue Attempts during the Holocaust,* ed. Yisrael Gutman and Efraim Zurof (Jerusalem: Yad Vashem, 1977), 527–28; Gerhard Hirschfeld, "Niederlande," Dimension des Völkermonds, *Die Zahl der jüdischen Opfer des Nationalsozialismus,* ed. Wolfgang Benz (Munich: R. Oldenbourg Verlag, 1991), 165.

BACKGROUND

1 *Though millions wanted to do something* This can be deduced from the prevalence and wide readership of Resistance newspapers. The other estimates come from de Jong, 47. See also Bob de Graaff, "Collaboratie en Verzet" in: J. P. B. Jonker et al. *Vijftig jaar na de inval* (Amsterdam: SDU, 1985), 95.

2 *Through the use of paratroopers* Gordon Craig, *Europe Since 1815* (New York: Holt, Rinehart and Winston, 1961), 721.

2 *"I saw the planes still diving"* Ralph Boucher, *Miracle of Survival* (Berkeley: J. L. Magnes Museum, 1997), 45.

2 *Closer to ground zero* This is based on the unforgettable description by Sebald of a similar, albeit larger, firebombing perpetrated later in the war by the Allies, combined with the statistics for Rotterdam provided by Shirer. See W. G. Sebald, *On the Natural History of Destruction* (New York: Random House, 2003), 27; William L. Shirer, *The Rise and Fall of the Third Reich: A History of Nazi Germany* (New York: Simon & Schuster, 1960), 722.

3 *"WE THE GERMAN PEOPLE"* Recalled by survivor Jack van der Geest, *Was God on Vacation? A World War II Autobiography,* written with Carol J. Ordemann (Arvada, Colo.: Van der Geest, 1995), 2.

3 *more than a hundred Jewish people committed suicide* See Werner Warmbrunn, *The Dutch under German Occupation 1940–1945* (Stanford: Stanford University Press, 1963), 166; Mark Klempner, "Navigating Life Review Interviews with Survivors of Trauma," *Oral History Review* 27, no. 2 (2000 Summer/Fall), 67–83.

3 *utmost restraint and compliance* See Gordon A. Craig, "'Schreibt und Farschreibt!'" *New York Review of Books* (10 April 1986).

3 *"We shall hit the Jews"* B. A. Sijes, *De Februaristaking, 25–26 Febrari 1941* (The Hague, 1954), 179–80.

4 *Though there was some protest* See Van Galen Last, 195; B. A. Sijes, "Several Observations Concerning the Position of the Jews in Occupied Holland during World War II," in *Rescue*

Attempts during the Holocaust, ed. Yisrael Gutman and Efraim Zuroff (Jerusalem: Yad Vashem, 1977), 535.

4 *"From the German point of view"* P. Romijn, 302.

5 *do away with the Jews most quickly* Christopher R. Browning, conversation with the author, 5 April 2002.

5 *The Nationaal Socalistische Beweging* See Albert Van der Mey, *When a Neighbor Comes Calling* (Ontario: Paideia Press, 1985), 40.

5 *Within a couple of years* Van Galen Last, 198.

6 *"tight network of identification and movement controls"* Hilberg, 371.

6 *only about fifty Jews refused* B. A. Sijes, "Several Observations Concerning the Position of the Jews in Occupied Holland during World War II," in *Rescue Attempts during the Holocaust,* ed. Yisrael Gutman and Efraim Zuroff (Jerusalem: Yad Vashem, 1977), 536.

7 *on the board of this and another major Jewish organization* The Committee for Jewish Special Interests (1933) and the Jewish Coordination Committee (Fall 1940). See Jozeph Michman, "Historiography of the Jews in the Netherlands," in *Dutch Jewish History: Proceedings of the Symposium on the History of the Jews in the Netherlands, November 28–December 3, 1982,* ed. Jozeph Michman and Tirtsah Levie (Jerusalem: Tel-Aviv University, 1984), 26–27.

7 *After being marched in columns* Moore, 71–72.

7 *"For the first time, the Germans had shown"* Ibid.

8 *eighteen thousand workers were absent* Hilberg, 373.

8 *that cut through the isolation* Ibid., 56.

8 *Nevertheless, about fourteen hundred Jews* de Jong, 20.

9 *nearly nine million people* Ibid., 30.

9 *it may be seen as a natural trap* Hilberg, 365.

10 *functioned parallel to other groups* In the uniquely pillared Dutch system of *verzuiling* or "vertical integration," religious groups choose to remain apart with separate but equal status, while maintaining their own political representation. Out of this, "integrated subcultures (*zuilen*) emerged that cut across class lines,

uniting disparate economic and social groups on the basis of their religious affiliation." See Moore, 23, 161.

10 *enthusiastic quorum of fifteen* Hannah Arendt, *Eichmann in Jerusalem* (New York: Bantam, 1965).

11 *"beyond the belief and comprehension"* de Jong, 6–7.

11 *"apparatus of total destruction"* Martin Gilbert, *The Holocaust: A History of the Jews of Europe during the Second World War* (New York: Holt, Rinehart and Winston, 1985), 274.

12 *One indication of this* Hilberg, 407.

12 *a kind of Nordic-Germanic people* Christopher R. Browning, conversation with the author, 5 April 2002.

12 *Dutch civil servants . . . Westerbork.* Paraphrased from Elma Verhey, "Anne Frank and the Dutch Myth," in *Anne Frank in Historical Perspective*, ed. Alex Grobman and Joel Fishman (Los Angeles: Martyrs Memorial and Museum of the Holocaust of the Jewish Federation Council of Greater Los Angeles, 1995), 24.

12 *Police Inspector Schreuder* Personal correspondence with Dr. Maurice van der Pol of Newton, Massachusetts, whose life was saved as a result of one of Schreuder's tip-offs, 30 May 2002.

12 *some non-Jews donned homemade stars* Martin Gilbert, *The Holocaust: A History of the Jews of Europe during the Second World War* (New York: Holt, Rinehart and Winston, 1985), 283.

13 *seventy thousand different issues* de Jong, 46.

13 *"The blindness of the Jews"* Elie Wiesel and Philippe-Michäel de Saint-Cheron, *Evil and Exile,* trans. Jon Rothschild (Notre Dame, Ind.: University of Notre Dame Press, 1990).

13 *"set off for the streets"* P. Romijn, 314.

13 *To expedite turnover* Elma Verhey, "Anne Frank and the Dutch Myth," in *Anne Frank in Historical Perspective,* ed. Alex Grobman and Joel Fishman (Los Angeles: Martyrs' Memorial and Museum of the Holocaust of the Jewish Federation Council of Greater Los Angeles, 1995), 24.

14 *a two-day raid on Rotterdam* Van Galen Last, 205.

14 *over ten times that many* B. A. Sijes, "Several Observations Concerning the Position of the Jews in Occupied Holland dur-

ing World War II," in *Rescue Attempts during the Holocaust,* ed. Yisrael Gutman and Efraim Zuroff (Jerusalem: Yad Vashem, 1977), 547. See also Henri A. van der Zee, *The Hunger Winter* (Lincoln: University of Nebraska Press, 1988), 305.

14 *"I have now been here"* de Jong, 16.

14 *"Tens of thousands of such letters"* Ibid., 17.

14 *"When you lie, tell big lies"* Adolf Hitler, *Mein Kampf,* trans. James Murphy (London: Hutchinson, 1939), 198–99.

15 *As Browning points out* Christopher Browning, conversation with author, 5 April 2002.

16 *"was thought to present special problems"* Moore, 171.

17 *"Few Jews survived in Holland"* Hilberg, 365.

17 *more than four thousand young lives* According to the *Encyclopedia of the Holocaust,* vol. 3, ed. Israel Gutman, (New York: Macmillan, 1990), 1005, about forty-five hundred children were hidden in the Netherlands during the Holocaust, and "only a very few were discovered." Additional children were helped to escape to Switzerland, Israel, Spain, France, and elsewhere. See Moore, 168.

Chapter 1 HETTY VOÛTE

21 *"the stubborn ounces of my weight"* Bonaro Overstreet, *Hands Laid upon the Wind* (New York: Norton, 1955), 15.

21 *One Führer, One Reich, One Egg* The source of this story is an unpublished interview with Hetty conducted by Bert Jan Flim in 1989, and contained in the archives of Beit Lohamei HaGetaot in Israel. A transcript is available in Hebrew.

23 *Once we went to the room of a fellow student* Jan Meulenbelt tells this story himself in *Nieuw Utrechts Dagblad,* March 17, 1955. An English version is included in Flim, 21.

27 *my legs were shaking* This detail from Hetty's interrogation came out in Bert Jan Flim's unpublished interview with Hetty, contained in the archives of Beit Lohamei HaGetaot in Israel. A transcript is available in Hebrew.

42 *By then, nine out of ten of Poland's 3.3 million Jews* Hilberg, 126, 767.

Chapter 2 HEILTJE KOOISTRA

46 *"It attacks unexpectedly"* De Telegraaf, 13 December 1944. Available at the Netherlands Institute for War Documentation.

46 *"Those who are hungry shout"* Henri A. van der Zee, *The Hunger Winter* (Lincoln: University of Nebraska Press, 1988), 146.

59 *The Spanish Crown sank millions of ducats* G. Parker, *Spain and the Netherlands 1559–1659* (London, 1979), 185, 188.

60 *"If you didn't have an onderduiker"* Moore, 177.

60 *"broke the bloody scepters"* John Calvin, *Calvin Institutes of the Christian Religion,* ed. John McNeil, trans. Ford Lewis Battles (Louisville: Westminster John Knox Press, 1960), 669.

60 *Indeed, his exhortations* Lawrence Baron, "The Dutchness of the Dutch Rescuers" in *Embracing the Other,* ed. Oliner and Oliner (New York: New York University Press, 1992), 319.

61 *though numbering only 8 percent* Moore, 165.

61 *seven hundred Catholics* Gordon F. Sander, *The Frank Family That Survived* (London: Hutchinson, 2004), 143. For the source of "five hundred Protestants" consult the Sijes reference cited next.

61 *These Catholics and Protestants* Paraphrased from B. A. Sijes, "Several Observations Concerning the Position of the Jews in Occupied Holland during World War II," in *Rescue Attempts during the Holocaust,* ed. Yisrael Gutman and Efraim Zuroff (Jerusalem: Yad Vashem, 1977), 550.

Chapter 3 RUT MATTHIJSEN

65 *what I had in my suitcase* I have relied in part on Flim's account of this incident, 40.

65 *my stamp collection* Flim, 26.

66 *One photo went* This matter of the purpose of the second photo was clarified by Flim, 6.

67 *"A cell is just two meters long"* The poem contains seven stanzas, but I have included only four. This free translation is based on the more literal one of Rena Minkoff, which I then modified.

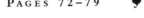

72 *Professor Scholten, a jurist*   Quoted by Presser, 21.

72 *The petition was signed*   Ibid.

73 *which amassed as many as two thousand signatures*   Ibid.

73 *"Naturally, it is far easier"*   Ibid., 20.

73 *"Their actions are beneath contempt"*   Ibid., 27.

73 *"this noble son of our people"*   Ibid., 27–28.

73 *Cleveringa was arrested*   Ibid., 28.

73 *thousands of copies of his speech*   Ibid., 28.

73 *Before dying*   Flim, 34.

73 *On 6 February 1943*   These statistics come from "Van Studentenverzet naar Universitaire Gemeenschap?" by Fjodor Molenaar. Online at http://www.kriterion.org/content/Meer Geschiedenis.html.

74 *Despite the additional threat*   This was told to me by Pieter Meerburg. The statistic comes from Flim, 34.

74 *the raiders*   Flim, 34.

Chapter 4 GISELA SÖHNLEIN

78 *a dull blow*   Flim, 184.

78 *"What do I do now?"*   Ibid.

79 *What I learned in Ravensbrück*   In this passage, Gisela paraphrases a favorite quote of hers by Arthur Koestler, one that he wrote about his imprisonment during the Spanish Civil War, but that Gisela feels captures her experience in Ravensbrück: "The life we led was a proof of man's capacity for adapting. I think that even the condemned souls in purgatory after a time develop a sort of homely routine. That is, by the way, why most prison memoirs are unreadable. The difficulty of conveying to the reader in his armchair an idea of this nightmare world from which he has emerged, makes the author depict the prisoners' state of mind as an uninterrupted continuity of despair. He fears to appear frivolous or to spoil his effect by admitting that even in the depths of misery, cheerfulness keeps breaking in." See

Arthur Koestler, *Arrow in the Blue: An Autobiography* (London: Hutchinson, 1969).

80 *"Come along, mates* This and the other lyrics by Gisela and Hetty have been translated by Martinja Briggs, professor of Dutch at Cornell University, and the author.

Chapter 5 CLARA DIJKSTRA

86 *"When father looks through his photographs"* In Han van der Horst, *The Low Sky: Understanding the Dutch* (Schiedam: Scriptum Books, 1996), 149.

99 *extreme and horrible circumstances* From a lecture by Ervin Staub at Amherst College, 29 March 2001.

99 *"They had been spared"* Simon Wiesenthal, *The Murderers among Us: The Simon Wiesenthal Memoirs,* Joseph Wechsberg, ed. (New York: McGraw-Hill, 1967), 48.

100 *In addition to the one hundred thousand people* All these statistics are from Henri A. van der Zee, *The Hunger Winter* (Lincoln: University of Nebraska Press, 1988), 305.

100 *The German children of 1918* Henri A. van der Zee, *The Hunger Winter* (Lincoln: University of Nebraska Press, 1988), 146.

101 *"the Germany which Britain now faces"* Clarence Pickett, "America's Food and Europe's Need," an address given to the American Academy of Political and Social Science, summarized in the Fellowship of Reconciliation's journal, *Fellowship* 6, no. 9 (November 1940), 135–37.

101 *The idea was to starve out the enemy* R. R. Palmer and Joel Colton, *A History of the Modern World* (New York: Knopf, 1963), 674.

102 *"the terrifying momentum of diplomacy"* From jacket copy to Sidney Bradshaw Fay, *The Origins of the World War, Volume 2,* 2nd ed., rev. (New York: Free Press, 1966).

102 *"a dictum exacted by victors"* Ibid., 549.

102 *the exchange rate* John R. Barber, *Modern European History* (New York: HarperPerennial, 1993), 270.

102 *In 1923, the mayor of Berlin* Gordon A. Craig, *Europe Since 1815* (New York: Holt, Rinehart and Winston, 1961), 613.

102 *"rose from the ranks"* Ibid., 525.

102 *"If a man's bare existence"* Inge Scholl, *The White Rose: Munich 1942–1943* (Hanover: Wesleyan University Press, 1983), 12.

103 *"the chains of Versailles"* Gerhard Ritter, "Nazism Arose from Democratic Radicalism," in *Critical Issues in History: 1848 to the Present,* ed. John Rule, David Dowd, John Snell (Boston: D.C. Heath, 1967), 730.

103 *"honestly hoped Hitler"* Luigi Barzini, *The Europeans* (New York: Simon and Schuster, 1983), 80.

103 *"every institution that under democracy"* Franz Neumann, quoted by Gordon A. Craig in *Europe Since 1815* (New York: Holt, Rinehart and Winston, 1961), 641.

103 *"Now that we have discussed the political situation"* Entire anecdote contained in Luigi Barzini, *The Europeans* (New York: Simon and Schuster, 1983), 80.

103 *"was as efficient in the techniques of control"* Gordon A. Craig, "Facing Up to the Nazis," *The New York Review of Books* (2 February 1989).

103 *When the Great Depression* Gordon A. Craig, *Europe Since 1815* (New York: Holt, Rinehart and Winston, 1961), 643.

103 *"The question of the treatment"* Quoted in *Nazi Conspiracy and Aggression: Opinion and Judgment* (Washington: Office of United States Chief of Counsel for Prosecution of Axis Criminality, 1947), 12–13, 16–21, 27–34.

Chapter 6 KEES VEENSTRA

105 *have remained almost completely unknown* Kees has not received the Yad Vashem award, or been recognized in any public way.

123 *"Death's Stairway"* See http://www.mauthausen-memorial.gv.at/engl/Geschichte/f.Geschichte.html

123 *"The 'work' took its toll"* Hilberg, 373.

123 *"On the third day"* Presser, 53.

123 *The Chief Rabbi of The Hague"* Ibid., 54–55.

124 *the Jewish Weekly* This is *Het Joodse Weekblad,* 7 August 1942. Available in the archives of the Netherlands Institute for War Documentation.

124 *"police-controlled labor contingents"* This anecdote comes from Peter Hellman, *Avenue of the Righteous* (New York: Atheneum, 1980), 69.

124 *"conscientious, much admired physicians"* Robert Jay Lifton, *The Nazi Doctors: Medical Killing and the Psychology of Genocide* (New York: Basic Books, 1986), 457.

125 *"Quite a few killed themselves"* Ibid., 458.

Chapter 8 PIETER MEERBURG

136 *"Once those fanatical Frisians"* Wouter expresses this sentiment directly and at more length in Flim, 32.

139 *The woman went ahead and took her* Mia Coelingh tells this story directly in Flim, 31.

142 *a message from Esmée van Eeghen* Piet provided this detail in his United States Holocaust Memorial Museum video interview. See USHMM Archives RG-50.030★0154, 19.

152 *Fifteen percent for Mr. Le Pen!* Jean-Marie Le Pen, roughly the equivalent of David Duke in the United States or Jörg Heider in Austria, won second place in the 2002 French presidential election with five million votes.

153 *"At best, they gave the odd fugitive"* Quoted in "Kroniek der Jodenvervolging" (Chronicle of the Persecution of the Jews) in *Onderdrukking en Verzet, Part 3* (Amsterdam, 1949–54), 160.

153 *"crowding on a small piece of wood"* Etty Hillesum, *An Interrupted Life: The Diaries of Etty Hillesum 1941–45* (New York: Washington Square Press, 1981), 188.

153 *were appointed by the Romans* See Alan Segal, *Rebecca's Children: Judaism and Christianity in the Roman World* (Cambridge: Harvard University Press, 1986).

154 *"will represent a natural selection"* International Military Tribunal, *Protocol of the Wannsee Conference,* Nuremberg: document NG2586F, 6.

154 *"they couldn't even conceive"* Christopher Browning, "An Insidious Evil," *The Atlantic Unbound* (online), 11 February, 2004. www .theatlantic.com/doc/prem/200402u/int2004-02-11.

154 *When someone discovered* Yad Vashem testimony of Sam de Hond, in file of Walter Suskind, Yad Vashem Department of the Righteous, Israel; also personal correspondence with Dr. Maurice van der Pol, 21 September 2005.

155 *slip yellow armbands* Mordecai Paldiel, *Saving the Jews* (Rockville, Md.: Schreiber, 2000), 277.

156 *"Over there, he wanted to do"* Ibid., 279.

Chapter 9 MIEKE VERMEER

158 *Naamloze Venootschap* In addition to information provided by Mieke Vermeer, this synopsis is based on Flim, 40–41, and Moore, 183–84.

158 *"a unity in all human minds"* Paramahansa Yogananda, *Auto-biography of a Yogi* (Los Angeles: SRF, 1956), 44.

160 *one newborn even passed through* I have supplemented Mieke's recollections with Lisette Lamon's direct testimony, contained in the Walter Suskind file at the Yad Vashem Department for the Righteous, Israel.

Chapter 11 THE HEART HAS REASONS

193 *if you observe one thousand white seagulls* Karl Popper, *A World of Propensities: Towards an Evolutionary Theory of Knowledge* (Bristol [England]: Thoemmes, 1990).

193 *at a crossroads where ethical action* Zygmunt Bauman, *Modernity and the Holocaust* (Ithaca: Cornell University Press, 2001). See also István Deák, "The Incomprehensible Holocaust," *New York Review of Books* (28 September 1989).

193 *"the hand of compassion"* Otto Springer, quoted in Eva Fogelman, *Conscience & Courage: Rescuers of Jews during the Holocaust* (New York: Doubleday, 1994), 57.

194 *"the ability to feel life"* *NOW with Bill Moyers,* Public Affairs Television, New York, 20 February 2004.

194 *Many even had parents or siblings* Heiltje Kooistra; Kees Veenstra; Mieke Vermeer; and Piet Meerburg, whose mother took in many Jews after his father died in 1942.

196 *"loving and creative participation"* Duane Elgin, *Voluntary Simplicity,* rev. ed. (New York: William Morrow, 1993), 38.

197 *simply acted from the heart* I will not attempt to further explain what "acting from the heart" is, because, in the words of novelist Robert James Waller, "Some things, magic things, are meant to stay whole. If you look at their pieces, they go away." Social scientists, however, do not share my qualms, and I would recommend the work of Pearl and Samuel Oliner to those who desire a rigorous analysis.

201 *"All people make their own decision"* From Miep Gies's speech at the College of St. Rose in Albany, New York, on 3 March 1996.

201 *Jews killed Christian babies* This was a revival of a medieval anti-Semitic myth known as the blood libel. See James Carroll, *Constantine's Sword* (New York: Houghton Mifflin Company, 2001), 268–77.

202 *without the purposeful inattention* See the new preface to Philip Hallie, *Lest Innocent Blood Be Shed: The Story of the Village of Le Chambon and How Goodness Happened There* (New York: Harper-Colophon, 1994).

202 *"Few among the perpetrators"* Christopher R. Browning, personal correspondence with the author, 10 June 2002.

203 *"truth-in-reconciliation"* Bill Moyers has made a fine video about these hearings: *Facing the Truth* (Princeton: Films for the Humanities and Sciences, 1999). See also Desmond Tutu, *No Future without Forgiveness* (New York: Doubleday, 1999).

204 *raised to mistrust the fabricated atrocity tales* R. R. Palmer and Joel Colton, *A History of the Modern World,* 8th ed. (New York: McGraw Hill, 1995), 859.

204 *Human beings will often substitute illusion* See M. Scott Peck, *The Road Less Traveled: A New Psychology of Love, Traditional Values, and Spiritual Growth* (New York: Simon & Schuster, 1997).

205 *it can be heard as a variation* See Kees Veenstra, page 116 and Pieter Meerburg, pages 147–48.

207 *"we cannot wait for our leaders"* From Miep Gies' speech at the College of St. Rose in Albany, New York, on 3 March 1996.

Chapter 12 REFLECTIONS

209 *every other nation was offered* Found in the *Avodah Zarah* 2b; Sifra; Brachah.

210 *William James may have described* William James, *The Letters of William James,* ed. Henry James, vol. 2 (Boston: Little, Brown, and Company, 1926), 90.

COMMENTS AND ACKNOWLEDGEMENTS

217 *when the genocide is referred to* James Carroll, *Constantine's Sword* (New York: Houghton Mifflin Company, 2001), 11.

218 *"I never use the word"* Amos Oz, *Under This Blazing Light* (Cambridge: Cambridge University Press, 1996), 81.

218 *In composing this work* Bert Jan Flim, *Omdat Hun Hart Sprak: Geschiedenis van de georganiseerde hulp aan Joodse kinderen in Nederland, 1942–1945* (Kampen, The Netherlands: Kok, 1996).

218 *The dissertation was published* Ibid.

218 *A condensation of that tome* Bert Jan Flim, *Saving the Children: History of the Organized Effort to Rescue Jewish Children in the Netherlands 1942–1945* (Bethesda: CDL Press, 2005).

218 *Jacob Presser, a Jewish survivor* J. Presser, *Ondergang. De vervolging en verdelging van het Nederlandse jodendom 1940–1945,* pt 1 (The Hague, 1965).

218   *based on a lecture series he gave*   Louis de Jong, *The Netherlands and Nazi Germany* (Cambridge: Harvard University Press, 1990).

218   *available in English as*   J. Presser, *Ashes in the Wind: The Destruction of Dutch Jewry,* trans. Arnold Pomerans (Detroit: Wayne State University Press, 1988).

218   *His book* Victims and Survivors . . . *explains*   Bob Moore, *Victims and Survivors: The Nazi Persecution of the Jews in the Netherlands 1940–1945* (London: Arnold Press, 1997).

218   *Finally, I owe a great professional debt*   Christopher R. Browning, *Ordinary Men: Reserve Battalion 101 and the Final Solution in Poland* (New York: HarperCollins, 1996).

218   *and whose most recent book*   Christopher R. Browning, *The Origins of the Final Solution* (University of Nebraska Press, 2004).

SOURCE MATERIALS BIBLIOGRAPHY

⁊

Flim, Bert Jan. *Saving the Children: History of the Organized Effort to Rescue Jewish Children in the Netherlands 1942–1945*. Bethesda: CDL Press, 2005.

Hilberg, Raul. *The Destruction of the European Jews*. Chicago: Quadrangle Books, 1967.

de Jong, Louis. *The Netherlands and Nazi Germany*. Cambridge: Harvard University Press, 1990.

Moore, Bob. *Victims and Survivors: The Nazi Persecution of the Jews in the Netherlands 1940–1945*. London: Arnold Press, 1997.

Presser, J. *Ashes in the Wind: The Destruction of Dutch Jewry*. Trans. Arnold Pomerans. Detroit: Wayne State University Press, 1988.

Romijn, P. "The War, 1940–1945." In *The History of the Jews in the Netherlands*. Ed. J. C. H. Blom, R. G. Fuks-Mansfeld, and I. Schöffer. Portland: Littman Library of Jewish Civilization, 2002.

Van Galen Last, Dick. "The Netherlands." In *Resistance in Western Europe*. Ed. Bob Moore. New York: Berg, 2000.